THE USE OF WEB IN LIBRARIES

THE USE OF WEB IN LIBRARIES

Edited by
KUSUM VERMA

AKANSHA PUBLISHING HOUSE
NEW DELHI - 110 002 (INDIA)

AKANSHA PUBLISHING HOUSE
R-37B, Vani Vihar, Uttam Nagar
New Delhi-110 059
E-mail: ektabooks@yahoo.com

Showroom:
4649/21B, Ansari Road,
Daryaganj, New Delhi-110 002
Phone: 9212065579, 9811582579

The Use of Web in Libraries

First Published, 2004

ISBN 81-87606-66-5

PRINTED IN INDIA

Published by M.P. Misra for Akansha Publishing House, New Delhi-110 002 and Printed at Tarun Offset Press, Delhi.

Preface

We live in a time when libraries will see their missions expanded as they continue to collect and preserve analog materials while at the same time participating wholeheartedly in the digital revolution. With multimedia technology we have image libraries, audio libraries, digital video libraries and web libraries. We might also think of libraries when we refer to collections that now reside in databases, text bases, gopherspace, or the World Wide Web (WWW). As digital storage costs go down relative to cost of library shelf space, and as electronic services become more useful, affordable, available and usable, there is a move towards the grand challenge of a global digital library system.

Libraries are using web to create gateways to what has been termed a massive library system, where people can roam through the electronic equivalent of book stacks via a desktop workshop. The electronic equivalent offers the ability to integrate text with charts, graphs, photographs, sound, video and other forms of multimedia. Librarians are now playing a vital role in identifying, evaluating and making available quality electronic documents. Criteria such as accuracy, comprehensiveness, balanced and accurate presentation and currency as well as style and functionality are being utilized to select Internet sites of value for their users.

This book discusses the extent of web usage in libraries. From the analysis of the use of web, it appears that there is no end point to which the web can be utilized by libraries. Librarians must be made aware that a sense of permanence is elusive in the web environment and a continuous investment in training for skills development, software construction approaches and computer technology must be made. Only then can this enabling technology be utilised for information access, communications, and education.

The present book describes and roles and responsibilities of world wide web in digital libraries. It enables the readers to understand the process of electronic dissemination of information, the impact of web on libraries and the changing responsibilities of library professionals. Besides library professionals, students and teachers of library and information science will find this work of utmost use.

Editor

Contents

1

Library Automation

Today, the computer has a central role to play in library systems. As a reliable, competent, accurate, and cheap manipulator or library information it can bring to fruition many idealistic concepts about flexible library services. It has the capacity to free human beings from much of the repetitive labour that is a necessary concomitant to library work, it can also give us the opportunity to provide personal service to real people. The necessary prerequisite to the wise and proper use of computing machinery in libraries in the future is a body of wise and informed library managers now. It is possible to distinguish two general directions in which computer-aided services will develop. Printed lists prepared by computer processing of a basic corpus of bibliographic records will increase in number and in diversity, and facilities for online interrogation of files held in machine memories will become more widely available.

Presently computer-aided library systems almost invariably produce as their end-product some sort of printed list for human consultation or scanning. In the future, then, we can expect to see more such lists prepared in circumstances where they can be justified either by reducing costs or increasing services. A number of experimental online library projects are either operational or under development. It is reasonable to suppose that these will be successful and will eventually find application in certain circumstances.It is possible to divide present-day online projects into two broad categories: those involving the automation of one or more library housekeeping functions, and those concerned with information retrieval and the processing of natural language text.

While the technological advancements which transformed the cataloging function into an automated process took place some years ago, the changes being witnessed in the area of acquisitions are generally a recent phenomenon. Acquisitions automation is becoming more sophisticated and at the same time electronic publishing is adding an entirely new dimension to acquisitions service. These two developments are bringing about major changes in acquisitions, in terms of both process and organisation. The future is in the way libraries adapt to the electronic environment that is increasingly surrounding them.

Much progress has been made in recent years in the development and enhancement of automated acquisitions systems. At one time the focus of development was on replicating manual ordering and receiving routines within a comparatively isolated context. The integration of the acquisitions component with other internal library systems and with external bibliographic utilities was considered ideal but not reality. With the advent of low cost microcomputers, the libraries and information centres are now encouraged to switch over to computerisation. There is also an enthusiasm among the professionals to get trained in library automation.

Automation has affected most library processes to some extent, and in many cases has influenced the development of library policy. In the area of cataloging, however, the effects of library automation have been so far-reaching and profound that a separate discussion of their impact seems warranted. The effects may be seen in four general areas:

— Extent of cataloging information presented to the users
— Choice of information given

— Arrangement of information
— Typographical presentation of such information.

Automation of Acquisitions

Automation of acquisitions has been slow in development. There are a number of reasons, two of which are the complexities of acquisitions tasks which have demanded time and expense in development of systems, and the evolving organisational structure in the performance of the acquisitions tasks. In a 1985 survey of 28 libraries, it was interesting to learn that only seven libraries used an automated acquisitions system but 75 per cent had an online catalog. Of those libraries with automated acquisitions systems, six had automated ordering, four used automated serials check-in and two, automated binding. Automation itself will cause further changes in the organisational structure of acquisitions, something which the in-house systems and early vendor-developed systems have indicated.

There are very labour-intensive tasks in acquisitions which require much typing and filing. In the current period of library financial retrenchment and with smaller percentages of the operating budget going to acquisitions, there has been tremendous pressure on acquisitions personnel in the acquiring of materials.Just a few years ago, all acquisitions work was performed manually. In general, it is still performed manually. Out of desperation and a desire to provide online acquisitions information service to the library's clientele a fair number of libraries developed in-house automated acquisitions modules. Some of these are still in use; however, their efficiency varies greatly. These were developed mostly as an interim step until turnkey systems became available. A majority of these systems are in batch mode and operate on a general purpose mainframe computer. Most of these early systems were not comprehensive acquisitions systems in their development because of technological, financial or political problems.

Automation of acquisitions has received less attention than other library functions. Although there are many elements that enter into the slow development of the automation of the acquisitions function, two of those reasons are the non-realisation of the service benefits of the acquisitions function, its complexity, and the lack of a uniform organisational structure for performing the acquisitions task. "The move toward integrated systems is belated in some ways since acquisitions automation in libraries is now more than two decades old. But it is now coming very quickly and will play a very significant role in our future activities." This statement was made in 1980 by one of the most knowledgeable librarians in the field of automation. Acquisitions automation of a sophisticated sort began in the mid-1960.

Today there are several automated acquisitions systems in the market, a few of which interface with a library's system if the library uses the same system for other library functions. There are others which perform most of the tasks needed in the acquisitions operation but which do not interface with a library's online catalog. Now that other service functions have been automated and are in the process of becoming highly developed, attention is focusing more on the automation of serials check-in and acquisitions functions for fully-integrated library systems. However, software vendors have not been willing to devote the time and expense necessary to develop the complicated software to handle the complex tasks of acquisitions. Until recently there was little available in vendor or network-supplied acquisitions systems or services. There are systems on the market for both functions; however, these are rare considering the length of time that has elapsed since the beginning in the mid-1960s. Several well-known systems available are NOTIS, GEAC, INNOVAQ. Several of the other early acquisitions were the Baker and Taylor BATAB system of 1969, WLN in 1978, CLSI, and OCLC. NOTIS, first operational in 1971, included both acquisitions and cataloging. Serials receiving was designed into the system as an integral part of acquisitions. Although automated acquisitions functions are a giant step forward, when software cannot interface with a library's online catalog, it deprives a library's clientele of valuable information.

The traditional tasks of acquisitions have included participating in collection development activities, serving as liaison with academic faculty in selection, bibliographic searching, ordering receiving and checking in all materials ordered, payment authorisation, and mail receipt and distribution. In some libraries, other activities include receipt and acknowledgement of gifts, binding and book repair, and disposition of discards. Although there have been arguments for decentralised acquisitions, to achieve efficiency and accountability, ordering, receipt and payment must be monitored by a single entity.After bibliographic searching and order information are entered into a part of a library's database, the interim file must be given a final review by Acquisitions prior to ordering. After revision by Acquisitions, the record then may become part of the online catalog/database and searchable by normal index keys. This would provide for centralised management of bibliographic and financial information and may also assist in the transition from manual to an automated environment.

In a 1984 survey, it was reported that 57 per cent of responding libraries stated that monograph and serial acquisitions are organisationally separate and at one time, proponents of serials departments argued that advanced bibliographic skills were necessary to handle problems with title changes, frequency changes, and claiming. According to the 1984 survey, integrated acquisitions areas performed somewhat less of preorder searching and did more work in marking, editing, and so on. In this survey, of 28 libraries, 19 respondees performed the functions of bibliographic searching, ordering, receiving, check-in, and payment. Eleven received and distributed mail, ten handled discards, and only six performed the binding function. It is interesting to note where some libraries have dispersed some of the traditional acquisitions functions in other library areas. For instance, at one library in California, the acquisitions librarian has the title of Collection Development Librarian; ordering and receiving are performed in that department.

Monographic materials are searched, verified, and ordered by the order section, a division of the cataloging department. A separate serials department handles ordering, receiving and check-in of all serials. However, the cataloging department catalogs all serials. At a college in New York, bibliographic searching is performed in the cataloging department and payments are authorised by a separate payment department.Mail receipt and distribution is performed by the department that handles payments and, binding, although formerly in the cataloging department, is now part of public services. The binding unit is near the area where all currently received periodicals are shelved.

Other acquisitions functions have been dispersed to various other areas of the library, but the library is now planning to return all ordering and receiving and check-in to a single acquisitions department. These are only a few, medium to large-sized, libraries that have chosen different ways of fulfilling the acquisitions function. However, the overwhelming majority of libraries responding to the 1985 survey maintained the acquisitions functions in the traditional way by an acquisitions department with a librarian as head. Twenty-two libraries responding to the survey employ one or more professional librarians in acquisitions with a range of one to ten. Forty-one per cent believe the greater part of acquisitions tasks is professional, 35 per cent believe the greater part of acquisitions tasks is business or management-oriented, and 23 per cent believe that acquisitions tasks are evenly split between professional and business-oriented tasks. When this question was posed differently, 68 per cent felt acquisitions tasks were an even combination. Twenty-two acquisitions librarians responding to the questionnaire participate in selection of materials for the library, act as liaison with other librarians who participate in collection development, make budget decisions, and negotiate with publishers and vendors. Fifty per cent of the acquisitions librarians believe that collection development differs from acquisitions, that collection development is the actual selection of materials and collection measurement, the analysis of and policies for these functions. The same 50 per cent believe acquisitions is the function of physically acquiring materials and participating in collection development. Four respondees believe collection development and acquisitions are the same function. In 81 percent of the libraries, librarians other than the acquisitions librarian participate in collection development and 54 per cent of acquisitions librarians serve as liaison with academic faculty in collection development. With decentralisation, "the role of acquisitions librarian would require greater coordination and communication with other library areas."

Automated acquisitions module is designed for batch processing and runs on the IBM 3084. The database used is IMS and the program is primarily written in COBOL. Much typing and filing is eliminated with the use of this system, and, also, by the use of only a few vendors from whom to acquire library materials instead of ordering direct from thousands of publishers. After entering orders into a database, they may be edited, status reports added and receipts recorded. Bibliographic searching is performed by using an online bibliographic utility and transferring the information into the acquisitions database by rekeying. Orders are edited by the acquisitions department, part of which includes assigning a search code for duplication, a fund check code, a claim date, and a vendor code. These are then verified the first part of each week and mailed to suppliers. The acquisitions department monitors each fund account by accessing a separate accounting database. Upon arrival, all materials are checked in on the acquisitions database. Status reports are also entered into the online order record. However, none of this information is available to the public service area. Although the biggest advantage in using this in-house developed acquisitions module is the termination of some paperwork, other benefits have been the automatic claiming and batch printing of purchase orders. However, batch processing of these purchase orders slows the process of ordering. The whole ordering process requires three full weeks.

It would not be too complex a task to define the information that libraries need, and to devise an automated acquisitions system that could store, manipulate and report the necessary data as well as manage purchase orders, claims and the other housekeeping tasks associated with the acquisitions process. Even within this publicly funded system, of the nine universities that theoretically follow uniform procedures, the libraries' acquisitions departments manage their funds and collections quite differently internally. They all prepare reports for a variety of departments and organisations at the library, university, state, and national levels. These reporting requirements influence what data is stored, how it is manipulated, and how it is reported for each library.

Several options are available to a library to automate its acquisitions procedures. A library can develop locally a dedicated acquisitions system to suit its requirements; such a project requires a considerable commitment in time and money for development and maintenance, however. If a vendor-produced dedicated system is used instead, development cost savings are offset by the compromises that are usually necessary to use the pre-defined records and reports, although some customising is usually possible, depending on the system. If the acquisitions module of an integrated library system is used, the acquisitions department must coordinate activities and prioritise needs with other departments in the same library or with other libraries within the same institution.

Acquisition of Electronically Publications

Electronic publications have become an important factor in the acquisitions process of most academic libraries. In the years since Lancaster's landmark study, debate has waned over the demise of the printed word and research supports the widely recognised view that traditional print publishing and electronic publishing will continue to co-exist in the information environment. As the two formats complement each other, they require an "integrationist approach" to their handling. How has the electronic publishing phenomenon affected the acquisitions process? As electronic resources play an even greater role in the information industry, how will acquisitions adapt in the future? These questions warrant an examination of the issue of access instead of acquisition, and of the policy and service implications inherent in the redefinition of the acquisitions process.

Electronic publishing encompasses a wide range of computer-produced media, from products such as CD-ROM to online, text databases. Acquiring microcomputer diskettes, CD-ROM, and so on has introduced new factors to the acquisitions process and to some extent has resulted in the loss of control. Since these computer-based resources must be used with some kind of equipment, acquisitions staff must be able to recognise and communicate equipment specifications to the supplier. Many products are available only from the publisher or producer and staff must deal with suppliers that have little or no understanding of library practices. This is particularly evident from the widespread use of licence agreements.

The acquisitions department as the purchasing agent is usually not aware of the legal terms of the purchase until the product is received, the package is opened and contents reviewed. There is little control over contractual obligations since the terms of liability are not known at the time of order placement. The issue of quality control of receipts is another example of loss of control. Without access to the proper equipment, there is virtually no way to check the quality of the contents beyond observing obvious physical damage. As is, the case with other nonprint formats such as sound recordings and microforms, the acquisitions department must rely for the most part on staff at the housing location to check for defects and promptly report problems.

The acquisition of electronically produced resources has posed no insurmountable problems for acquisitions departments. "Parallel" publishing, where information is available in hard-copy format as well as online, has further complicated the picture. Historically the online publication has been treated as a service, usually in the reference department, and not as property to be acquired. Intner argues that computer-based services should be coordinated with the parallel hardcopy acquisition in order to achieve some measure of control and avoid unnecessary duplication. The issue then becomes one of access versus acquisition. Electronic journals are accessed online and only "published" on demand. There is virtually nothing for libraries to acquire for the collection, at least as far as the physical piece is concerned. The end user will create his or her own product through facsimile transmission of individual journal articles, preprints, and so on.

Electronic journals are limited at present. Butler asserts that most will continue to be published in print form as long as their level of use demands it and as long as there are subscribers without the ability to use electronic services." However, the worldwide adoption of a standard for the production of electronic manuscripts may provide incentive to book and journal publishers alike. What libraries must address is the issue of who pays for access to electronic information and its on-demand product. It is likely that access to full-text electronic resources will be funded from the library acquisition budget and on-demand prints will be paid for by the end user.

Online publishing developments have important implications in terms of the scope of acquisitions activities, budgetary policies and sources of supply. Acquisition policies are broadening to include what have traditionally been considered the realm of reference and circulation—access to databases and document delivery. Additionally, as the academic library continues to integrate and make accessible information that is "no longer packaged in neat bibliographical bundles, it has gone beyond the traditional print boundaries of the library." At some institutions the library and the computer centre have been combined administratively to form a scholarly information centre.

In such an environment the acquisitions department must participate in campus-wide information resource policies. Even in more traditional settings many acquisitions departments are involved in cooperative purchases with academic computing units, not only for microcomputer software but also for mainframe-supported data files. With the advent of institution-wide access to online information, the potential is great for acquisitions departments to help formulate institution-wide policies. There are implications for library budgetary policy. The traditional acquisitions budget has become a comprehensive "information resource budget" which supports not only the purchase of print and nonprint material, but also the access to online publications. The latter have expanded the services of libraries but reduced the amount of money available for the purchase of books and journals.

With the spiraling increases in costs for all types of resources the library must maintain a careful balance among expenditures in all categories. Libraries may charge a fee for the use of some databases, but this has been regarded largely as a fee for service, particularly for bibliographic databases. As acquisitions funds are increasingly used for access to electronic sources, the distinction between a service and a resource in electronic format will become clouded.Service implications exist in terms of the nature of the relationship between libraries and suppliers. Use of the academic book vendor and subscription agent continues but the traditional sources of supply for print and nonprint materials are not as yet offering their services for online publications. It may be preferable to bypass the vendor and deal directly with the publisher or producer, but as the number and sources of online publications increase, the industry may respond with the emergence of a library vendor specialising in online resources.

Brownrigg *et al*. note that "as the library stores less and less material in-house on a permanent basis, it will become more and more reliant on the smooth continuance of its relationship with external suppliers." The traditional criteria governing sources of supply such as discount, service charge, fulfilment rate and turnaround time, may be inappropriate in an online environment. New criteria will no doubt be established. Online electronic publications and their unique requirements present some interesting challenges to traditional acquisitions policy, practice and service.

Electronic publishing and the development of automated acquisitions systems have had and will continue to have a significant impact on both the process and the organisation of acquisitions in academic libraries. What is the likely result in the long term? Acquisitions will operate within a distributed environment which may extend to virtually all units in the library; the traditional organisation will focus on specialised services and may require fewer clerical staff. Acquisitions departments will continue as policy-setting units, will work closely with other units on campus and may become the primary negotiator involved in the business aspects of information handling.

Application of Distributed Acquisitions

A distributed environment for some aspects of the acquisitions process is possible because automation has made acquisitions and accounting data widely accessible and because electronic publishing has made new forms of communication available online. The process of acquisitions can be distributed among various departments and service units within the library which have the equipment to support it. Because an integrated library system allows for access to national bibliographic databases as well as databases of library holdings, orders, and items expected on approval, pre-order bibliographic searching would not need to be done centrally. Automation also allows sophisticated links between acquisitions and account data, system monitoring of budget balances and access to accounts by dispersed users. Interfaces with library suppliers could facilitate the online ordering of certain categories of materials such as in-print US trade books, technical reports, journal article reprints, and so on from approved library suppliers, or if local micro-computer-based options are available, using designated electronic ordering services. Authorised users in public service units could order these kinds of items because they are relatively easy to obtain and do not require specialised acquisitions knowledge. Budget monitoring would be controlled by the system.

Electronic links to supplier systems would facilitate the sharing of status information on outstanding orders, as well as claiming activity. The application of distributed acquisitions could be extended to include receipt of those items not requiring, further processing or, in an environment where the cata-loging function is also distributed, it could include receipt of all the above-mentioned categories of materials. Acquisition of specialised materials, overall management of the resource budget, policies pertaining to supplier selection and ordering service selection, and the negotiation of contracts would remain the responsibility of the acquisitions department.

The impetus for the shift toward distributed acquisitions is electronic publishing. Access to full-text databases by end users will surpass the acquisition of print materials in some disciplines, particularly the science, where electronic journals will become an essential resource. Access to online information is not location dependent; once the acquisitions department initiates a contract with the supplier, the end user may access online journals from the home, office, and so on. However, access to online information is equipment dependent and it may be quite some time before most users have access from remote locations. A library's commitment to online publishing implies a commitment to client-centred service units.

Effects of Automation on Cataloging

One of the greatest effects of automation on cataloging practice to data has been in the arrangement of entries in relation to each other. Virtually all book catalogs are divided catalogs, abandoning the so-called dictionary arrangement that interfiles all types of entries in a single sequence. The type of division is not consistent from one catalog to another. Some have separate author, title, and subject sections; some combine author and title entries in one catalog with a separate subject section; and at least one combines titles and subjects, with the author entries separate. Regardless of the method of division, however, two principal reasons are usually given for the arrangement: users make different uses of subject entries as opposed to author and title entries, according to a number of user studies, and the filing or sequencing of entries can be simplified if all types of entries are not interfiled. The latter reason is normally the more urgent when automation is involved. Catalogs can be divided without being automated, and if ease of use were the only justification for division there would be no reason to attribute the popularity of the practice to automation.

Filing, however, is another matter, and simplification of filing for automation purposes is undoubtedly the main reason for the predominance of the practice. Computers can sequence and arrange data with extreme speed and accuracy if given explicit rules for doing so, but traditional library filing arrangements are a mixture of alphabetical, chronological and other sequences presumed to be "logical", with numerous general and specific exceptions. In addition to the complexity of the rules, many of them are based on the ability of human filers to recognise information that is only implicit, not explicitly stated, and computers can work only with explicit data. At least five categories of difficulty may be identified:

a) Information in the headings must be ignored or removed in order for computers to sort it acceptably. Honorific titles such as "Sir" in proper names are also commonly disregarded, so that "Drake, Sir Francis" files as "Drake, Francis."

b) Information that is implicit must be made explicit. A common example is "U.S.—History—Civil War," which as a subdivision of "U.S.—History" files not alphabetically under "C" but chronologically, as if it were "U.S.—History—1861-1865." This category of problems is perhaps the most difficult for computers to deal with because there are no clues for most such instances, and the number of "as if" situations in most current filing practices is large. It is also the least defensible. "Dr." is filed "as if" spelled "Doctor" or "Doktor," depending on the language of the text, but if the reader does not know the rule, or has only a title such as "Dr. Jacob Dubs" to go on, he may miss the entry entirely. "Mrs.," (and presumably "Mac," although McKenzies insist they are not Mackenzies). Numbers are a special example of the "as if" problem; they file as if spelled out (again depending on the language of the text) at the beginning of titles, but file as numbers, in numerical sequence, in headings for numbered conferences, series and so forth.

c) Information in headings must be rearranged in order for machines top sort it into the desired sequence. "Charles II, King of England" must be read as 'Charles, King of England, II"—or actually, since there is also a numeral in this case and the second category of difficulty comes into play, as "Charles, King of England, 2."

d) Exceptions must be made to alphabetic order. Some rules require that entries beginning with the same word or phrase be sub-arranged not alphabetically by the next filing element but by bibliographic function (authors, then subjects, then titles, for example), or according to the type of entity the heading describes (persons, then places, then things).

e) Punctuation is even a problem, because of complications introduced both by the machines and by filing rules. Computers regard punctuation marks as character just as letters and numerals, and sort them into a certain order (differing to some extent by brand of machine) unless programed to do otherwise. Extra spaces inadvertently inserted by humans will affect machine filing order as well. Existing rules differ on the treatment of certain marks, for example, whether "Brewer's Dictionary of Phrase and Fable" should be filed as "Brewer's" or "Brewer's," and "Mott-Smith" as "Mott Smith" or "MottSmith."

The ideal solution to these various problems is unclear, but attempts to solve them in automated catalogs have produced a significant amount of change as compared with manually filed catalogs. Most projects have used a combination of four basic approaches:

a) Continue to follow present filing rules, using people to assign additional codes to headings as necessary to allow computers to arrange the headings as desired.

b) Abandon present filing rules, and use the arrangements produced by the computer's sorting sequences with a minimum amount of change.

c) Change the headings themselves as necessary so that computers can arrange them in accordance with very simple filing rules.

d) Attempt to program computers so that they will arrange headings automatically, either by present filing rules or by modifications of them.

In 1968, Stanford University's on-line BALLOTS project had evolved a technique of filing machine-readable catalog entries not by any of the usual rules, but in an arbitrarily arranged file with indexes by various bibliographic elements, such as author, title, topical subjects, and so forth. By itself, this was not new. The significant and important aspect of the technique, however, was that the position of each entry in the author and title indexes was computed directly from the data itself, using the first three letters from the author's last name and the words of the title. The computer, of course, followed the same procedure in retrieving the index entries on command. In effect, the actual filing arrangement of the "catalog" was transparent to the user.This technique of "derived keys" was being studied by several researchers at about this time. Nugent described four different "compression coding" techniques, and Kilgour and Ruecking reported the results of separate tests using various combinations of characters from author and title entries for retrieval purposes.

In 1970, Kilgour and two associates analysed the effectiveness of derived keys varying from four to eight characters in length for retrieval of name and title entries taken from a sample of 132,808 entries. They concluded that a "3,3" key—that is, the first three characters of the author's last name and the first three character of the title—would retrieve five or fewer entries 99 per cent of the time. Further experiments with titles only (using the first three letters of the first two words, or the first three characters of the following three words) produced similar results.The results of this research led to the use of 3,3 keys for name and title searches and 3.1,1,1 key for title-only searches in the design of the Ohio College Library Center (OCLC) system, and the technique has been one of the major factors in OCLC's success.

Library Networks

Information network are a set of interrelated information systems associated with communication facilities, which are cooperating through more or less formal agreements and institutional agreements, in order to jointly implement information handling operation, with a view to pooling their resources and to offer better services to the user. They generally follow identical or compatible rules and procedures. A library network consists of six major components:

a) Information resources.

b) Reader or users of information.

c) Schemes for intellectual organisation of data/documents.

d) Methods for the delivery of information to user—the output.

e) Formal organisation—cooperation, whether voluntary or obligatory, in information exchange and utilisation.

f) Bidirectional communication links.

Based on these components, the essential requirements of INFLIBNET can be identified as:

— Libraries.

— Computer facilities.

— Machine-readable databases (Library holdings, Union catalogues, National & international database).

— Reprographic facilities.

— Communication link (Telephonic, postal or satellite communication channel).

The services provided by library network include:

— *Shared cataloging*: Cataloging has three parts : descriptive cataloguing, subject cataloging and locational information. The objective of this service is to share by a library the work of cataloging of publications already done elsewhere in the INFLIBNET. It will enable a librarian to use the catalogue information available in a major, nearby university library or regional centre for cataloging new publications added to his library. In other works, a document is cataloged only once at the time of first input into the network.

— *Union Catalogue of Books, Serials and Non-books Materials:* The objective of this service is to provide a union catalogue of books, serials and non-book materials held in different libraries in the country, with a mechanism for maintaining it uptodate all the time. For serials, besides title information, holding data of back volumes would also be provided. The union catalog will be compiled and made available in four regions. Each regional union catalogue, besides featuring the holding of libraries in the concerned region, will also show the holdings of libraries in other regions. This is achieved in a manner that when a new catalog record is added by a participating library, it will first be incorporated into the union catalog of its region and that the incorporation is further carried out subsequently into other three regional union catalogs. A user will be able not only to locate precisely the library(ies) where his sought document can be had but also to limit his search to a particular geographical region which is proximate to him. Several efforts have been made in the country towards developing union catalog of serials—such as by INSDOC for serials in science and technology and NASSDOC (ICSSR) for social sciences. While developing a union catalog of serials for INFLIBNET, due attention will be paid to utilise, to the extent possible, the existing union catalog compilations.

— *Online Catalog Access*: The objective is to provide online catalogue access to the user/library staff at local library level, as well as library staff at higher than local level (university/ proximate regional centre/other regional centres) for purpose of shared cataloging or to identify location of one or more books among participating libraries. The flow chart for online catalog access is given in.

— *Catalog production, book processing and preparation:* Catalog production may be in the form of card, book, magnetic tape/floppy/optical (CD-ROM) or COM form. Book processing and preparation include generation of spine labels, book cards, list of additions, etc.

— *Bibliographic database services:* These services would enable library staff to search bibliographic databases developed/ mounted at one or more sectoral and other information centres, in order to disseminate current information and retrieve retrospective information. Anticipatory services like S.D.I. and current awareness service and responsive services like literature search and bibliography compilation by downloading could be offered with the help of the databases. Bibliographic databases may be considered as of three types:

  — retrospective databases in core areas, built on the computer facility at the sectoral and other information centres. The databases comprise bibliographic citations/ abstracts of world information on magnetic tapes, which are acquired from foreign database producers as well as locally produced machine readable databases of Indian bibliographic information.

  — retrospective databases in peripheral/low usage areas, available through international search systems like DIALOG, BRS and ESA which can be accessed through appropriate gateways.

  — retrospective databases on CD-ROM for secondary information, whenever they are available for useful and trust areas, from which service could be generated nationally.

— *Document Supply Services*: Information dissemination services by themselves are of no avail unless they are backed up by actual provision of copy of source documents. The user is invariably interested in going through the original source document of his interest. For that matter, document supply service assumes a great importance and the INFLIBNET has to play due attention to it.

— *Inter-library Loan Request:* This service enables a library to request another library through the network, for one or more books on inter-library loan basis for meeting the demands of its users. This may also include facility for reserving a book, if it is on loan in the leading library. The actual transmission of the book itself will be through postal mail or other physical delivery mechanism like inter- and intra-city courier services (e.g., using document pick-up and delivery vans). An efficient and effective mechanism for physical delivery of the document needs to be developed. Success of this service depends upon the cooperative spirit of participating libraries. A code for inter-library loan transaction may have to be evolved and adopted by all the libraries. Libraries having a richer collection will be major providers of this service. Such libraries may need additional support for administering the inter-library loan service satisfactorily.

— *Document Delivery (fax)* : This service enable a library to request another library for a copy of a document, to be transmitted via telefacsimile. This service may be largely used for transmitting a few pages from documents, say, journal articles. It is to be provided by the Document Resource Centre which are to be identified for this purpose within the INFLIBNET. Problems associated with copyright regulations need to be considered in consultation with concerned organisations like, the Department of Education, Ministry of Human Resources Development. It may, however, be noted that the major users of INFLIBNET belong mainly to research and academic community and that reproduction to a single copy of journal articles for bonafide academic/research pursuits may not meet with any serious problem in regard to copyright regulations.

Currently, the paper used for fax reproduction cannot be preserved for more than a year due to the chemicals used in its preparation. It is also expensive. In view of the anticipated high growth in demand for document copy supply service in the INFLIBNET, alternatives for more economical document reproduction methods like image capturing through a video camera to a PC and reproduction using a high speed dot matrix or laser printer should be explored.

— *Document Delivery (non-fax):* It refers to supply of hard copy of documents required by users, by exploiting/ mobilising the document resources in the country through the Document Resource Centres. Supplying xerox copies of documents is the most convenient method, even though microfilm/microfiche may be preferred occasionally for certain reasons. The Document Resource Centres are to be equipped with one or more heavy duty xerox machines and supporting facilities to handle a large volume of demand for document copies. The INFLIBNET is a vast network and a major part of the demand for document copies could be met from some library in the network. Still, there will be a residual demand for documents that are not available in the country within and outside the INFLIBNET. There would be a need to procure documents from foreign libraries and documentation centres. Organisations like INSDOC are offering national level document delivery service and these facilities could be availed to meet the demand for documents not available within the country. Alternatively, the British Library Lending Division at Boston, Spa, which is well known for its international document delivery service, can be approached in such cases. The task of procuring documents not available within the country may be centralised at and handled by the Document Resource Centres and the Regional Centres.

— *Collection Development*: The objective is to help the libraries to identify and select publications which are worthwhile acquisitions. This can be based on usage data available at different levels in the network (e.g., circulation, inter-library loan statistics, document copy supply service, citation studies, SDI user profiles, etc.). After examining the strengths and weaknesses in the document collections in the libraries as well as duplication and based on the specialisation of libraries which are to be designated as Document Resource Centres, the INFLIBNET will gradually evolve a cooperatives acquisitions system. The libraries will be enabled to develop their collection on the basis of mutually agreed upon profiles assigned to each of them, so that duplication in acquisitions is minimised. The INFLIBNET's objective of resource sharing implies also sharing responsibility in acquisition, in order that the available total book purchase fund of the INFLIBNET is allowed to go the longest way for acquiring maximum number of documents in the network as a whole.

— *Referral service*: Requests for actual provision of information which cannot be satisfied by service library are referred to another source wherefrom the information can be had. In this service, the users are informed of the sources to the approached to get the required information. The users are put into direct contact with the sources of information. The libraries will be required to maintain a representative stock of referral directories and tertiary tools for undertaking this service. The referral function will get maximised progressively in the libraries at higher levels of the hierarchy. The communication system of the INFLIBNET will be used to send referral queries and receive answers.

— *Electronic mail:* This gives an ability to transfer/receive message among the participants in the network. This is an important facility in the network through which other services like inter-library loan requests, location search in union catalogs, document delivery requests transmission, referral and reference service and academic communication are implemented. This service will reduce communication delays in switching information among the constituents of the INFLIBNET.

— *Bulletin board:* This is as facility to display/view in an electronic bulletin board, news, announcements, etc. with constant updating of information. Several bulletin boards can be made available in the network for each of specific categories of users, node types, staff, disciplines, etc.

— *Academic communication:* The INFLIBNET can be extended to meet the communication requirements of the academic and scientific community. This may be accomplished through electronic mail, file transfer and bulletin board. Computer conferencing can be also carried out through the network facilities. More sophisticated instruments will be needed by the network to support services like teleconferencing.

Managing the Automation Process

A successful library automation project depends on good management. The manager must know and understand the task to be performed and the individuals involved in the project, and must have the confidence of his or her staff and manager. A manager can receive valuable assistance in planning and implementing a library automation system from a few key individuals in an organisation, but consultation within a wider group is critical. Any organisation considering automation should create a group that represents the constituencies that will manage, fund, use, operate, and maintain the system. Such a group serves many functions and may exist for a long time. The group can provide valuable information on specific requirements for the system, evaluate the comments of others about the necessity and feasibility of certain features, and serve as a sounding board for the individual who manages the automation project.

The importance of such an advisory group cannot be minimised, because systems are neither selected nor used in a vacuum. The sooner, all can participate in the process, the more likely its success. The duration of such a policy group can vary widely. It might be formed to provide advice on functions and features of a proposed system, but could remain active to evaluate alternative designs, vendor proposals, prototype systems, testing, and implementation. Such a committee may also be reformed after implementation to give continuing advice on systems operation.

When any type of computer system is installed in an organisation, it changes the way operations are performed, the tasks of the staff, and the relationship between the library and external units. Staff that work on the automation project are involved in the day-to-day tasks of bringing the system to operation. Staff that have to use the system once it is operational need to know about it and how it will impact their lives. The way these staff members conduct themselves within the organisation and while providing services to users is a complex process which requires thoughtful management. This is especially true when the changes raise the possibility of economic insecurity and fear of the unknown or threaten social relations and habitual practice. The organisation must take into account that individuals perceive events around them differently, that people are motivated in widely different ways, and that attitudes are formed by complex sets of variables and events. The project team staff face other issues. They are part of a group whose members have certain roles and status. The group as a whole is accountable for the project, but the members of the group must do the work. Individuals on the team may have personal goals different than the group goals or they may be in complete harmony with the project team.

The structure of an organisation may change as a result of automation activities. The installation of a new system or change over from one system to another requires skilful management. Departmental structures may change and some departments may disappear. New organisational units may be formed and new staff functions created. Such changes may be difficult to implement because of organisational inertia.

Realignment of departments represents a threat to existing managers, but may present an opportunity to improve performance and service. For example, a streamlined piece of software may render existing organisational task divisions illogical. If boundaries need to be redefined, managers must consider the needs of individuals as well as the goals of the organisation. Patterns of communication between departments may also change. For example, usually the library is not a discrete enough unit to manage its own pool of funds, but relies on another organisation to handle the burden of management and disbursement of funds for an acquisitions system, for instance. The link between the library and the unit that manages the bank accounts must be renegotiated to take into account the effect of the new computer system. This link may involve routine exchanges of data, but managerial intervention in the initial stages is crucial to success.

The steps to implementing a library automation system are generally the same whether converting an existing system or introducing an automation system for the first time. Both begin by problem identification and planning. The next steps involve determining the objectives of and constraints on the project, an analysis of existing systems or processes, design or selection of a new system, testing the system, conversion to the new system, staff and user training, and evaluation of the system. It begins with an assessment of the need for an automated solution or recognition that an existing automated system is inadequate. This assessment uses informal techniques (conversations with staff, management, users, or funders) and/or formal methods (surveys, questionnaires, or indepth interviews). Whatever the method, the result is recognition of the need for change or acceptance of the status quo. Planning activities are not confined to development of functions and features. Once need is determined and required features have been defined, the manager of the project can decide how to proceed, with the help of top-level managers, the library board, executives of other governmental units, staff, and the advisory committee. A timeline is developed, funding obtained, staff recruited, physical space obtained, contracts issued, and the system installed, tested, and implemented. Staff must be trained to use it and library users educated in its features, if appropriate.

An organisation needs a clear statement of what it wants to accomplish in terms of a needs or requirements assessment. If there is a need for a new library automation system, the next planning task is to assess the functions and features that this system should contain. If a new online catalog is considered, what should be the nature of the user interface? Should the catalog be accessed through computer networks? How many bibliographic records should the catalog be designed to manage? How many terminals should be attached to it? This type of list is endless. The examples given here are general, but a completed list is much narrower and more specific. Assessing the system requirements, defining them precisely, and testing the acquired system's fulfilment of the needs are critical to a successful automation venture. A statement of objectives includes the desirable functions and features of the system such as user, management, hardware, and software requirements. A particularly desirable approach to this task is to be guided by what one wants to accomplish, not by what one thinks is feasible.

Given a set of objectives mediated by constraints, the next step is to analyse the operation of the existing system to see how it works and to determine its functions and features. The system to be analysed is either one currently used in the organisation, such as a manual circulation function or an automated circulation system or one proposed by a vendor. The desired outcome of this phase is a good, well-documented understanding of how the existing system works, its acceptable features, and those needing redesign. The resulting document serves as a basis for the next phase of the project—the design of a new system or the selection of a specific vendor's offering. System design is often a long and complex operation that assesses user requirements and existing system operations and constraints. It should result in a schematic for a new system that meets formal requirements and individual needs. Since most libraries do not develop their own automation systems, the process of developing an entirely new system is omitted.

However, some design activities are often encountered in configuring vendor systems to meet specific user requirements.

Testing is a continuous process when a programer develops a code, when other programers use the code, when the staff informally review the system, and when the product goes through various stages of quality assurance. Testing continues even on a complete configured product ready to be delivered by the vendor. Whether a system is designed within the organisation or purchased, it must be implemented on a trial basis to test that it meets the objectives and the design specifications established at the outset. Sometimes preliminary testing of a system configured to the library's specifications is done in the vendor's offices using the library's data. Sometimes a vendor's system is shipped to the library and the system is configured there. The testing process can be informal or extremely rigorous depending on the demands of the organisation. Both hardware and software must be tested. While there are relatively standard methods for ensuring that hardware is functioning properly, the testing of library automation software is less codified.

There are mechanisms for testing large online systems which involve a computer system being connected to another computer whose function is to emulate a set of terminals all submitting requests to the machine being tested. The emulator stores scripts of commands to issue and expected responses; it logs and date and timestamps all communication with the test machine. By adjusting the mean time between requests, the emulator ascertains how the tested machine responds to varying loads. Usually testing is not this formal. Often a group of library staff members are assigned the task of informally trying out the functions of the system. They log on paper or with screen dumps any anomalies that occur. Problems are then communicated to the designers or vendors.

If the library converts from a manual system to a computerised one, considerable conversion activities are required. For a circulation system, all borrower records are keyed into the automated system, new user library cards are issued with barcode ID numbers attached, the bibliographic description for each book in the collection is recorded in a computer file, a barcode is placed in each book to identify it uniquely and each barcoded book is linked to a bibliographic description. Borrower categories must be identified and borrowing privileges for each borrower type and materials category must be established. These tasks are not trivial and may take hundreds of hours for a large library. The results must be almost error-free.

During preparation for automation, the manual system must continue operation. When use of the automated system begins, backup safeguards must be in place to protect the integrity of transactions. Conversion may seem simpler when a library moves from one automation system to another, but there are advantages and disadvantages to this scenario. On the plus side, the staff has experience using an automated system and may understand the underlying concepts. On the down side, no two vendor software or hardware systems operate the same way, load or unload information in the same format, handle all fields (like dates, quantities), or structure their files in the same way. The conversion becomes difficult when it requires intimate knowledge of not one but two library automation systems. Often it demands knowledge of two operating systems and two hardware platforms as well.

Once a stable system exists, can be placed in operation. The staff must understand the system thoroughly and procedures must be written and followed. Among the more important activities to be documented are how to start and stop the system, how to shut it down under emergency situations, how to make backups of the files, how to detect problems (and to determine if they are with communications equipment connected to the system), and who to notify under a variety of circumstances.

The many individuals who will operate the system need training. At the beginning, management needs to know the general characteristics of the system, how it works, if it is working well, and how it differs from the current system. Management also needs periodic status reports on system operation. Systems managers need training in the hardware on which the system will run, the operating system, and the library automation application itself. There is a temptation on the part of libraries to shift the burden of responsibility for understanding a library automation system onto the developers, vendors, or consultants. This is a mistake and can lead to an implementation problem when the library thinks the system should perform in a certain way which is different from how the vendor/developer believes it operates.

The staff that will operate the system needs extensive training in its use, despite the fact that developers often think that the operation of the systems they have created is self-evident and once in use will be problem-free. Generally, this is not the case. Therefore, the more documentation available in written form, in videos, and in assistance programs built into the system from vendor-technical support staff and from human beings serving as tutors, the greater is the likelihood that the staff will accept and use the system successfully.

Once a system is installed and has been operating for a reasonable period of time, inferences can be made about its performance, reliability, and capacity. Most library automation systems generate reports such as the number of orders processed, overdue notices sent, serial titles checked in, and so forth. But other measurements give important information about the internal operation of the software itself, such as response time for online requests, percentage of space on the system disk drives that is filled, central processor capacity utilisation by time of day, disk input/output operations performed by time of day, memory utilisation, and communications line utilisation and error rates. A more qualitative form of evaluation should also be undertaken that involves comparing the objectives established for the system with results from its operation. This evaluation takes place at least twice, once when the library is about to accept delivery of the system and again after the system has been running. During acceptance testing the library can reject the system based on its failure to meet library needs.

After the system has been accepted, the library should continuously evaluate the system to see if it continues to meet its needs. Most library managers will choose to purchase rather than build their own library automation system. Since a wide variety of systems is available on the market for tiny, small, medium, and large libraries, only libraries that are very large, have special requirements, or have the interest and funds are likely to pursue designing and implementing their own systems.

Automation Scenario

International programmes like UNISIST/UNESCO, Universal Availability of Publications (UAP) and Universal Access to Information (UAI) of IFLA and a few others have helped in promotion and coordination of information services throughout the world. IDRC, Canada, EEC, Brussels and similar other have helped developing countries to strengthen their information infrastructure. Global information systems, characterised by decentralised input, centralised processing and decentralised distribution, such as INIS, AGRIS, and DEVSIS have been evolved towards universal bibliographic control and dissemination of literature.

Major producers of secondary information services have become international information/database centres for their respective subjects/disciplines. International information network/ centres such as Lockheed/DIALOG, SDC/Orbit and ESA/IRS hold 100 or more databases in several disciplines and offer online services to users throughout the world. Communication networks like TYMNET, TELENET and ESANET offer communication facilities to international information centres that offer database services. Towards promoting cooperative endeavours, regional networks like ASTINFO, RINSCA and TECHNONET and specialised networks like AIBA, INNERTAP, SEAMIC and others have come about. These are all useful international efforts in transborder flow of information and in diffusion of knowledge throughout the word.

The library networks in USA are in a most advanced level of development. The favourable factors responsible for successful development of library networking in USA are long tradition of cooperation among libraries, introduction of library automation as early as from 1960's, advances in information science during 1970's and 1980's and introduction of MARC format by the Library of Congress in 1968. The experiences of USA in library networking are valuable to our efforts in designing the INFLIBNET. Three foremost bibliographic utilities and networks in USA are the Online Computer Library Centre, Dublin, Ohio (OCLC), Research Libraries and Information Network, Stanford, California (RLIN) and Washington Library Network, Olympia, Washington (WLN). In addition, there are networks of different types, levels, etc.

The library networking is based on three major areas of technology, viz., creation of bibliographic information in machine readable format for storage and retrieval, hardware/software for database use and services and telecommuni-cation mechanism for transmission of information. The major point of success of library network depends upon availability of machine-readable catalogs in the constituent units. A great progress has been made by USA in this regard. The latest trend is to use CD-ROM technology for storing the catalog data. The OCLC, established in 1967, and has a staff of 812 persons (as on 1987) is a non-profit organisation and supports resource sharing among more than 6,700 libraries in USA, besides countries in Europe, Saudi Arabia and Australia. Its union catalog database contains 13 million records; some 30,000 records are added every week. With the steady growth of OCLC, there has been a progressive decline in the amount of original cataloging to be done by the participating libraries. The system hit rate has increased from 66 per cent in 1971 to 94 per cent in 1983.

RLIN, established in 1978 and which has as staff of 81 persons, supports the cooperative programmes of Research Libraries Group, comprising 36 major libraries and other research institutions. It maintains 6 databases online. The catalog database holds more than 20 million records. WLN, established in 1972 and which has a staff of 51 persons, provides, more than 250 libraries in seven states of USA, online computerised services to promote resource sharing and automated library functions. The bibliographic file contains more than 3.5 million catalog records.

In India, nearly 100 library and information centres are known to be computerising their activities. The number is steadily increasing. Some of the major organisations engaged in computerised information handling are:

- Indian National Scientific Documentation Centre (INSDOC)
- Documentation Research and Training Centre (DRTC)
- Indian Institute of Science, (I.I.Sc.)
- Indian Institute of Technology, (IIT), Madras
- Indian Institute of Technology, (IIT), Kanpur
- National Informatics Centre (NIC), New Delhi
- Bhabha Atomic Research Centre (BARC), Bombay
- Tata Institute of Fundamental Research (TIFR), Bombay
- Physical Research Laboratory (PRL), Ahmedabad.
- Indira Gandhi Centre for Atomic Research, Kalpakam, Madras.
- Defence Scientific Information and Documentation Centre (DESIDOC), Delhi.
- NISSAT Sectoral Centres: NICDAP, Lucknow; NICLAI, Madras; NICFOS, Mysore; NICMAP, Bangalore; and NICRYS, Madras.

Automation being carried out by libraries is usually in acquisition, serials control, cataloging, circulation and management statistics. Some progress has been made by the libraries in these areas. A few institutions are cresting and maintaining bibliographic databases in machine readable form and bringing out lists, catalogs, union catalogs, etc. They offer current awareness service. NISSAT is engaged in promoting the development of sophisticated all purpose library application software packages. However, some important packages now available for use in India libraries are CDS/ISIS (microversion) developed by UNESCO and MINISIS developed by IDRC, Canada. Private software firms have recently started to develop library application software packages and they are made available on a commercial basis. Some libraries and information centres have developed softwares in-house for specific application, with local expertise. Serious attention is now being paid to training aspect for developing skills in computer application among the library and information manpower. While, there are long term requirements, training institutions like DRTC and INSDOC place emphasis on information technology in their course curriculum, and the library schools in the universities have begun to introduce computer application in the courses being offered by them, towards short term requirement of training the existing personnel, numerous training programmes are being launched by professional associations, institutions and others. NISSAT, UGC, etc. are promoting/sponsoring such training programmes in a big way. A favourable feature is that the library and information personnel are now increasingly interested in getting trained for acquiring skill and knowledge in computer application

2

Information Retrieval

Information retrieval (IR) deals with the representation, storage, organization of, and access to information items. The representation and organization of the information items should provide the user with easy access to the information in which he is interested.

Data Retrieval

Data retrieval, in the context of an IR system, consists mainly of determining which documents of a collection contain the keywords in the user query which, most frequently, is not enough to satisfy the user information need. In fact, the user of an IR system is concerned more with retrieving *information* about a subject than with retrieving data which satisfies a given query. A data retrieval language aims at retrieving all objects which satisfy clearly defined conditions such as those in a regular expression or in a relational algebra expression. Thus, for a data retrieval system, a single erroneous object among a thousand retrieved objects means total failure.

For an information retrieval system, however, the retrieved objects might be inaccurate and small errors are likely to go unnoticed. The main reason for this difference is that information retrieval usually deals with natural language text which is not always well structured and could be semantically ambiguous. On the other hand, a data retrieval system (such as a relational database) deals with data that has a well defined structure and semantics.

Data retrieval, while providing a solution to the user of a database system, does not solve the problem of retrieving information about a subject or topic. To be effective in its attempt to satisfy the user information need, the IR system must somehow 'interpret' the contents of the information items (documents) in a collection and rank them according to a degree of relevance to the user query. This 'interpretation' of a document content involves extracting syntactic and semantic information from the document text and using this information to match the user information need. The difficulty is not only knowing how to extract this information but also knowing how to use it to decide relevance. Thus, the notion of *relevance* is at the center of information retrieval. In fact, the primary goal of an IR system is to retrieve all the documents which are relevant to a user query while retrieving as few non-relevant documents as possible.

Information Retrieval

In the past 20 years, the area of information retrieval has grown well beyond its primary goals of indexing text and searching for useful documents in a collection. Nowadays, research in IR includes modeling, document classification and categorization, systems architecture, user interfaces, data visualization, filtering, languages, etc.

Despite its maturity, until recently, IR was seen as a narrow area of interest mainly to librarians and information experts. Such a tendentious vision prevailed for many years, despite the rapid dissemination, among users of modern personal computers, of IR tools for multimedia and hypertext applications. In the beginning of the 1990s, a single fact changed once and for all these perceptions — the introduction of the World Wide Web.

The Web is becoming a universal repository of human knowledge and culture which has allowed unprecedent sharing of ideas and information in a scale never seen before. Its success is based on the conception of a standard user interface which is always the same no matter what computational environment is used to run the interface. As a result, the user is shielded from details of communication protocols, machine location, and operating systems. Further, any user can create his own Web documents and make them point to any other Web documents without restrictions. This is a key aspect because it turns the Web into a new publishing medium accessible to everybody.

As an immediate consequence, any Web user can push his personal agenda with little effort and almost at no cost. This universe without frontiers has attracted tremendous attention from millions of people everywhere since the very beginning. Furthermore, it is causing a revolution in the way people use computers and perform their daily tasks. For instance, home shopping and home banking are becoming very popular and have generated several hundred million dollars in revenues.

Despite so much success, the Web has introduced new problems of its own. Finding useful information on the Web is frequently a tedious and difficult task. For instance, to satisfy his information need, the user might navigate the space of Web links (i.e., the *hyperspace*) searching for information of interest. However, since the hyperspace is vast and almost unknown, such a navigation task is usually inefficient. For naive users, the problem becomes harder, which might entirely frustrate all their efforts.

The main obstacle is the absence of a well defined underlying data model for the Web, which implies that information definition and structure is frequently of low quality. These difficulties have attracted renewed interest in IR and its techniques as promising solutions. As a result, almost overnight, IR has gained a place with other technologies at the center of the stage.

Basic Concepts

The effective retrieval of relevant information is directly affected both by the *user task* and by the *logical view of the documents* adopted by the retrieval system, as we now discuss.

The User Task

The user of a retrieval system has to translate his information need into a query in the language provided by the system. With an information retrieval system, this normally implies specifying a set of words which convey the semantics of the information need. With a data retrieval system, a query expression (such as, for instance, a regular expression) is used to convey the constraints that must be satisfied by objects in the answer set. In both cases, we say that the user searches for useful information executing a *retrieval* task.

Consider now a user who has an interest which is either poorly defined or which is inherently broad. For instance, the user might be interested in documents about car racing in general. In this situation, the user might use an interactive interface to simply look around in the collection for documents related to car racing. For instance, he might find interesting documents about Formula 1 racing, about car manufacturers, or about the '24 Hours of Le Mans.'

Furthermore, while reading about the '24 Hours of Le Mans', he might turn his attention to a document which provides directions to Le Mans and, from there, to documents which cover tourism in France. In this situation, we say that the user is *browsing* the documents in the collection, not searching. It is still a process of retrieving information, but one whose main objectives are not clearly defined in the beginning and whose purpose might change during the interaction with the system.

User's task might be of two distinct types: information or data *retrieval* and *browsing*. Classic information retrieval systems normally allow information or data retrieval. Hypertext systems are usually tuned for providing quick browsing. Modern digital library and Web interfaces might attempt to combine these tasks to provide improved retrieval capabilities. However, combination of retrieval and browsing is not yet a well established approach and is not the dominant paradigm.

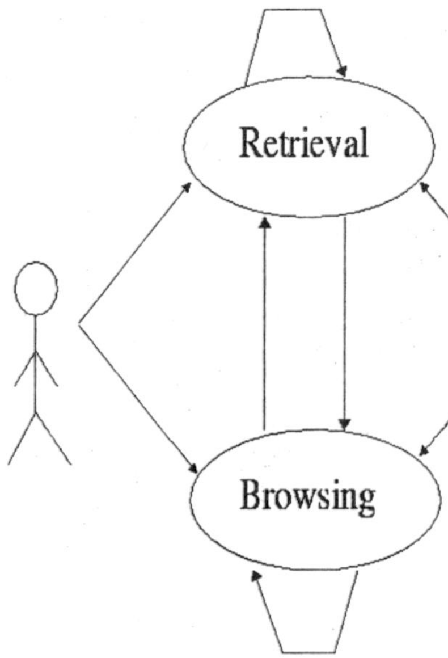

Fig 1. Interaction of user with retrieval system through distinct tasks

Figure illustrates the interaction of the user through the different tasks we identify. Information and data retrieval are usually provided by most modern information retrieval systems (such as Web interfaces). Further, such systems might also provide some (still limited) form of browsing. While combining information and data retrieval with browsing is not yet a common practice, it might become so in the future.

Both retrieval and browsing are, in the language of the World Wide Web, 'pulling' actions. That is, the user requests the information in an interactive manner. An alternative is to do retrieval in an automatic and permanent fashion using software agents which *push* the information towards the user. For instance, information useful to a user could be extracted periodically from a news service. In this case, we say that the

IR system is executing a particular retrieval task which consists of *filtering* relevant information for later inspection by the user.

Logical View of the Documents

Due to historical reasons, documents in a collection are frequently represented through a set of index terms or keywords. Such keywords might be extracted directly from the text of the document or might be specified by a human subject (as frequently done in the information sciences arena). No matter whether these representative keywords are derived automatically or generated by a specialist, they provide a *logical view of the document*.

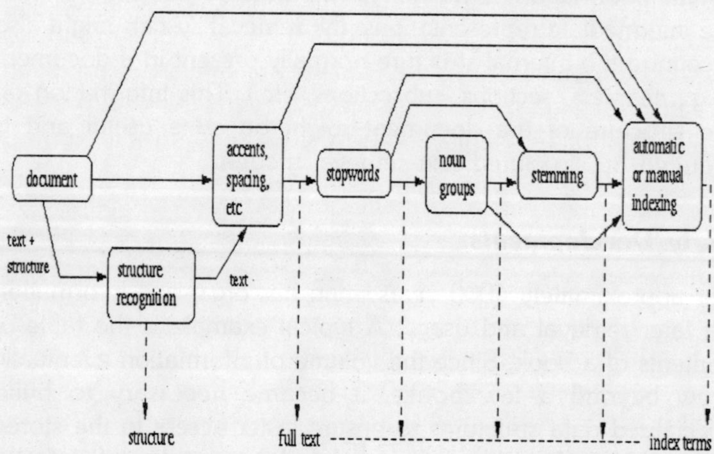

Fig.2 Logical view of a document: from full text to a set of index terms.

Modern computers are making it possible to represent a document by its full set of words. In this case, we say that the retrieval system adopts a *full text* logical view (or representation) of the documents. With very large collections, however, even modern computers might have to reduce the set of representative keywords. This can be accomplished through the elimination of *stopwords* (such as articles and connectives), the use of *stemming* (which reduces distinct words to their common grammatical root), and the identification of *noun groups* (which eliminates adjectives, adverbs, and verbs). Further, compression might be employed. These operations are called *text operations* (or transformations). Text operations reduce the complexity of the document representation and allow moving the logical view from that of a full text to that of a set of *index terms*.

The full text is clearly the most complete logical view of a document but its usage usually implies higher computational costs. A small set of categories (generated by a human specialist) provides the most concise logical view of a document but its usage might lead to retrieval of poor quality. Several intermediate logical views (of a document) might be adopted by an information retrieval system. Besides adopting any of the intermediate representations, the retrieval system might also recognize the internal structure normally present in a document (e.g., chapters, sections, subsections, etc.). This information on the structure of the document might be quite useful and is required by structured text retrieval models.

Early Developments

For approximately 4000 years, man has organized information for later retrieval and usage. A typical example is the table of contents of a book. Since the volume of information eventually grew beyond a few books, it became necessary to build specialized data structures to ensure faster access to the stored information. An old and popular data structure for faster information retrieval is a collection of selected words or concepts with which are associated pointers to the related information (or documents) — the *index*. In one form or another, indexes are at the core of every modern information retrieval system. They provide faster access to the data and allow the query processing task to be speeded up.

For centuries, indexes were created manually as categorization hierarchies. In fact, most libraries still use some form of categorical hierarchy to classify their volumes (or documents). Such hierarchies have usually been conceived by human subjects from the library sciences field. More recently, the advent of modern computers has made possible the construction of large indexes automatically. Automatic indexes provide a view of the retrieval problem which is much more related to the system itself than to the user need. In this respect, it is important to distinguish between two different views of the IR problem: a computer-centered one and a human-centered one.

In the computer-centered view, the IR problem consists mainly of building up efficient indexes, processing user queries with high performance, and developing ranking algorithms which improve the 'quality' of the answer set. In the human-centered view, the IR problem consists mainly of studying the behavior of the user, of understanding his main needs, and of determining how such understanding affects the organization and operation of the retrieval system. According to this view, keyword based query processing might be seen as a strategy which is unlikely to yield a good solution to the information retrieval problem in the long run.

Libraries were among the first institutions to adopt IR systems for retrieving information. Usually, systems to be used in libraries were initially developed by academic institutions and later by commercial vendors. In the first generation, such systems consisted basically of an automation of previous technologies (such as card catalogs) and basically allowed searches based on author name and title. In the second generation, increased search functionality was added which allowed searching by subject headings, by keywords, and some more complex query facilities. In the third generation, which is currently being deployed, the focus is on improved graphical interfaces, electronic forms, hypertext features, and open system architectures.

Traditional library management system vendors include Endeavor Information Systems Inc., Innovative Interfaces Inc., and EOS International. Among systems developed with a research focus and used in academic libraries, we distinguish Okapi (at City University, London), MELVYL (at University of California), and Cheshire II (at UC Berkeley).

The Web and Digital Libraries

If we consider the search engines on the Web today, we conclude that they continue to use indexes which are very similar to those used by librarians a century ago. What has changed then? Three dramatic and fundamental changes have occurred due to the advances in modern computer technology and the boom of the Web.

First, it became a lot cheaper to have access to various sources of information. This allows reaching a wider audience than ever possible before.

Second, the advances in all kinds of digital communication provided greater access to networks. This implies that the information source is available even if distantly located and that the access can be done quickly (frequently, in a few seconds).

Third, the freedom to post whatever information someone judges useful has greatly contributed to the popularity of the Web. For the first time in history, many people have free access to a large publishing medium.

Fundamentally, low cost, greater access, and publishing freedom have allowed people to use the Web as a highly *interactive* medium. Such interactivity allows people to exchange messages, photos, documents, software, videos, and to 'chat' in a convenient and low cost fashion. Further, people can do it at the time of their preference (for instance, you can buy a book late at night) which further improves the convenience of the service. Thus, high interactivity is the fundamental and current shift in the communication paradigm.

In the future, three main questions need to be addressed.

First, despite the high interactivity, people still find it difficult to retrieve information relevant to their information needs. Thus, in the dynamic world of the Web and of large digital libraries, which techniques will allow retrieval of higher quality?

Second, with the ever increasing demand for access, quick response is becoming more and more a pressing factor. Thus, which techniques will yield faster indexes and smaller query response times?

Third, the quality of the retrieval task is greatly affected by the user interaction with the system. Thus, how will a better understanding of the user behavior affect the design and deployment of new information retrieval strategies?

Practical Issues

Electronic commerce is a major trend on the Web nowadays and one which has benefited millions of people. In an electronic transaction, the buyer usually has to submit to the vendor some form of credit information which can be used for charging for the product or service. In its most common form, such information consists of a credit card number. However, since transmitting credit card numbers over the Internet is not a safe procedure, such data is usually transmitted over a fax line. This implies that, at least in the beginning, the transaction between a new user and a vendor requires executing an off-line procedure of several steps before the actual transaction can take place. This situation can be improved if the data is encrypted for security. In fact, some institutions and companies already provide some form of encryption or automatic authentication for security reasons.

However, security is not the only concern. Another issue of major interest is privacy. Frequently, people are willing to exchange information as long as it does not become public. The reasons are many but the most common one is to protect oneself against misuse of private information by third parties. Thus, privacy is another issue which affects the deployment of the Web and which has not been properly addressed yet. Two other very important issues are copyright and patent rights. It is far from clear how the wide spread of data on the Web affects copyright and patent laws in the various countries. This is important because it affects the business of building up and deploying large digital libraries. Additionally, other practical issues of interest include scanning, optical character recognition (OCR), and cross-language retrieval.

The Retrieval Process

To describe the retrieval process, we use a simple and generic software architecture as shown in Figure 3. First of all, before the retrieval process can even be initiated, it is necessary to define the text database. This is usually done by the manager of the database, which specifies the following:

(a) the documents to be used,

(b) the operations to be performed on the text, and

(c) the text model (i.e., the text structure and what elements can be retrieved).

The text operations transform the original documents and generate a logical view of them.

Once the logical view of the documents is defined, the database manager (using the DB Manager Module) builds an index of the text. An index is a critical data structure because it allows fast searching over large volumes of data. Different index structures might be used, but the most popular one is the *inverted file*. The resources (time and storage space) spent on defining the text database and building the index are amortized by querying the retrieval system many times.

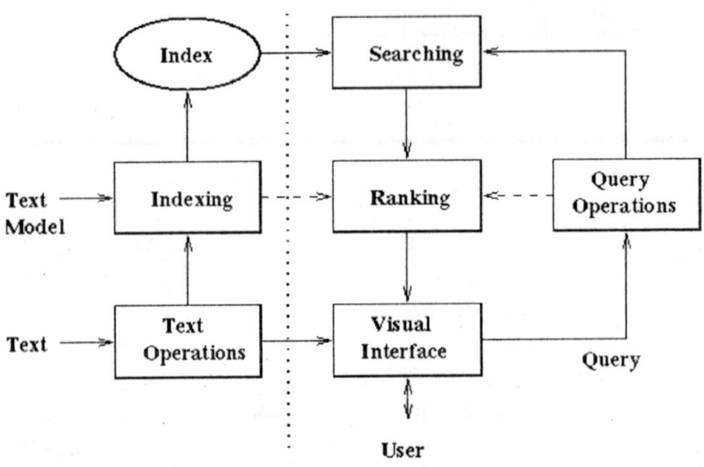

Fig. 3: The process of retrieving information

Given that the document database is indexed, the retrieval process can be initiated. The user first specifies a *user need* which is then parsed and transformed by the same text operations applied to the text. Then, *query operations* might be applied before the actual *query*, which provides a system representation for the user need, is generated. The query is then processed to obtain the *retrieved documents*. Fast query processing is made possible by the index structure previously built. Before been sent to the user, the retrieved documents are ranked according to a *likelihood* of relevance. The user then examines the set of ranked documents in the search for useful information. At this point, he might pinpoint a subset of the documents seen as definitely of interest and initiate a *user feedback* cycle. In such a cycle, the system uses the documents selected by the user to change the query formulation.

Stages of Information Retrieval

Retrieval is the process whereby data or documents are found in the attempt to deal with inquiries that have been posed. The following are the important stages in information retrieval.

— The analysis of search question.

— The translation of the question into the indexing language of the system.

— The formulation of the search strategy.

In addition, a lot of service problems occur, such as, how to provide copies of documents, how to display them, how to manage search and retrieval, how to protect, copyright and how to manage loans. To avoid these problems, in electronic environment interface design is very important issue. There are various ways, for example :

— *Plain text interface*: Electronic documents are presented as plain (ASCII) text, without images or other multimedia elements.

— *Image based interface:* The material is presented in image form of only some relevant parts.

— *Hypermedia based interface:* Electronic documents are presented following the paper book metaphor and the electronic library design reproduces the main features of the physical library.

Retrieval Systems

The catchwords in the retrieval systems are Online, Internet, Fidonet, etc.

— *Fidonet*: Fidonet is just one form of electronic communication that provides a means to bridge time and distance, to facilitate interpersonal communications. The simplest is a bulletin board system. In its basic form, the idea of the system can post a message in a public area. Any other member of the system can bowse through the bulletin board reading items of interest.

— *Main services*: Electronic Mails (one to one), Conference Mails (many to many) and File Transfer (can handle both text and binary files) when these services are integrated with an interactive electronic bulletin board system, such as remote access, they can be accessed by people using only a modem and ordinary phone lines.

— *Internet*: The Internet is a cooperative computer network of networks that links libraries, schools, governments, corporations, individuals and others to each other and to vast information resources. The internet protocol links many independent networks together so that they appear as a single network to the user. The Internet currently consists of about 28,000 registered networks, about 2 million host computers and an estimated 15 million users. About 149 countries have connections to some sort of an international computer network; of these about 63 countries have direct connections to the Internet. Internet can be used to send and receive electronic messages, to contact and search other computers—Telnet—to copy files.

The Internet is an open network. Anyone or any group is welcome to use it as long as that person or group has a terminal or a computer with the correct software and the ability to pay the costs. Since most users of Internet are affiliated with institutions, the computers they use are attached to LAN which are in turn connected by a router (a device that connects networks together and passes information among them) to a regional or wide area network.

You may also be limited in the applications you can use since the Transmission Control Protocol/ Internet Protocol (TCP/IP) does not really come to your own computer, it stops at the host. For this type of connection, you will need a modem and access to a standard voice grade telephone line. Gopher, Archie, Veronica, Jughead, WAIS and the WWW are the tools supported by Internet that help users to find and retrieve information.

— *Online*: Online makes information available in different formats. It is a means of constant access to databases around the world from any location using an inexpensive telecom link and a PC terminal.

— *Eliron*: Eliron is one of the first electronic library developments in the UK. It has given the user aspects of the electronic library a high priority in the research program. In fact, from the outset it included a user-friendly interface as one of the important selection criteria, on which the electronic library system (ELS) could be based. The basic objective of eliron is to set up a large image database of complete books, journals and course materials which can be directly accessed by students and teaching staff via Windows-based IBM and Macintosh PC's. ELIRON ELS employs current Graphical User Interface (GUI) technology, the basic feature of which is WIMP, i.e., Window, Icon, Mouse and Pull-down menu. It may be divided into broad aspects such as:

  — *Finding document:* Browsing and searching the electronic library database are two possible routes to find a document, which may be either a known citation or any relevant document related to a topic. The browsing-related interface provides graphical presentation of the hierarchial structure of the data fileroom, e.g., books, computer, computer architecture, from logic to page. The searching and browsing routes may be combined to find a relevant document, e.g., the user can first select certain drawers in the electronic library fileroom and then enter a free-text search clue to find relevant documents in the selected drawers.

— *Reading a document:* The PIX/TEX/EFS system links OCR'ed text page of a document with its corresponding image page. The user can, therefore, switch the display between the text and the image pages. Within the text pages, the user can enter simple searches on terms, which is similar to the "Find" function commonly available in word processors. For image viewing, the user can easily drag the page up/down and right/left. He can also reduce or enlarge the size of the image by simply double clicking the mouse. It is also possible to zoom into a particular area of the image page. Images may be rotated to 90, 180, 270, 360 degrees for viewing. The user can flip through the pages by clicking the next or previous buttons, or the 'go to' button to select any given page. It is also possible to lock up to four windows, each displaying an image page of one or several books. The user can, therefore, compare different parts of a book or read several books on the screen. Because the user station runs on Windows-based interfaces, the user can create notes with any Windows-based editor while viewing a page. The above two procedures can, to a certain extent, be used interchangeably. The user can highlight a term or sentence in the text page being read and go on to

The Process of Infroamtion Retreival

A person is likely to advance only those inquiries which he or she thinks the system may be able to cope with. This is no more than rational behaviour on the part of the user. The expectations with respect to the system may not be accurate. Indeed, they might be wildly unrealistic. Nevertheless, we can expect the user's decision to advance the inquiry to be conditioned by:

— the importance and urgency of the request,

— the perceived effort involved in using the system, and

— the perceived ability of the system to yield a worthwhile response.

Librarians may be correct in asserting that users are often unaware of the power and scope of the retrieval tools available. However, it is also possible for librarians who are intimately familiar with the bibliographical power of their libraries' apparatus to underrate the efforts involved from the users' perspective and to overrate the relevance, range, and accuracy of the retrieval systems.

The manner in which the inquiry is presented will be influenced by the linguistic, cultural, and technical orientation and personal knowledge of the user; and the user's expectations as to what form of inquiry will be acceptable and/or intelligible to the retrieval process. The user will have sufficient understanding of the retrieval system to know exactly what form of expression will produce the response most appropriate to the inquiry. Indeed, only the designer of the retrieval system or someone intimately familiar with it could be expected to approach such knowledge.

Since every individual has a particular conceptual framework and vocabulary, since the retrieval system has its own technical vocabulary, and since the user cannot be expected to have an intimate knowledge of the retrieval system, a greater or lesser degree of distortion is to be expected in the transformation of the inquiry into the language of the retrieval system. Librarians recognise that some degree of distortion is to be expected. The short-term solution is for the librarian to initiate a dialogue or negotiation with the user. This is commonly referred to as the reference interview. Inevitably, as in any human interaction, there is more involved than a simple exchange of verbal statements. At some stage the inquiry is expressed in the language of the retrieval system, since there is no other way of using it. In a sense a retrieval system can be regarded as responding to any inquiry addressed to it. But, if alien terms are used, there is no positive response. The retrieval system will only be responsive to terms it recognises. The yielding of a set of retrieved signals in response to an inquiry in the language of the retrieval system is an important transformation. The word 'set' is used advisedly since the retrieval system may yield nothing.

Once the inquiry has been posed in the language of the retrieval system, the outcome is automatic. The search is predetermined. Headings in the catalog lead directly or indirectly to catalog records. In this sense, retrieval systems are automatic devices, machines, in which any given input will yield one and only one output, which is predictable given a sufficient understanding of how the system works. The only exception to this is that there may be mechanical failures: a connection may be lost in a computerised system, or a card misfiled or overlooked in a card catalog.

Barring temporary mechanical failures, retrieval systems are like automata in that the same inquiry repeated will yield the same predictable response. This may seem contrary to experience in that two different people with the same initial inquiry can and often do end up with different results. There are two explanations for this:

a) *Retrieval systems are usually in a state of continuous, gradual revision*: data are added or withdrawn; new index points inserted; syndetic relationships changed. A library catalog may seem to be a particularly undynamic object, but the appearance is misleading. It follows that, when the same inquiry is presented at different points in time to what is ostensibly the same retrieval system, the system has, in fact, changed somewhat. It is, therefore, in an altered state—updated, most likely—and, therefore, while still an automaton, it has become a slightly different automaton.

The slight difference may well be significant for some inquiries.

b) There is scope in sophisticated retrieval systems like most online bibliographical search systems and complex card catalogues for changes in the expression of the inquiry. For example, one might conclude that the rendering of the inquiry in the language of the retrieval system has not been done well and that a modification of the phrasing would improve it. Another possibility is that the initial formulation of the query may yield too little by way of retrieved signals.

Online bibliographical retrieval systems are usually post-coordinate systems wherein complex searches are formulated from their constituent concepts at the time of searching instead of depending on selecting complex descriptions composed when the document was catalogued. It is, therefore, comparatively easy to expand searches. One can add restrictions. In pre-coordinated systems, such as library card catalogues, one can simply decide to exclude some of the richness offered. Alternatively, one can expand the expression of the search by formulating it more broadly in the language of the retrieval systems. In both cases, the change in the set of retrieved signals from one posing of the inquiry to another represents not an unreliability on the part of a stable retrieval system but a change in the state of the retrieval system or in the formulation of the inquiry.

Data Retrieval vs. Document Retrieval

A data retrieval system is one in which specific data are retrieved—the specific information requested in the inquiry. The term document retrieval refers simply to systems in which a document is retrieved. Ordinarily, however, it is used to refer to a retrieval system in which the data retrieved are the description and address of one or more documents; and it is these documents that will contain the data desired. A basic distinction between a data retrieval system designed to provide directly what one thinks one wants and a document retrieval or, better, a reference retrieval system that merely points one toward the desired data in one or more steps. The inquiry could have been formulated in the same way and posed to the same bibliographic retrieval system in the same way. The exact same response might well have been received as that given above. The difference is that the desired datum has been retrieved, without further searching being needed.

We can classify a retrieval system as being a data retrieval system or a document retrieval system on the basis of the intention of the person using it, and can define retrieval systems according to whether they are capable of functioning as a reference retrieval as well as a data retrieval system. This capability would appear to extend to any system in which the data stored are capable implicitly or explicitly of indicating further sources of data. From this perspective, we can consider data retrieval systems as a limited, primitive category within the larger class of retrieval systems.

The ability of a retrieval system to retrieve signals can be illustrated by considering some the many examples of retrieval mechanisms in a library. One user might treat the subject arrangement of the documents on the shelves as a retrieval mechanism and go directly to the shelves associated with the Dewey number(s) expected to contain the signals (books) desired. A second user might approach the library catalog and examine subject headings and note the bibliographical data recorded on the cards there. That may be all that the user wanted if verifying a bibliographical citation and willing to rely on card catalog data instead of inspecting the documents themselves. A third user might do exactly the same as the second user but the data recorded on the cards do not constitute the goal, only the directions to he document on the shelves. A fourth user might go to the librarian and express the inquiry verbally.

The librarian, acting as a retrieval system, would endeavour to convert the inquiry into the terms of the library system and deliver the data required, whether this is a whole document or merely a mention of specific data from within a book. When a document is found, further retrieval mechanisms—index, table of contents—may be used to identify more specifically what is wanted. Dictionaries, encyclopedias, and bibliographies—all examples of retrieval mechanisms—may well be used independently or in conjunction with other means of searching.

Retrieval Languages

Describing things is a linguistic problem. Even concepts in formal logic have to be defined linguistically at some stage. One readily recognised distinction in descriptive labels is between natural language and artificial languages. For example, in a bookshop texts on economics are likely to be shelved by a sign bearing the label ECONOMICS. The very same books in a public library might bear the sign '330', the symbol denoting Economics in the artificial notation of the Dewey Decimal Classification. From the point of view of achieving an acceptable address, the labelling doesn't matter very much so long as it is intelligible and accurate.

From the point of view of achieving acceptable definition, the choice of notation, language, or meta-language doesn't matter very much as long as the description is sufficiently precise and intelligible for the purposes intended. It is common for a major distinction to be made between classification schemes based on artificial notations and natural language indexes. In natural language indexing systems, words or terms from the language of choice are used as descriptors. The simplicity is highly attractive. However, as increasing numbers of terms are used, various problems emerge.

Since terms in natural languages overlap in meaning and in appearance, some kind of control is usually imposed. Examples of these include homographs: two or more words spelled the same way but different in meaning. For example, the word CHARACTER means different things to a playwright, a typewriter mechanic, a theologian, and an architect. Similarly, information about a TANK that would interest a general would not necessarily help a plumber. In these cases, the terms need to be expanded or differentiated in some way, or else inappropriate signals are likely to be retrieved.

Different words for the same concept or entity cause other problems. A retrieval system with information under AGRICULTURE might yield nothing in a search under FARMING. Straightforward one-to-one relationships can be handled by imposing further control. Typically, one term becomes the 'preferred' term and the other term is used only for redirection. 'For FARMING see AGRICULTURE'. In practice, more difficult to handle are near-synonyms where the overlap is incomplete, e.g., AGRICULTURE and LAND USE. A list of subject headings, or thesaurus, enumerating terms and relationships between them and other terms is used. The process of control is usually known as vocabulary control or authority control.

Another complexity has to do with hierarchical relationships where material on a topic, such as dairying, can be found not only in books specifically on dairying listed under the heading DAIRYING, but also within more general books on agriculture listed under AGRICULTURE. Alternatively, there might be no general work on agriculture but books dealing with aspects of agriculture such as dairying, horticulture, aquaculture, and so on.

Retrieval systems vary in the extent and manner in which they contain references to narrower (more specific) topics and to broader (more general) ones. In practice, the topics of inquiry often require some complexity in description. Consider, for example, 'TEACHING METHODS IN INDIAN UNIVERSITIES FROM 1918 TO 1939.' Natural language indexing systems can handle such combinations (coordinations) of concepts in either of two ways. In a manual system, it is convenient to compose (pre-coordinate) a single (but complex) entry following agreed conventions concerning the order of the aspects of the concept.

In a traditional library subject catalog one would expect to find a book on this topic listed under a heading of the following form "INDIA, Higher education, 1918-1939. Teaching methods" and probably only under that heading. If this pre-coordination were not done, one would need to look at each item listed under INDIA, under HIGHER EDUCATION, under 1918-1939, and under TEACHING METHODS and select only those items which had been entered under all those labels. Technically, this is known as 'post-coordination' since the expression of the relationship the coordination—is done at the time of the inquiry, after the time of indexing.

In computer-based systems, where the computer can take on the chore of doing the 'coordinating', it is customary not to express the coordination at the time of indexing. Various appropriate index terms would be assigned. In a post-coordinate search, the searcher enumerates the index terms that are expected to be helpful in identifying desired material, and the computer assumes the task of finding the books which have been assigned whatever combination of terms the searcher has specified. In this example, one might try the following terms:

— HIGHER EDUCATION or POST SECONDARY EDUCATION or UNIVERSITIES

— TEACHING METHODS

— INDIA

One might also be able to specify the historical period though, in this case, it would probably be quite convenient to browse among the items retrieved by the above terms. These coordinate relationships can be ambiguous, since the mere occurrence of words may be insufficient to define the topic. A textbook example is the difference between a venetian blind and a blind Venetian. Similarly with the three words 'bites,' 'dog,' and 'man'—'dog bites man' is not the same syntactical relationship or meaning, nor is it as newsworthy, as 'man bites dog.' These relationships can properly be described as syntactical in exactly the same way that syntax denotes grammatical relationships. On the whole, syntactical relationships tend to be ignored in indexing languages, but there are notable exceptions. An often overlooked attribute of natural language indexing systems is that each system is natural to a particular time, place, and cultural environment. Subject headings used in the British

National Bibliography are different from those assigned for a comparable purpose by the U.S. Library of Congress.

Special groups of any kind—professional, social, technical, cultural, regional—will tend to use their own particular vocabularies. A natural language indexing system appropriate to one group is likely to be more or less unnatural and inappropriate to another. This limited applicability is also true to a lesser degree in the case of indexing languages with artificial notation in that they too reflect the conceptual arrangements of a particular group.

Classification schemes with artificial notation tend to have characteristics similar to those of natural language systems.

— Homographs are avoided since the concepts are identified and distinguished prior to the assignment of the labels.

— Synonyms should also be avoided since, having established a label for a concept, subsequent labels for the same concept need not be created.

— Hierarchical relationships need to be handled in the same sort of way. The relationships are typically embodied in the notation, e.g.,

942 History of India

942.7 History of Northwestern India

942.76 History of Bangladesh

942.769 History of Pakistan

— With complex topics such as "teaching methods in Indian Universities, 1918-1939," the same solutions are available as with natural language, e.g. 378.1709436 in the Dewey Decimal Classification.

Since most existing classification schemes are designed for human rather than computer use, complex precoordinate labels are used. Pre-coordination, however, is not a necessary characteristic of classification schemes with artificial notation any more than it is with natural language indexing schemes. It is true that most existing schemes are precoordinate, but in recent decades most thinking about classification has been based on analysis into a number of facets, which, in combination, define the topic concerned.

This faceted approach, which is detectable in revisions to existing schemes such as the Universal Decimal Classification (UDC), lends itself to post-coordinate searching by computer, because the elements which have been pre-coordinated remain identifiable could, therefore, be used for a post-coordinate search also. Natural language indexing systems and classification schemes with artificial notation are substantially similar in structure, controls, and uses.

A natural language indexing system with a fully worked-out relationship between topics will require the same degree of analysis and control as a classification scheme for the same range of topics. From this perspective, it seems helpful to regard them both as part of the generic category of indexing systems. The difference in notation is just one of the differences between them and not necessarily the most important. Other differences are as follows:

— Since the construction of a classification scheme with an artificial notation implies analysis of the relationships between topics, such schemes ordinarily have a great deal of syndetic control, i.e., rules concerning the preferred choice of indexing term and the relationships between terms. The development of syndetic control is not a necessary part of using natural language indexing systems, although it may be desirable. Consequently, the amount of syndetic control varies in practice from essentially none to very detailed control. Intuitively, it seems needed; in practice, there is some question as to whether the benefits justify the costs.

— A classification scheme with artificial notation will need a natural language index to it—a "relative index"—if it is to be conveniently used.

— Classification schemes with artificial notation permit the designer to arrange topics that are similar or related to be collocated. In natural language indexing systems, the juxtaposition of concepts will depend on accidents of spelling in the language concerned.

— The labels used in classification schemes with artificial notation tend to be shorter, though there can be considerable variations in this.

Indexing systems vary in several ways: in fineness of detail; in degree of vocabulary control; in syndetic structure; and in choice between pre- and post-coordination. The principal conclusions from tests of retrieval systems are that, despite these variations and the ingenuity of their designers, there is little difference between them in effectiveness, even though they tend to retrieve different material even when the same inquiries are posed in identical circumstances.

Categories of Information Retrieval Languages

The many information retrieval systems that exist can be divided into four major groups. Three of these groups index and retrieve works on the basis of their subject, that is, what they are about. The fourth works on other bases, for example, on the basis of having one work list another work as a source, such as in a footnote (citation indexing). Of the three groups that are based on the work's subject matter, the first indexes works with the actual words used in the documents themselves; that is, it uses their natural language. Since the terms used are not controlled in any way, this group is said to use an uncontrolled vocabulary. The other two groups use controlled vocabularies. One of these uses prescribed words to describe a work's subject. For example, for a work about professionals in the field of law, the prescribing authority might authorise the word lawyers as a retrieval term, but not the words attorneys or barristers. This group uses alphabetical systems. The third group uses notations, that is, numbers or letters or combinations to express subject matter: 723.1; *RpMsEn*; *NR716*. This group uses notational or classed systems.

Major systems from each group are discussed subsequently in this book, particularly in chapters five through eight, but it is essential at this point to visualise the basic differences between the alphabetical and the classed arrangements of a file, If the file is arranged alphabetically, works that are listed under the subject word lawyers are listed between works on lawns and works on lead poisoning. That is the nature of the alphabet. However, if the file is arranged in classed (grouped) order, works that are under the class notation for lawyers will be listed between other works on legal matters. In the Dewey Decimal Classification, for example, works on lawyers are listed between works on law in relation to groups of people, such as "The law and young adults", and works on law in specific countries. This is the nature of classification. Subsequent chapters will show that both arrangements serve useful purposes.

The rest of this chapter discusses the use of language in controlled and uncontrolled systems. Much will, perforce, be devoted to word-based systems.

The phenomenon of language, and of communication generally, may be considered at three levels:

1. The meaning or semantic level, that is, the meaning of the individual language element and of the complete statement.
2. The structural or syntactic level, which is concerned with the way in which the individual language elements are joined together to form statements.
3. The effective or pragmatic level, which is concerned with the effects that statements have. At the pragmatic level, there is need to concern ourselves not only with language itself, but also with its users, because their relationship to the language and to each other affects the result that a statement may have.

The individual elements of a language are usually referred to as words. Words themselves are often divisible into two parts. The first part is the stem, which is the semantic portion of the word. The second part, consisting of affixes and infixes, is syntactic in nature, because it indicates the relation of the stem to the stems of the other words in the statement or sentence. For example, in the phrase *its effect*, the *s* in *its* is an affix indicating the possessive relationship to the following word *effect*. For this and other similar reasons, the individual meaningful elements of a language are sometimes called semantemes. The totality of semantic elements in a language—all the semantemes—are referred to as its vocabulary. The structure of the language is its syntax or grammar. Our immediate concern is with the semantic and syntactical levels of language. However, in designing and evaluating online catalogues, we must pay considerable attention to the needs of the clientele for whom they are created and, therefore, we must pay significant attention to the pragmatic aspects of language as well. All three levels—syntactic, semantic, and pragmatic—are important in information retrieval, because they affect the use and the effectiveness of an information retrieval system.

The differences between semantic and syntactic relationships are not absolute and precise, but we can state simple rules based on our definitions. First, a syntactic relationship exists between two terms in a statement. Second, a semantic relationship exists between terms that are defined in a vocabulary as having meanings that are in some way related. Syntactic rules determine how words within a statement are sequenced and interrelated so that the statement becomes meaningful. The statements "They are eating" and "They eating are" exemplify where syntactic rules operate. Although both statements contain the same words, according to rules of syntax only one of them is correct and meaningful. Examples of semantic relationships appear among terms such as heating, electric heating, plasma heating, heat, and temperature. The meanings of these terms do not completely overlap with one another. Nevertheless, we recognise that they are related in some manner.

Semantic relationships exist independently of statements; that is, two terms may have a semantic relationship even if they are not used together in any statements. Conversely, syntactic relations exist only in statements. However, the same relationship may be regarded as either semantic or syntactic. For example, we may consider the phrase *high schools* to consist of two elements, *high* and *schools*, which are syntactically related; or we may consider it to be a single element, which is semantically related to a broader element, *schools*, and to a narrower element, *junior high schools*. In the following sections, the notions of semantics and syntax from the perspective of information retrieval are explored in detail.

Semantics is the study of meaning. Words have two kinds of meanings. First, words "mean" the things to which they refer (denotation), so that *cat* means a small furry domesticated animal. Denotative meaning is, and must be, shared among members of the society in which the words are used, for otherwise communication would be impossible. Second, words have a significance for the individual in personal terms. For some people, the word *cat* signifies pleasure; for others, it indicates unpleasantness. This is not usually because of the word itself, but because of the attitudes which individuals have towards the animals (connotation). The distinction between denotative and connotative meanings is reflected in the fact that some subjects have "hard" terminologies, in which there is little or no disagreement about what the words mean. These terms will have the same import for the author of the document, the indexer, and the inquirer. Other subjects have comparatively "soft" terminologies; there is little or no agreement on the meanings of words. The same word may be used in different senses by different users at different times. This obviously reduces the value of these words for indexing and retrieval purposes.

In literature, words may be used to convey ideas that do not directly relate to the author's purpose. To say that "The Rime of the Ancient Mariner" is about water, for instance, is to miss the point; to index it as though it were prevents those who want to see the poem from finding it, but may retrieve it when it is not wanted.An aspect of meaning that has particular relevance for indexing, because of its bearing on vocabulary control, is the relationships between meanings, and therefore between the denotations of words used to represent them. Foskett noted three categories of relationships:

Equivalent

Hierarchical

Affinitive/associative.

Two expressions are equivalent when they denote the same referent. Synonyms are an obvious case of equivalence, as are variations in spelling and wordform, and acronyms and abbreviations. Examples of such equivalences are 1. D. Cards and Identification cards; SDI and Strategic Defence Initiative; Colour pigeons and Color pigeons. Translated words are also (usually) equivalent. Note that there are degrees of equivalence: some words overlap the meaning of others but do not mean the same thing, such as animals and zoology.There are two hierarchical relationships: genus-species and whole-part. For instance, Homo sapiens is a species of the genus Homo. All of Homo sapiens belongs to the genus Homo, but only some of the species which belong to the genus Homo belong to the species Homo sapiens. An example of whole-part relationship is camera and camera lens. An example of a group of words that bears affinitive relationships is teaching, learning, education, training, and teachers. Education and teaching are concurrent activities, while teaching (one hopes) bears a cause-and-effect relationship to learning, and the teacher is the agent of this activity. The difficulty that arises with these kinds of relationships is that, unlike equivalence and hierarchical relationships, affinitive relationships are dependent on context. Education may imply training, and training is frequently a part of education, but it cannot be assumed that training necessarily implies education. Decisions about affinitive relationships cannot easily be built into the indexing language or into the system of which the language is a part; they must be made on an individual basis.

A statement consists of elements from the vocabulary of a language joined together in such a way that it has more meaning than a simple list of the same elements. The additional meaning is given to the statement by its structure, or syntax, because it shows the relationships between the elements. Syntactical relationships in statements may be shown in two ways. One of these is their order or sequence. A given group of words will make sense only in one sequence:

The lady is smiling

The smiling is lady

The order (syntax) can sometimes even reverse meaning:

Man bites dog

Dog bites man

The second method of showing syntactic relationships is the use of markers. In natural language, these may take the form of inflections or may be prepositions (such as of). For example:

The dog's hair

The hair of the dog

It should be noted that, although we can differentiate the two ways of showing syntactical relationships, we cannot necessarily separate them; we may have to use both together. The markers may determine the order of elements in natural language (we do not say "the hair dog's").

Vocabularies

An information system may help the user by explicitly assigning index terms (that is, words or notations) to the documents and controlling, at least in the case of alphabetical (word) systems, the semantic and often the syntactic relationships between these index terms. The words (which may be subject headings or descriptors) are assigned from nationally recognised subject heading lists or thesauri, and the notations from nationally recognised classification schedules, and thus use controlled vocabulary. The Library of Congress List of Subject Headings is an example of a controlled alphabetical vocabulary, and the Dewey Decimal Classification is an example of a notational vocabulary. An alternative to this approach is to let all meaningful words that occur in the title of the document, abstract, contents note, or even the text itself be index terms. In this case, the system does not impose any semantic or syntactic controls over the index terms. Such terminology is called uncontrolled, or natural language, vocabulary.

Controlled vocabulary

A controlled vocabulary is one in which there is only one term or notation in the vocabulary for any one concept: for example, the vocabulary might list relevant material under either the scientific nomenclature for species of animals, or under everyday terms (bovidae or cattle), but not under both. For word-based systems, the controlled vocabulary identifies synonymous terms and selects one preferred term among them. For homonyms, it explicitly identifies the multiple concepts expressed by that word or phrase. For example, the term Springs may represent either mechanical devices or sources of water. Therefore, the two notions must be distinguished by being described more precisely: "Springs (mechanical devices)", and "Springs (water sources)".Most, if not all, of the above-mentioned four tasks can be considered advantages. In addition, and perhaps more specifically, controlling an information retrieval vocabulary:

— Increases the probability that both indexer and inquirer will express a particular concept in the same way, so as to improve the matching process, and enable the inquirer to find what is being looked for.
— Increases the probability that the same term will be used by different indexers, or by the same indexer at different times, to assure consistency.
— Increases the probability that both indexer and searcher can be led to a desired topic, by the use of "see-also" references to related topics.
— Helps to speed the searching process by enabling the user to ascertain quickly that the item(s) of information sought are not available, since it ensures that there is no necessity to search under a wide variety of synonyms.

Bernier is a good example of the belief in "traditional virtues" of controlled vocabulary:

> the index assists the unknown searcher ... in bringing ... vocabulary into coincidence with that of the index by a proper choice of terms, by the use of accepted grammar, and by providing cross-references.... Word-indexing [that is, uncontrolled vocabulary] leads to omission of entries, scattering of related information, and a flood of unnecessary entries.

Users often come to information systems without a full realisation of what information it is that they need. For such cases, it is assumed that controlled vocabularies help users to focus their thoughts. Furnas *et al.* reported that random pairs of people use the same word for the same object only 10 to 20 per cent of the time. If there is such fundamental inconsistency in the use of vocabulary, uncontrolled retrieval vocabulary places burdens on users, because they must be aware of all the words other people might have used to describe one concept or thing. The problem of creating and using a controlled vocabulary is a very real one, because all the terms/ headings need to be linked syndetically into a single structure.A quite typical statement of the case for not controlling vocabulary was put forward by Klingbiel, who wrote:

1. Highly structured controlled vocabularies are obsolete for indexing and retrieval.
2. The natural language of scientific prose is fully adequate for indexing and retrieval.
3. Machine-aided indexing of natural language text is within the state of the art.
4. Natural language retrieval can be conducted online if the request can be stated in a phrase or a sentence.

Klingbiel pointed out that experiments conducted in the 1960s appeared to show that the use of controlled vocabulary did not increase the effectiveness of retrieval systems. At the same time, too, it appeared to be the consensus that even if controlled vocabulary did improve retrieval performance, it did not do so to an extent that justified the added costs involved. Klingbiel stated in his point 2 that "scientific prose" is adequate for indexing. The language of science is highly controlled and standardised, because all sciences tend to be taxonomic In nature, taxonomy implies definition and, therefore, control of the meaning of words. However, it is wrong to generalise from science in particular to written language in general, because research has also shown that precision of terminology used in a text, or in the title of a text (and therefore needed for uncontrolled retrieval), varies with the field. Buxton and Meadows, for example, showed that the use of informative words in titles of articles (that is, the kinds of words that would be logical to use in uncontrolled retrieval) ranges from very high in journals of chemistry and of botany to very low in the social sciences, with philosophy lowest. Many similar findings have been reported since then.

Uncontrolled vocabulary

An uncontrolled, or natural language, or free-text, vocabulary is one that uses the actual words of a document as index terms. Indexing that uses uncontrolled vocabulary is also referred to as derived, because the terms used in the index are directly taken (or derived) from the text of the document, or from some description of it, such as its title or an abstract. In an indexing system that uses uncontrolled language, no effort is made to control the semantic relationships among the indexing terms. That is, a given concept may have been described, and therefore indexed, under two or more different terms, with no links among those terms available to the user of the retrieval system. Based on the nineteenth-century technique of catchword title indexing (that is, listing a work under the word in its title that best expresses what the work is about), uncontrolled vocabulary indexing was reintroduced by Hans Peter Luhn of IBM in 1959 in the form of KWIC (keyword-in-context). Each significant word in a title becomes an access point, printed in the middle of the line, with the surrounding words of the title on either side. Titles are thus listed under as many access points as there are "significant" words (keywords) in the title. Minor words such as articles, prepositions, and pronouns are not keywords.

Development of the computer permitted this technique to be expanded beyond the title. Keywords can now be taken from any term that can be fed into a computer: abstracts of documents, the text itself, and even words that are taken out of the controlled terms assigned to a document. The term keyword is now sometimes misused to include the concept of controlled terminology. Strictly speaking, however, keywords are uncontrolled derived vocabulary. An uncontrolled vocabulary will contain synonyms, near-synonyms, and variant word forms and spellings, including misspellings.

One of the advantages of using uncontrolled vocabulary is that the effort, and therefore the cost, required for indexing the document tends to be minimal. No personal examination of the document is needed to index it, no decision need be made as to what a document is about, and no effort need be expended to connect various synonyms by means of cross-references such as: "Inter-national politics, see World politics".The computer needs only to be programmed to accept every word in a given number of fields (such as the title or the abstract) as a keyword, except for selected minor terms, such as articles, which are put on a so-called stop-list. The user, in turn, who may look under one of several synonyms or near-synonyms (Parasites; Animal parasites; Entozoa; Epizoa; Pests) has, on the one hand, a good chance of finding at least something under whichever term he or she selects as a retrieval term. On the other hand, to get a full listing of relevant material on a topic the user must be aware of, and search for, all possible variations of a keyword, such as the variations of the keyword labor in the preceding example. This places a burden on the users of which they are not even likely to be aware. One way to get around this problem, at least to some extent, is the use of truncation: right-hand or left-hand truncation.

Right truncation allows a single expression to be used to represent a number of cognate words. For example, labo? can represent all variant spellings of the English-language term labour, laborers, etc., except, of course, for the misspelling labrer. The computer treats the question mark (or whichever symbol the programme requires) as a substitute for the missing characters in the various words which have the stem labo. By this means the user avoids the necessity of entering all variations of the truncated keyword, saving quite a bit of time.Similarly, left truncation can be used to allow for matching to be performed regardless of the presence of prefixes. For example, ?natal would match both prenatal and postnatal. Similarly, if the computer programme permits it, internal truncation can be used, so that lab?r matches both labor and labour- but not laborers.

Truncation, however, is not the full solution. It does not provide access to synonyms (Spectacles; Giasses) or to foreign-language equivalents, such as Arbeit, or travail for labor. Nor, if British documents are involved, does it provide access to British equivalents for American terminology, such as lift for elevator or, in the case of our labor example, trade instead of labour for terms such as trade unions instead of labor unions? For such cases, the user must think of appropriate terms if the vocabulary is uncontrolled.

Indexing Systems

Since the 1960s, much research has been done to test whether controlled or uncontrolled indexing languages provide better retrieval results and, in the case of controlled vocabularies, whether alphabetical (word) systems or notational (classed) systems provide better results One point that needed decision was the definition of "better" retrieval results. It is felt that a perfectly successful system retrieves all documents in a collection that provide the desired information (no only some of the documents) and provides only these documents (no also irrelevant ones). At first, researchers tended to think in either-or terms. A document either provided the desired information, or it did not; it either was or was not relevant. In the late 1960s, researchers like Saracevic began to introduce finer methods of distinction, such as relevant, partially relevant, and not relevant. This led to the use of the mathematical fuzzy set theory in information retrieval, by which it is said to be possible to list retrieved documents in probable order of relevance.

The first major comparative experimental study of indexing systems, the so-called Cranfield One study, concluded in 1962 that the performance of an indexing system depended not on whether it uses a classed or alphabetical indexing vocabulary, but on the power of the indexing language allied to the standard of indexing. It also introduced measurable concepts of retrieval performance in terms of precision (the proportion of retrieved documents that are relevant) and recall (the proportion of relevant documents retrieved as against those in the file that are not retrieved). Since that time, it has been generally accepted that these two measures have an inverse relationship: steps taken to increase recall decrease precision, and vice versa.

A second experiment, undertaken by the same researchers partly because the original project was criticised in reviews, concluded that natural language had a slight edge over controlled indexing vocabularies. For many years, this finding was accepted half-heartedly by most writers in the field, but experiments continued to be conducted. Interestingly enough, most of the actual online databases created since then, both files of documents such as the ERIC database and online public access catalogues (OPACs) like the University of Wisconsin-Madison NLS Catalogue, were programmed to accept controlled, or controlled and uncontrolled alphabetical subject vocabularies. This may have been an act of caution on the designers' part, or it may have been done merely because it is relatively easy to blend both systems in a computer programme.

In any case, by permitting access via both controlled and uncontrolled alphabetical indexing languages, the system designers anticipated at least some recent research results. Based on these results, controlled and uncontrolled—notational (classed) and alphabetical—vocabularies are not to be considered only as alternatives, but rather as complementary. Both have advantages in particular situations, and together they provide more comprehensive retrieval results than any one type of vocabulary by itself.

Raitt illustrated with numerous examples that neither the free text by itself, nor the controlled alphabetical vocabulary by itself, leads to complete retrieval of all pertinent documents. Based on experimental results Carrow and Nugent, Calkins, Schabas, Tenopir, and others found that controlled alphabetical and free-text vocabulary searches each produce unique, if overlapping, results. At the same time, OCLC, a large utility which controls millions of bibliographic entries, sponsored research on retrieval via the Dewey Decimal Classification (DDC), and found that this approach, too, has unique advantages. Conventional wisdom holds that searching by notation, and freetext searching, contribute to precision, and that controlled vocabulary serves primarily to promote recall. This theory is being increasingly challenged. For example, Svenonius pointed out that it has not been definitely proven, partly because so far most experiments have ignored the human factor when comparing the effectiveness of controlled versus free-text vocabularies; that is, they ignored relative searching skill or clumsiness.

Sievert and Boyce explained how, particularly in an online retrieval system, controlled indexing vocabulary becomes a precision tool rather than a broad recall tool. Svenonius also questioned, with a good deal of justification, the conventional belief that recall and precision must operate in inverse relationship. She suggested that "free-text and control led-vocabulary terms each contribute to precision and each to recall, but they do so in different ways, and it is the relative weight of the contributions that affects any given retrieval outcome." One undisputed fact is that, even at the expense of spending more time and money in a search, and at the risk of receiving marginal material along with truly relevant items, a combined classed vocabulary/controlled alphabetical vocabulary/ uncontrolled alphabetical vocabulary produces the most complete file. What needs much more testing is the precise advantages of each system, the precise situation in which each system shines, and the optimum combinations of systems for different retrieval situations.

Another way of classifying information retrieval systems is to group them by who or what builds the terms that permit retrieval. Who creates the semantics and syntax that permit retrieval: the indexer, the searcher, or the indexing language itself? The answer is, all three. If a controlled indexing language is used, a work on a plain topic such as weaving or ethics can be listed under a single subject label: under the word weaving, or ethics, or under the pertinent notations that mean, respectively, weaving or ethics. In the case of the Library of Congress Classification (LCC), this would be TS 1490 and BJ 37, respectively.Works that deal with the interrelationship of two topics, with more than one topic, or with special aspects of a topic, present greater difficulties. Four techniques exist for creating indexing terms for such situations.

1. A single subject label can express the interrelationship or special aspect.

   Subject heading:

   — Music and society (for a work on the role of music in daily life today)

   Descriptor:

   — Educational economics (for the economic aspects of education)

   DDC: 291.171 (for the role of religion in today's society)

   LCC: BF 56 (for the psychological aspects of economics)

These labels are called pre-coordinated indexing terms.

2. The system requires the indexer to combine language elements in order to create a viable index term.

   Faceted classification:

   The schedules contain the separate symbols G2 (College libraries), K4 (Periodicals), and M2 (Selecting resources), which the indexer combines into M2 K4 G2 (Selecting periodicals for college libraries) according to precise rules.

   String indexing:

   For a work on the uneasy relationship between the Sinhalese and the Tamils in Sri Lanka, the indexer analyses the various elements, and the computer program combines them into the string Sri Lanka. Tamils. Relations with Sinhalese, 1948-1984.

These systems are called pre-coordinated indexing systems, and the terminology is pre-coordinated indexing terms.

3. The system of limited pre-coordination does not permit the indexer to combine major, individually authorised language terms, but does permit combining a major term with a limiting auxiliary. Example: The system does not permit joining the separately authorised words or symbols for tennis and for gambling, in order to create the alphabetical or notational label for gambling on tennis games. It does encourage the joining of an authorised major term with an authorised limiting label to provide the desired accuracy of description, if the indexer judges it to be helpful to the searching process. Typically, in a small collection one tends to do less combining than in a large collection.

   Subject headings:

   Some labels listed in the authority lists are: Law; Labor supply; Windmills. Among terms that may limit the scope of these labels are: India; Periodicals; History. The indexer may combine these to result in: Labor supply-India; Law-Periodicals (for a periodical in the field of law); Windmills-History; Labor supply-History; Law-India; etc.

   DDC: The schedules contain symbols such as 070.4 (Journalism), 070.41 (Editorial Policy), Elements that can limit the meaning include 0207 (Humorous treatment) and 092 (Biography). The indexer can combine these into notations such as 070.40207 (a work ridiculing journalism) or 070.41092 (a biography of an editor).

Like the second technique, these systems are called pre-coordinated indexing systems, and the terminology is pre-coordinated indexing terms.

4. If it is linguistically not possible to combine language elements, the indexer may (or must) select more than one index term to describe the special aspect or the interrelationship.

Subject headings:

For a work on nickel and chromium plating, the two labels: 1. Nickel-plating. 2. Chromium-plating. For a work that describes tensions among the various social classes in France, the two labels: 1. Social classes-France. 2. Social conflict.

Descriptors:

Descriptor systems are designed to use separate indexing terms for each aspect of a document. A report on technology education in Oklahoma received the descriptors: *Curriculum development; Industrial arts; Program descriptions; Program development; Program implementation; Secondary education; State programs; Technology.*

Since it is only possible to retrieve a document with all of the characteristics described by the labels (such as nickel- and chromium-plating) by combining all indexing terms in the search, the searcher must construct the desired combination of terms. This technique is, therefore, called, post-coordination.

Note that in this technique one can assign pairs of pre-coordinated indexing terms as needed, such as Music and society and Black music for a work on the influence of black music on daily life. The various techniques affect the precision and recall of retrieval. For example, in technique 1, when a single phrase is used (Music and society) only material on that specific topic should be found, which is, of course, what is wanted. But in technique 4, use of the term Social conflict will return not only the work on social tension among social classes in France, but any work that deals with any aspect of social conflict. Recall will be high, precision low. String indexing and faceted classification schemes have precise semantic and syntactic rules that must be followed to have the system work. Other systems, such as subject headings and descriptors, have rather general syntactic rules and rather vague semantic rules—really more in the nature of guidelines that leave much to the designer of the specific vocabulary and to the indexer. This is not necessarily bad. The guidelines and rules are explained in works devoted to that topic. Sample semantic guidelines for subject headings and/or descriptors are:

— Use nouns or noun phrases. Use adjectives only as qualifiers: Democracy, not Democratic, But: Governmental investigations.

— For subject headings, find an indexing term that describes the work as a whole. If that is grammatically impossible, or if the work contains several separate topics, or if the topic can be viewed from different angles, assign more than one indexing term. The rule of thumb is "up to three terms", but use your judgement.

— In general, use the plural form for things that can be counted: Teeth, Stars, Students. Use the singular form for properties and things that cannot be counted: Executive ability; Cement; Conductivity.

With respect to pre-coordination of indexing terms (technique 1, above), the semantic rules for subject headings and descriptors are quite flexible and often subjective. For example, of a book on microbiological research, the authority list for the subject headings or descriptors for one field of study might authorise the two separate terms

1. Microbiology.
2. Research.

whereas the authority list for another field of study might authorise the pre-coordinated term

1. Microbiological research.

Both techniques are feasible. The decision is made on the basis of the authority list's policy (if there is one) or on the basis of frequency of occurrence: if several works exist, or are likely to be written, on microbiological research, the list will authorise the pre-coordinated term. Otherwise, it will authorise the two separate terms so that the searcher must post-coordinate. Pre-coordinated indexing terms have positive results, as previously mentioned. However, they also have negative results. For example, the term *microbiological research* separates that aspect of microbiology and of research from all other aspects of microbiology and from all other aspects of research. Specific, pre-coordinated indexing terms are not helpful to the searcher for broad topics.

Indexing systems which require or permit the indexer to build labels from individual language elements, in order to create a workable indexing term, are pre-coordinated and use pre-coordination. Indexing terms which combine several subjects in one label are pre-coordinated indexing terms. There are no post-coordinated indexing terms, but the searcher can, in some systems, combine individual language elements to produce a post-coordinated searching phrase.

A brief description of some major indexing systems are given below:

— *Descriptor system*. Word-based system, designed to assign controlled separate words or phrases to each aspect of a work, along with one or more terms that describe the work as a whole. May be pre-coordinated terms. Typically five to fifteen descriptors per document.

— *Enumerative classification system* (examples; DDC, LCC). Classification system that lists in the schedules whatever concepts it contains. The indexer may not combine concepts. For example, the concept "Mathematics for aviators" can only be expressed if it is listed in the schedules with a notation. Otherwise it must be classed either as Mathematics or as Aviation, depending on the rules of the system. Some enumerative classification schemes, like the DDC, also have limited synthetic features.

— *String indexing system*. A word-based system in which the indexer analyses the various aspects of a complex subject treated in a work, and records the aspects along with "role operators" (that is, instructions to the computer). The computer then combines these terms into a string of terms that is really a brief summary of the document's content. The computer automatically lists the string under each significant term that forms part of the string.

— *Subject headings system.* Word-based system designed to assign a controlled separate word or phrase to the work as a whole. If that is not grammatically possible, or if the work treats several independent topics, or a topic that can be viewed from several angles, more than one subject heading may be used. Subject headings may be pre-coordinated terms, usually one to three subject headings per document. The indexer may also assign additional, "analytical" subject headings which are designed to describe the content of a specific section in a work.

— *Synthetic classification system.* Classification system whose schedules tend to list not complete notations, but language elements, which the indexer is expected to combine into a complete notation. This permits the indexer to create notations that are as broad or as specific as seems suitable for a particular collection or database. The best constructed synthetic schemes are faceted classification schemes which break a field down into its component parts—that is, view it from all pertinent angles (like the facets of a diamond)—and assign symbols to each angle, which the indexer then combines into a notation according to precise guidelines.

Markers or Relators

Looked at from a grammatical point of view, each of the above-described indexing systems has semantic and syntactical rules. As mentioned, some of the semantic rules are rather casual and ad hoc. The syntactic rules are far more precise. The markers mentioned previously in the section on syntax, which decree the relationship of the various semantic elements and give them added meaning, also operate in information retrieval languages, where they have a variety of names. For the sake of simplicity, we use the term relators generically for all of them. A relator:

1. Indicates the relations between the semantic elements in an information retrieval statement.
2. May determine the order of the semantic elements.

3. Without itself being a semantic element, adds to the meaning of the statement (such as by avoiding ambiguity).

A precise relator rule for subject headings is, for example:

> For a topical work, use an indexing label that describes first the subject and then, as needed, the method of presentation: Education—Bibliography (for a biblio-graphy in the field of education), and Education—Periodicals (for a periodical in the field of education), not Bibliography—Education, not Periodicals— Education.

In this case, the dash is the relator between the subject and the dependent clause, the method of presentation. It has the effect of causing material on the same topic to be listed together, rather than material that is presented in the same format.

In PRECIS, which is a string indexing system, the relators are called "role operators". They show relationship and regulate the order in which the language elements will appear (without the relators) in the printed indexes that PRECIS is used to produce.

In the Universal Decimal Classification (UDC), which is a synthetic classification scheme, punctuation and mathematical symbols are used to distinguish otherwise identical symbols. The symbol 51 means mathematics, (51) means China, and (051) means 'in the form of a periodical'. A colon (:) between numbers means that both concepts are interrelated. Example:

Symbol for agriculture	63
Symbol for statistics	31

Therefore, Agricultural statistics 63:31

In the UDC, the relators clarify the meaning of a linguistic element and dictate their order. In faceted classification schemes, each aspect (facet) of a topic is typically described by a separate letter. For example, in a faceted scheme for ships and shipping, one facet might be for the purpose of the ships: pleasure craft, transport of goods, etc. The symbols for this facet might begin with the letter *P*: *P*1, *P*2, *P*2.3, etc. Another facet might be for the means of propulsion: by wind, by motor, etc. The symbols for this facet might begin with the letter *M*: *M*1, *M*5, *M*7.2, etc.

The standard letter/number symbols act as relators: they describe the aspect and regulate the order of combining facets into a complete notation.

Grammar of Post-Coordinate Searching

Austin distinguishes between two kinds of relationships, which he refers to as grammatical and logical. In the examples in the preceding section, the relationship, and therefore the role of the relators, is clearly grammatical; it affects the order of linguistic elements and enhances their meaning. In a post-coordinated system, grammar is less important; there, the logical relationships (the relators) are signified by the Boolean operators AND, OR, and NOT, and by parentheses. The terms Boolean operators, or Boolean logic, are named after the English mathematician and logician George Boole, whose set logic can be exploited for information retrieval purposes. The command languages used to activate computers, like other languages, have their own vocabularies and syntax. Although they generally do the same things, or enable the same things to be commanded, the commands vary widely with regard to both terminology and syntax.

It is not unusual for a reference librarian to have to learn five or six different command languages to be able to search in different databases. The differences are partly due to the origins of the command languages in, and their connections with, particular computer systems, and partly to attempt to improve the languages by making them easier to use or quicker in operation. Attempts are being made to create more uniformity among computer languages. The typical searching operation involves two steps or sets of steps:

— "Find" commands, which exist to show whether the database contains material on the desired subject(s), and how much.

— "Display" commands, which display the actual document descriptions on the screen.

A search for a simple topic may involve only one indexing term: "Find documents on the psychological aspects of education in general." This retrieves documents that have the Library of Congress subject heading label educational psychology. This retrieves documents that are listed only under this subject label, plus documents that have this label plus other subject labels such as Creative ability, Education- Nigeria, Problem children, Science-Experimentation, Sex differences in education, and others. Clearly, some of these documents are too specialised to answer this search question. They represent "false drops", that is, larger recall but less-than-perfect precision.

Unfortunately, most systems do not permit a command that says, "Find documents that are listed under term X and only under this term." Methods of broadening or restricting a search involve "ORing" and "ANDing." If a more precise topic, a smaller group of documents is desired, the search can be refined by using the Boolean operator AND. To check whether something is available on any possible connection between speaking more than one language and being a naughty child, one might use the command: "Find Problem children AND Bilingualism." "ANDing" limits search results. It cuts out all documents that are indexed under only one of these terms, but it includes documents that are indexed under both of these terms plus any others. Again, the search is bound to include some false drops.

To broaden a search, "ORing" is needed. This is especially necessary when uncontrolled vocabulary is used, since it is likely to include synonyms and near-synonyms such as Plant pathology as well as Plant diseases, and Pipe fitting as well as Plumbing: "Find documents indexed under the terms Space exploration OR Outer space research OR Planetary exploration OR Extraterrestrial exploration." This technique is also useful with controlled languages if several terms are likely to produce acceptable results.NOT is a limiting operator. It is used if material is wanted on a topic unless that topic is described with some emphasis on a specific other topic: "Find Recreational activities BUT NOT Social class," for a search for material that deals with recreational activities regardless of social class.

Contextual Attributes

Documents and data can have 'contextual' attributes assigned to them for the purpose of retrieval, such as author, publisher, and date of creation. Indeed, in academic libraries, more use is made of author entries in the catalogues than of subject entries. The principal means of arrangement and approach for archival materials is their administrative provenance.

Attributes of authorship and provenance can also have connotations of subject content. A citation, by means of which an author refers in one document to another document, implies a relationship between the two and constitutes *prima facie* evidence that if one document is relevant to an inquiry, so might the other be. Citation indexes can be viewed as a form of subject index even though the attribute that forms the basis for retrieval is citedness rather than a description of what the document is about. The argument is that the usual custom in scholarly research is to cite closely related work. Such citation is, therefore, indicative of a close relationship, usually in subject matter. Hence, the citation of one article by another generally implies similar subject matter.

Since the description is in the form of a citation, not in the inconstant terminology of subject indexes, a citation index has some advantages when it comes to the use of articles in foreign languages or on subjects without standardised terminology. A document description can be a surrogate description of a subject inquiry. This point has been stressed because of our assertion that retrieval is primarily a linguistic process, drawing on:

- *semantics*: the study of the elements of a language from the point of view of meaning;
- *syntax*: the study of the formal interactions that exist between the elements of language; and
- *pragmatics*: the study of the relationships between signs of linguistic expressions and their uses.

Since retrieval systems are based on indexing languages which share the attributes of ordinary languages, they derive from the culture of their context and their study can be asserted to be a form of linguistic study. We can note that this assertion assumes that linguistics does or can include the study of artificial languages. How far this assertion can be pushed is a matter for debate. It is suggested that all retrieval systems could be included on the grounds that all depend on indexing languages, that all indexing languages depend on the assignment of attributes and on the labelling of these attributes, and that a proper understanding of these systems depends on semantic, syntactical, and pragmatic analysis. This is more easily understood in the case of 'word'-based subject indexes than in others, but we speculate that it is also true of all 'non-word' indexes using artificial notation, all contextual indexes, all citation indexes, and even systems based on the statistical association of attributes of data or documents. So far, we have simply assumed that a 'descriptor', whether drawn from natural language or concocted in some artificial notation, can suffice to describe concepts. This is not the case. A descriptor can act as a label. It may also serve as an address. It may define the topic, more or less, but it is unlikely in all cases to provide sufficient definition to describe completely the topic in relation to other topics. The extent to which definition is needed will vary with respect to at least two considerations:

— The number of different entities to be described. In a trivial example of an information retrieval system that retrieves data concerning only two or three items, the need to define will be trivial.

— The definability of the entities concerned. It is clear that not all concepts are equally easily defined. Consider the following sequence of concepts:

    — Seat 34C on flight PA 6 from San Francisco airport on January 29, 1980.

    — An elephant

    — Heat

    — Lassitude

The airline seat is easily unambiguously defined. An elephant is quite difficult to describe but can be recognised from pictures. Once one knows what an elephant looks like, there is usually little doubt as to whether a particular object is an elephant or not. Heat can only be indirectly illustrated. It cannot be seen directly, though sometimes its causes or effects can be. It can be sensed, however, if one is close enough and it can be defined and measured in physical terms. Lassitude can be sensed and symptoms of lassitude can be observed. Not at all clear, however, is the relationship between lassitude and related concepts such as ennui, tiredness, weariness, exhaustion, boredom, etc.

Unlike the aircraft seat, the elephant, and heat, there would appear to be no precise accepted definition of lassitude. If one were to search in an information retrieval system for material about 'lassitude' one would probably have to try a variety of search terms, and the items retrieved as a result of the search would probably vary in the extent to which they were about lassitude. Areas of study appear to vary in the extent to which the concepts they deal with are definable.

Physical sciences tend to have 'hard', i.e., relatively definable concepts such as temperature, molecular weight, size, velocity, etc. This is reasonable since the physical sciences deal with physical objects and the physical relationships between them. The 'hardness' of these properties permits relatively easy measurement and calculation. One development can build upon another because the earlier achievements are clearly defined. The progress in achievement in the hard sciences is, in consequence, more palpable than in other areas of activity such as education, literature, political science, or social welfare.

The 'softer' areas tend to be those which deal with human behaviour and social values. Each area of study appears to have a characteristic degree of intellectual hardness/softness. There seems to be variation within areas and subjects may change in hardness/softness over time. In other words, definability does not appear to be itself a linguistic problem. If it were, then coining new words might solve many difficulties.

Rather, there appears to be something more basic that has effects which are difficult to handle linguistically. Bunge comments that vagueness or blurredness has no positive aspect and is a conceptual rather than a linguistic disease, hence it is rather more difficult to cure.

The extent to which formal, logical notation and quantification are used is an indicator of hardness. It is an imperfect one since the use of such notation and quantification is not necessarily appropriate or well rooted in realistic definitions. The terminology of hardness and softness is potentially misleading. One of the meanings of the word 'hard' signifies a firm consistency and its opposite is 'soft'. In that sense, the imagery of intellectual hardness and softness is appropriate. A different meaning of the word 'hard' is 'difficult'. For that meaning, the proper opposite is 'easy' rather than 'soft'. It is in the second connotation of hardness as an indicator of difficulty that this imagery is misleading with respect to intellectual hardness and softness.

The pages of formal notation and algebra which characterise writings in physics and chemistry look particularly unintelligible to the lay person. However, in an important sense it is even more difficult to make progress in fields where definitions are 'soft' and unreliable, than when they are relatively 'hard' and dependable. The foundations built by previous scholars cannot so easily be taken on trust but may need redefinition. New work may need to be built into rather than onto prior work. However one may view difficulty, let us simply accept that the definability of concepts—the intellectual 'hardness' and 'softness'—varies from one field of discourse to another.

To the extent to which terms are relatively low in definability, information retrieval is likely to be less satisfactory since retrieval, being a linguistic process, depends heavily on definitions. In view of the importance of definition in communication, one would expect definability to emerge as fundamental in information studies in general and information retrieval in particular.

Storer has referred to the distinction between hard and soft sciences as being possibly the most powerful single variable in explaining disciplinary differences in the cultural realm. So far, however, research appears to have been limited. Studies of the information gathering habits of social scientists indicate a general similarity with the habits of physical scientists. Hindle has suggested that in patterns in use of books and journals, softer subject areas are characterised by much more diffuse reading than harder subjects. Mooers describes information retrieval as 'communication through time'.

The image of information retrieval as communication through time helps explain the lack of direct link between the originator of the message and the recipient. One can readily imagine messages (data, documents) as having hooks (tags, labels, or descriptors) attached to them and then being placed in some timeless void where they remain until an inquiry in the form of a set of one or more hooks reaches into the same void and pulls back any messages which have one or more hooks coinciding with those of the inquiry.

However, as one starts to work around the edges of this definition it becomes a little frayed. In one special case of information retrieval, there is an attempt to minimise the lapse of time. This occurs when every new batch of marked and parked information is automatically searched for material pertaining to specific inquiries.

In professional jargon, a standing profile of reader's searches is routinely searched against a file in order to provide SDI. (selective dissemination of information). One might regard this as a sort of pre-emptive information retrieval, although the notion of a standing order would seem closer. Yet even here, some delay, even if minimised, is necessarily present because each of these processes of acquiring, marking, parking, and retrieving must take some time.

Even in prompt online processing, the indirectness and sequential, discontinuous, two-stage nature of the process necessarily involves some time. A different sort of problem emerges from other examples of communication which take time and which do not easily fit accepted definitions of informal retrieval. Although information retrieval can properly be regarded as communication through time, it is not the only form of communication in which time may be significant. Delay, one could conclude, is a necessary attribute of information retrieval but not exclusive to it.

In information retrieval, the indirectness or discontinuity of communication permits and, indeed, ensures delay over and above the time required for communication itself. The disadvantage of old catalogues is that older cataloging practice differs from contemporary cataloging in two ways. Descriptive cataloging has evolved over the years. More serious is the shift in terminology for describing things over the years. In all aspects of human activity, new terms are coined and existing words change their meaning. Language evolves. Objects themselves may evolve. Consider, for example, the computer. Its appearance, power, and function have all changed radically in less than half a century. Finding antiquated terminology in library and other sorts of catalogues can be a source of amusement, of irritation, and of failure to retrieve. Inevitably, the use of words reflects the parlance and perspectives of the day.

From the point of view of information retrieval, the shifting of word usage over time and the evolving of new concepts, objects, and terms will mean that the retrieval system itself tends to become less accurate and less effective over time. The already imperfect description and definition, which are pivotal to effective retrieval, get worse. Ideally, of course, the books should be recatalogued continually according to contemporary cataloging practice, especially with respect to the subject headings used to describe what they are about. This requires, however, relatively expensive intellectual labour and the cost and benefits need to be weighed against the alternative uses of such money as is available. Most library users would be properly upset if their librarians ceased to buy new books of current interest in order to divert resources to the recataloguing of old books which may be of limited interest.

Indirectness of information retrieval systems is the characteristic that the designers and operators do not know who will seek the indirect communication that the information retrieval system provides. Not only does one not know who, one also does not know why they will seek to use it or what perspectives and vocabulary they will have when they seek to use it. To some extent, this lack of prior knowledge is shared by other communication systems, notably in mass communication. One is, in general, unable to predict or later ascertain who heard a radio broadcast, read a newspaper, or heard a speech to a crowd how beneficial the message was to them.

In information retrieval situations, however, there is a further problem and that is that the user needs to define what it is that needs to be retrieved. The vocabulary of the would-be user is necessarily somewhat different from that of the designer of the retrieval system, since no two persons' vocabularies are exactly alike, and may be substantially different especially if the designer is distant in time, education, and culture from the would-be user.

This problem of predicting rather than knowing what each future user of the system is likely to ask for and how he or she is likely to ask for it has long been recognised. Indexing and cataloging are, in part, predictive pastimes since the formal description of what data represent and what documents are about has to be modified by estimation of the probability that they will be sought and of the probable ways in which they will be sought.

In practice, the importance of this indirectness varies according to the circumstances and, we suspect, with the degree of definability. The factors affecting definability are:

- The range of choices available: limited in most management information systems; unlimited in general libraries and archives.
- The definability of the things that might be retrieved: from specific aircraft seats to vague cultural concepts.

— The extent to which the individual seeking to use the system can describe what he or she needs to reduce distressing ignorance: from a telephone number to, say, background material on stoicism in modern Western culture.

It is the fact of indirectness which permits the matching of definitions and it is the fact of time which inhibits adaptation of the system to the user. The user can, heuristicly, learn to understand the system better and the system, if computer-based, might be programmed to facilitate this heuristic learning. With either manual or computer-based systems, other humans can, and often do, play a mediating role, as, for example, in doing a literature search on behalf of someone else who is too busy or less familiar with the retrieval systems available.

Design, Use, and Evaluation

Design, use, and evaluation of retrieval systems depend heavily on various sorts of relatedness. There have been two problems in discussions of this area: the elements and relationships have not always been analysed in enough detail; and the terminology has not always been clear and consistent. The utilisation of retrieved data has not always been adequately distinguished from the retrieval process and the term relevance has been loosely used for more than one sort of relatedness.

The mechanism by which retrieval systems operate is the association of arbitrarily chosen but predetermined attributes of the set of data that is to be susceptible to retrieval. The attributes that are used include authorship, date of publication, age, occurrence of words, and so on. The list of possible attributes that could be used seems endless: location, size, chemical process, origin, etc. Nor need attributes be used alone: systems retrieving bibliographical data, for example, commonly operate on two or more attributes in combination, e.g., authorship, date of publication, language, and subject matter.

Writings about retrieval and especially about the evaluation of information retrieval systems have been dominated by just one of the apparently unlimited range of attributes: subject matter, i.e., what documents are about. The term 'aboutness' can be conveniently defined as referring to a coincidence of concepts, that is to say, if a book is 'about' India, we infer that the book contains concepts that we associate with the subject 'India.' If it did not do so, we should deny that the book is 'about' India. This is not entirely an objective matter since concepts have to be perceived and there may be some scope for disagreement in the perceptions by different people as to the concepts they perceive in a book and even in the concepts they associate with the subject 'India'.

Hence, there is scope for honest difference of opinion as to what a book is about. Consider, for example, an allegory. A person who fails to perceive the allegorical symbols will have a different opinion concerning what the text is 'about' than someone who does perceive them.

In an extreme case, most persons who saw a book on Buddhist mythology written in Tibetan would be able to perceive so little of the concepts that they would, if honest, have to say that they did not know what the book was about. This is a matter of conceptual perception as well as a linguistic problem. If the book on Buddhist mythology were translated into a language they could understand, then, if the concepts were unfamiliar, they would probably still understand little of what the book was about. It is unwise to assume that a document has a single subject matter.

There is also the problem of the definability of the concepts. Even with accurate perception, if there is not a rigorous, exclusive, unambiguous use of terms, the defining of the concepts perceived in the book may vary from one reader to another. This might simply be a matter of using alternative and equivalent synonyms.

However, to the extent that concepts are not susceptible to description in unambiguous terms—they are vague or 'soft'—then it is to be expected that statements by different individuals as to what a book is about, i.e., which set of concepts they perceive to be represented, will vary. The scope for honest disagreement concerning what something is about is important.

However, in any given point in linguistic and cúltural time and space, there is likely to be a great deal of agreement. If there were not, then subject indexes would not work. On the assumption that indexes are expected to indicate what things are about, one can state that the effectiveness of indexes depends on and is determined, in part, by the degree of uniformity in perception of concepts, and common definition and labelling of those concepts.

Retrieval using the attribute of what documents are about has been and can be expected to be of primary importance since subject access is difficult, useful, and technically interesting. It has dominated so much that it has, perhaps, hindered clarity of thought about the foundations of information retrieval theory. Retrieval by 'aboutness' has to be seen as the use of one attribute among many.

If reading a document and being informed by it leads to an enhanced state of knowledge which enables one to achieve some goal, then we can describe that process as having been beneficial or useful—as having utility. We need to note two other outcomes: having a harmful effect, sometimes referred to awkwardly as a 'negative utility', 'disutility', or 'disbenefit'; and having no known effect that could be regarded as useful or harmful—no utility or benefit.

Utility is meaningful only in terms of some objective, explicit or implicit. Giving somebody money has the property of utility if becoming wealthy or purchasing things are goals for that person; if that person were trying to achieve spiritual growth through poverty, then the gift of money would be unhelpful—of negative utility. Utility, then, is in all cases dependent on an objective. People have objectives. Inanimate objects do not. Organisations have objectives only to the extent to which individuals and groups have objectives which they seek to achieve through the organisation. Hence, utility is dependent not only on an objective but on the objective of one or more persons.

Let us look how information retrieval and the manner in which it might have utility. In principle, it would seem that being informed might assist in any of the objectives that one or more individuals might have: spiritual, physical, intellectual, professional, or social. These objectives might also be hindered. An obvious example of harmful information would be information that was, in fact, misinformation. The objective of getting from San Francisco to New York is likely to be hindered if one receives inaccurate information about the departure time of the airline flight and, as a result, misses the plane. Even so, although inaccurate information is likely to be the major cause of disutility associated with information retrieval, it is not necessary or proper to equate disutility with inaccuracy since it can happen that accurate information can also hinder the achievement of objectives. If the utility derived from information retrieval can pertain to any human objective, then it is only to be expected that some of these objectives will appear obscure. They might seem irrational to other people. They might be kept a secret. They might lie deep in the subconscious and not be recognised even by the individuals concerned. They can be expected to reflect values of a very private nature as well as publicly proclaimed ones. There may be inconsistencies between professed objectives and those actually pursued.

Implications for Information Retrieval

An ideal information retrieval system would retrieve data and documents that would assist individuals in the pursuit of their objectives, i.e., values. This implies that the information retrieval system should be concerned with the utility of what is retrieved rather than what it is about, since utility, not aboutness, is the goal. In order to achieve utility, the ideal information retrieval system would need to know the objective(s) and value(s) of each user.

Since redundant information does not help achieve goals and may hinder their achievement, the information retrieval system would, ideally, also have to know the state of knowledge of the inquirer—both its extent and its limitations. Avoiding the retrieval of unneeded and unusable data is, after all, a major purpose of information retrieval systems. If a researcher sought material relevant to an inquiry concerning Freud, it is unlikely that it would be helpful to retrieve a document that had been written by that same researcher, even though it may be related to the subject of the inquiry. It is not practical by any known technique to expect to know all of the objectives of people currently using an information retrieval system. It is still less reasonable to expect to be able to predict what future users' objectives and values might be. Even if one could, the most useful set of retrieved documents is likely to be unique for each inquiry.

Since each person's mind is unique, even objectives that are ostensibly the same for different people may be different in practice. What is more, since redundant information is to be avoided, subsequent inquiries concerned with the same person's objective would call for different responses since the individual's state of knowledge will probably have changed in the meanwhile. Some things will have been learned, others forgotten.

An ideal information retrieval system based on utility would have a formidable set of design requirements. It would need to understand objectives that present inquirers might not be willing to admit to or might not consciously understand fully themselves; it would need to predict which persons might use the system in the future and what their objectives might be in that future; and it would in each case need to know not only what the individual's objective is but also that same individual's state of knowledge not at the point in time that the inquiry was made but at the point in time that the data are retrieved. This would have to be true for each and every individual who may come to use the system.

What should be retrieved should vary even for different posings of the same question by the same person. All this is quite apart from the fact that the concepts and definitions used may be more or less ambiguous. Although such an ideal system would seem to be what is needed, the compounding of inherently improbable achievements one upon another means that this ideal system is most likely to remain an inspiring but unrealised achievement. The notion of imagining what future inquiries might be posed may very well be a useful device, but the combination of needing to know objectives, values, and future states of knowledge casts grave doubt on the achievability of such an ideal system.

Indexing and retrieving books according to what they are currently perceived to be about is, therefore, a more practical matter than indexing them in relation to potential future inquiries. If indexing and retrieval based on aboutness is more practical than indexing with respect to predictions of future inquiries and future knowledge, how does aboutness relate to utility? The answer would appear to be two-fold:

— If we hold relentlessly to the importance of utility, we can still regard aboutness as a sensible predictor of utility to the inquirer. If we seek to reduce our ignorance about Freud, a document about Freud is likely to make us more fully informed about Freud. Further, although this process does nothing to minimise the retrieval of knowledge that we already know, this redundancy is at worst inefficient rather than misleading since we can, presumably, ourselves filter out subsequently that which is already known to us.

— The attribute used as a basis for retrieval would be its subject aboutness. Although a subject retrieval system could operate in isolation, this is a singularly unrealistic and unnecessary assumption, since constant use is in fact made of other attributes of identifying documents which might be useful.

In libraries, a common mode of approach is to use the author's name as a means of identifying books on a subject on which it is thought that person might have written. Citations, by means of which an author refers in a document to another document, imply a relationship between the documents. The success of the various citation indexes is clear evidence of their value in supplementing subject indexes. Further, a part of the formal information system is the information specialist who operates and may have designed it. Users of archives depend heavily on the archivist for guidance. Librarians have always included in their role the drawing on their experience with bibliography, with their collections and with their users in order to assist users. Information retrieval based on what documents are deemed to be about can be expected to work moderately well in practice because there is more or less consensus on what documents are about, because 'aboutness' can plausibly be regarded as predictive of utility, and because, in practice, subject indexing is supplemented by other indicators of probable utility.

Information retrieval based on 'aboutness' lends itself to automatic indexing since the occurrence and more especially the co-occurrence of terms in the text can indicate the apparent subject content of the document. This may be expensive and error-prone, but results likely to be of some use can be achieved. The very same reasons which make the ideal information retrieval system unlikely also make implausible the concept of an 'information counsellor' in any sophisticated sense. Any person knowledgeable about sources of information can, in general, be helpful.

Quality Issues

Manually, bibliographic publishers and indexing firms created their products. But with the introduction of mainframe computing, obvious application of the technology was to automate the publication of these types of products. The original use of their computers was for publishing in print, but some early online industry visionaries saw that the by-product electronic file could be used for Boolean searching. This was pretty much the model in the 1970s—bibliographic files were the foundation, and some directory-type files followed. The publisher of Nexis launched Nexis, a service with the full-text of newspapers, magazines and newsletters. Besides enabling a user to search on every word of every article in the publications it carried, Nexis allowed for the retrieval and printing of the entire article in ASCII format. Why has full-text online caught on so dramatically? Its importance has become much more apparent since the spiralling cost of serials has undermined many institutions' ability to own and archive several years of various titles. Access to articles has overtaken the need to *own* them. Full-text online solves several problems, including space constraints, copyright compliance and royalty payments, and precision of searching. While ASCII full-text may seem to be the focus today, we can look to a future where exact images and searchable full-text will somehow be combined. Most publishers of newspapers, magazines and newsletters are primarily in the business of producing print products, even if they are automating that process or using an in-house desktop publishing system. These publishers must consider many factors when deciding whether and how to allow the public electronic access to their products.

Factors Controlling Online Availability

Among the factors controlling online availability are legal, financial and technological concerns, as well as data integrity and quality. While some of these may seem irrelevant to customers, they can determine if and where a title becomes available electronically.

Technological Factors

Much to the amazement of some online searchers and end-users, for many publishers the technology is nowhere nearly as sophisticated as one would imagine. Automating the publication of print products was undertaken to get the product to press more productively. Thus, some publishers cannot yet provide electronic copy to online services due to complex coding in the copy which needs additional programming to strip down to ASCII. One major search service in particular has eight pages of file formating specifications. FORBES is currently photo-composed electronically using Atex software, a fairly standard system for publishing. Atex was created to assist in layout, photo-composition and delivery to printing plants, not for creating machine-readable and text-searchable databases. Thus, the electronic copy has all the Atex photo-composition codes embedded in the files and would require a separate software routine to strip them out. It would then require programing for each of the ten different database producers to meet their specifications.

With only one bi-weekly title, there is no economy of scale. Therefore, arrangements with seven of these producers call for a slightly lower royalty rate when electronic copy is not provided, meaning that seven companies *each* key the title in manually. Publishers take great care to make sure their publications go to press as error-free as possible, and have reputations riding on this commitment, so they are naturally concerned about errors made by others.

Although the original magazine is perfectly spelled, it is possible for each of the seven different companies to make separate but equally damaging typographical errors. This, in turn, means that you may not be able to retrieve articles from FORBES because someone else typed a name or company incorrectly—and different errors might be made on each system. To give an example of this, there are three places on one host system where Forbes had correctly spelled the name of Mr. Mitterand, but the name was keyed in wrong by the database producer. In two of these cases, it is a unique mention of the name, which means that neither of these articles would be retrieved when a searcher inputs the name correctly. Where FORBES is accepted electronically by a database producer, such as Ebsco Publishing, the process is begun at Forbes. When an issue is released for publication, the files or 'stories' are down-loaded from the Atex system onto a DOS platform. They are then copied onto floppy diskettes and mailed—not sent via modem—to Ebsco. At this point, the files are in Atex/ASCII format. Ebsco down-loads the files onto its network, strips the Atex type-setting codes from the data, and adds special text tags which allow elements of the articles to be recognised electronically. Several software routines are run on the files to ensure accuracy, including, in certain cases, a visual comparison with the hardcopy. Finally, the files are sent to Ebsco's production facility. This process can take up to two weeks, the span of one FORBES publishing cycle. The process described is similar to that used by the other database producers to upload the text onto their systems. Forbes is in the process of implementing a new editorial system which will have the capability of providing better electronic copy, but this feature is one of the lower priorities in getting the new system up and running.

Quality concerns arise when publishers employ certain typesetting fonts that can 'confuse' the scanner. Consider the word 'modern'. When the type is set tightly, the n and the 'r' and the 'n' are quite close together; often, this causes the scanner to read the word as 'modem'. Since 'modem' is a word in the English language, a spell-check would not necessarily catch this error. When errors show up in articles from a reputable magazine, the reputation of the editorial product suffers, through no fault of the original publisher. As one can imagine, this is not an attractive scenario to most publishers.

Economies of scale have enabled some publishers to produce in-house tapes for vendors. One publisher in particular, which has almost thirty titles available online, employs a licence negotiator and technical staff to produce tapes according to the specifications of each online host they work with. Thus, you will find their combined file of publications on Dialogue and Dow Jones News/Retrieval, and each of the titles as a separate file on Nexis. In this case, any "selected" full text will be decided by the original publisher, not by an intermediary database producer's editorial department. In this instance, the publications are online cover-to-cover. Each publication cycle, tapes are produced for each vendor. Any typographical errors in these files will be found in the print originals as well. The only 'quality' issue encountered here is making certain the fight tape reaches the right vendor. A mistake will delay loading of the files and their availability within the advertised time period. Of course, when the publisher does not have to pay an intermediary company a portion of the royalties paid by the host system for the file, this kind of venture becomes more profitable for them. Companies in this position will probably be quicker to adapt, in the future, to technology that allows for image transmission as well.

Newsletters are primarily found online in two places, NewsNet, a freestanding online service, and the predicasts family of databases (on Dialogue, Nexis and Data-Star). Each company approaches the business differently. In the case of Predicasts (now owned by IAC/Ziff Davis), the files are transmitted electronically to the database producer (Predicasts), which formats them for their own files, adds index terms, and then does the negotiation and loading with the search services. Publishers run the gamut of technical sophistication and Predicasts has several options for them. About 10 per cent of Predicasts newsletters are keyed in. Another 25 per cent or so are shipped on floppy disks in ASCII. If necessary, Predicasts will convert data into ASCII from a publisher's file. The remaining 65 per cent of publishers send the ASCII text via modem. Once the copy has reached Predicasts, it is tagged, coded, indexed and loaded onto the next release to each of the host services. NewsNet, by contrast, is a search service in its own right. Like Nexis, it mounts each title as a separate file.

Almost every file is created from full-text ASCII files telecommunicated directly to NewsNet's data centre by the original publishers. These files are then processed by the publishers themselves through a proprietary error-checking program resident on the NewsNet mainframes. If the program detects errors, they must be corrected by the publisher and the file reprocessed until it is 100 per cent effort-free. To this point, each publisher has control over file integrity. Once released by the publisher, the files are processed further by NewsNet.

The availability of newspapers online has increased in the past several years. Dow Jones, Dialogue, NewsBank and Nexis carry the full-text of many years DataTimes full-text of many newspapers, online and/or on-disc. In England, the *Financial Times* has been online for years, as have the *Independent* and other major newspapers. For information on which newspapers are available on what search services, reference can be made to BiblioData's *Newspapers Online*, which covers major international newspapers with articles online in full-text. As of the 1993 edition, international papers must be accessible through a US host in order to be included, but their entry will carry references to non-US hosts that also carry that title. The primary reason that one can find newspapers online and on-disc in full-text is because the technology for producing the print copy—the publisher's primary business—was automated to enable the print product to go to press more easily.

After a number of years, the hardware and software developed to allow for more sophisticated uses of this automation, and newspapers began using the technology to replace their expensive, labour-intensive clip files with an electronic in-house 'morgue'. This enabled journalists and editors to perform research on their own newspaper electronically. In fact, both DataTimes and Vu/Text began as newspaper service bureau which developed software specifically for the newspaper morgue function.As of the end of 1992, Vu/Text was relieved of the search service function by its corporate owner, Knight-Ridder, and now exists only as a service bureau. Dialogue, another Knight-Ridder subsidiary, has taken over almost all the newspaper data bases from Vu/Text. Generally, newspaper libraries have staff who index each article in every version of the paper, as part of the process of publishing the paper and storing it archivally. Field tags are consistent for internal and database publisher requirements, as are index terms. The index terms are created by each newspaper for its writing staff to use in retrieving past articles, rather than for external database searchers. There is little consistency from one newspaper to another, even on the same search service, which is why using index terms on this type of full-text file is usually not productive.

Newspapers are now engaged in developing or purchasing the technologies for their futures. This should produce even more changes in this sector of the text retrieval business. The transmission of data will probably be much faster than we could have imagined a few years ago. Data compression techniques will continue to be improved, and new infrastructures will allow for larger masses of data to be sent simultaneously. Many papers already transmit via satellite to remote plants. Information intermediary companies such as NewsBank and Dialogue have acquired licence agreements for newspapers for CD-ROM products. When a title becomes available on CD-ROM in full-text, publishers are often apprehensive that the market for their online version will be cannibalized, but this has not yet come to pass. At this time, much of the major US press is available on CD-ROM in libraries, universities and corporations all across the country. While it varies from vendor to vendor, the searching of ASCII text at a customer-owned work-station is a fairly new concept. Financial, legal and business factors will determine how widely available such systems become. But once those factors are ironed out, the ability for a worker to search the full-text of a newspaper at a fixed price will begin to have the same type of effect that CD-ROM index products had.

Once the product can be transmitted with graphics, what information practitioners, and probably most end-users, will really want is to be able to search the text as well. This is known as 'text-searchable image'. Sooner or later, it will be a part of our lives; whether sooner or later is the only variable. Images will be easier to digitise for transmission and/or storage. Instead of keeping physical copies of photographs or charts, the system will be able to store them digitally. With the correct indexing and location mapping, retrieval will be not only more accurate, but perhaps even enhanced. This will be part of the production phase of the publication itself, not an afterthought for which indexers and searchers will have to clamour. Customers are likely to see image-based, full-text searchable products for newspapers sooner than for magazines. Companies are very involved in automating the publication of journals and books with graphics, and it is likely that European and Far Eastern companies are in the game as well.

The trade association for newspaper publishers and some newspaper librarians are working on standards for this image-based future, but the technology has moved so fast that many papers are not waiting to create their own files. What we will probably see is a UMI Business Periodicals On-disc model, with an ASCII-based database front end which can be free-text searched, and an image file behind it for retrieving. Whether the file is prepared by an indexing/abstracting company or by the publisher, once it is sent to the host system, there may be further problems which affect the retrieval of the full-text. Some service bureau used by publishers for processing data still are not equipped to handle tape cartridges, which have become the preferred way of storing files. This can cause delays in delivery to search services. Even though most providers have migrated from magnetic tape to tape cartridges, and most use overnight delivery services as opposed to the postal service, some tapes still arrive physically damaged. This is less common than it used to be, but it can still affect online availability. Another factor might be the widespread availability of a file on many host systems, each of which has a different loading priority for that file. For example, it stands to reason that a Swiss newspaper database might have loading priority at DataStar over a file with Australasian newspapers. However, on a US or a Japanese host, that Swiss paper might be very far down the priority list. A search service must rank the priorities of its clients. This reality, while not always on the mind of the seeker of information, certainly affects perceived availability. If one seeks to read the latest issue of FORBES online, one finds that it is available on certain services faster than on others, depending on whether that service accepts the electronic copy, and on how high a priority they think the title is for their customers.

In a series of interviews performed in 1990, we learned of several other interesting matters concerning online host services which affect the timely availability of files. One host service reported that they load files around the clock, in three eight-hour shifts. This includes reloading entire files as well as updates. The loading queue is so long that the process is performed nonstop. The scheduling for this queue must be done fairly far in advance, which can have a negative effect on publishers who are considering back-loading full-text to increase the coverage of a title. It also means that corrections to current full-text files may take longer to get on us. The other primary factor is the cost incurred by publishers. If the royalties collected do not cover the cost of maintaining and loading the files, the publishers will not get, or remain, involved in the online process. The inherent limitations of this software have begun to hamper the implementation of full-text files. Since the software was designed for files with size-delineated fields, adding full-text does not allow for effective searching by limiting terms to the same text paragraphs. A capability that might normally be assumed by people seeking to search and print full-text is not easily implemented by software that was originally designed to do something entirely different. There is a long way to go before we see the ideal search environment for full-text files.

Legal factors

Most publishers are attracted by the promise of royalties from information providers and search services, but do not realise the overhead expenses involved in this business.

Licence agreements must be drawn up which are practical for both parties. This is a time-consuming process, since many print publishers do not really understand the issues which must be addressed. Obvious issues include setting the royalty rate, the dates the agreement is in effect, and the embargo period from the time of publication until it can go online. It becomes even more difficult when one must consider whether to make the arrangement an 'exclusive', whether or not a contract can be assigned in case the ownership of one of the parties changes, and when dealing with warranties and indemnifications, deletion and correction policies, and the delivery of electronic copy according to the search service's specifications. Questions like who is responsible for errors, whether there is to be a 'breach of contract' clause, and extent of coverage must be considered as well. This process can take a very long time. We have engaged in negotiations with three separate organisations, each of which took 18 months to complete, even though both parties were friendly to the deal and the negotiators understood the issues fully. One reason we sometimes see files come and go, or become spotty in coverage, has to do with poorly-written contracts entered into by parties not fully aware of all the relevant issues. The publisher has to decide whether the potential royalties are worth the time that must be devoted by the attorneys and the licence negotiators.

Copyright considerations are another area of legal concern. While online full-text delivery solves the users' copyright compliance problems, it may expose the publishers to additional liability, since they may not actually own more than first serial fights to the contents of a publication. Contracts in force may be so old that print fights are the only ones referred to. In some cases, the selective nature of the database may give rise to the argument that 'this isn't XYZ magazine, it's just five articles per issue', and that negotiations fall under rights and permissions per article, not generic publication rights. The publisher may have to renegotiate many contracts with individual writers and freelancers; in fact, the author community is catching on to a possible revenue enhancer for itself. Intellectual property is the bottom line—'Who owns the content' will be a growing consideration in this arena over the next few years, and we may see changes in online file configurations as technology allows individuals and smaller publishers to bypass some of the current intermediaries. Another set of copyright-related considera-tions has to do with other kinds of material the publisher does not own.

Royalties: If the party publishing the database owns the contents online pricing is set the same as the company that owns the data. In other cases, publishers will load their titles one or more online files of their own and have the tapes loaded directly of second-party online search service. In most cases, information providers, Information Access Company or UMI/Data Courier, will act as intermediary between the publishers and online search services such as DataStar, Dialogue or Mead Data Central. Obviously, the more intermediaries between the original publisher and the customer, the less revenue the publisher will see, since the intermediaries take a share of the royalties. Royalties are set by publishers when they draft the original agreement to license the product to the next party, whoever it is. The information provider, if there is one in the deal, then charges the online host a certain royalty of its own, completely independent of the publishers, in order to recover costs and produce a profit. In most cases, the intermediary company has a licence with the publisher to load other titles as well, and the publisher has nothing directly to do with the search service. Until Forbes finds that it is profitable or even cost-effective to produce the formatted product internally and absorb the costs involved, it will remain financially attractive to use such an intermediary.

Pricing: A number of factors go into the pricing of a product, which may affect online or on-disc availability. These include, in addition to licencors' demands for royalties, the intermediary company's own business plan, the costs of the technology, various customer requirements and the competition. Of course, pricing also depends on the market for the product, with differing levels for an online homework helper for students, a database mounted on the wide area network of a major research university, or a dial-up system used by the technical information centre of a multinational pharma-ceutical firm.

Publisher priorities: If electronic publishing is not a primary business or a part of the future business plan of the organisation, the company must consider long and hard whether staff time and technology is being put to good use in developing revenues in optical and electronic products.

Editorial factors

Some indexing/abstracting companies that load full-text onto their services are not including every article. In some cases, only articles covered by the intermediary's indexing and editorial policies are included in full-text. In other cases, only articles longer than a certain length are included.

3

Library Networking

Computer networks come in many different shapes and sizes. Over the years, the networking industry has coined terms like "LAN" and "WAN" attempting to define sensible categories for the major types of network designs. The precise meaning of this terminology remains lost on the average person, however.

For historical reasons, the industry refers to nearly every type of network as an "area network." The most commonly-discussed categories of computer networks include the following:

— Local Area Network (LAN)

— Wide Area Network (WAN)

— Metropolitan Area Network (MAN)

— Storage Area Network (SAN)

— System Area Network (SAN)

— Server Area Network (SAN)

— Small Area Network (SAN)

— Personal Area Network (PAN)

— Desk Area Network (DAN)

— Controller Area Network (CAN)

— Cluster Area Network (CAN)

LANs and WANs were the original flavors of network design. The concept of "area" made good sense at this time, because a key distinction between a LAN and a WAN involves the physical distance that the network spans. A third category, the MAN, also fit into this scheme as it too is centered on a distance-based concept.

As technology improved, new types of networks appeared on the scene. These, too, became known as various types of "area networks" for consistency's sake, although distance no longer proved a useful differentiator.

A LAN connects network devices over a relatively short distance. A networked office building, school, or home usually contains a single LAN, though sometimes one building will contain a few small LANs, and occasionally a LAN will span a group of nearby buildings. In IP networking, one can conceive of a LAN as a single IP subnet (though this is not necessarily true in practice).

Besides operating in a limited space, LANs include several other distinctive features. LANs are typically owned, controlled, and managed by a single person or organization. They also use certain specific connectivity technologies, primarily Ethernet and Token Ring.

As the term implies, a wide-area network spans a large physical distance. A WAN like the Internet spans most of the world! A WAN is a geographically-dispered collection of LANs. A network device called a router connects LANs to a WAN. In IP networking, the router maintains both a LAN address and a WAN address.

WANs differ from LANs in several important ways. Like the Internet, most WANs are not owned by any one organization but rather exist under collective or distributed ownership and management. WANs use technology like ATM, Frame Relay and X.25 for connectivity.

Home networkers with cable modem or DSL service already have encountered LANs and WANs in practice, though they may not have noticed. A cable/DSL router like those in the Linksys family join the home LAN to the WAN link maintained by one's ISP. The ISP provides a WAN IP address used by the router, and all of the computers on the home network use private LAN addresses. On a home network, like many LANs, all computers can communicate directly with each other, but they must go through a central gateway location to reach devices outside of their local area.

A Metropolitan Area Network connects an area larger than a LAN but smaller than a WAN, such as a city, with dedicated or high-performance hardware.

A Storage Area Network connects servers to data storage devices through a technology like Fibre Channel.

A System Area Network connects high-performance computers with high-speed connections in a cluster configuration.

To the uninitiated, LANs, WANs, and the other area network acroymns appear to be just more alphabet soup in a technology industry already drowning in terminology. The names of these networks are not nearly as important as the technologies used to construct them, however. A person can use the categorizations as a learning tool to better understand concepts like subnets, gateways, and routers.

Networking in Libraries

Digital libraries aim to provide ready access to the storehouse of humanity's information. They combine technology and information source and allow remote access of its resources to other libraries by breaking down the physical barriers through national and international computer networks. They rest upon:

— Basic human need for timely and relevant information,

— Accumulation of information and all the supporting infrastructure which includes users, professional associations, library and information centres and publishers; and

— Advances made in networking, information science, information storage and retrieval, hypermedia, human-computer interaction, artificial intelligence, etc.

The components of a digital library system may include:

- Personal library system for the users,
- Organisational library system for serving groups of individuals or activities,
- New as well as existing local or distant databases,
- Database servers to handle remote requests, and
- A variety of system functions to coordinate and manage the entry and retrieval of data.

Networks implies putting together subsets of information centres and libraries in order to act in a cooperative manner with a predetermined obligation. The network concept is an old one found throughout the world popularly in the form of inter-library loans and centralised cataloging. But now there is a widespread interest in the possibility of improving operations interconnecting information systems and services, as well as inter-library operations.

Networking means a formal organisation of a group of digital libraries following common pattern or design for information exchange and communication with a view to improve efficiency and effect economy in an overall manner. The digital library networking concept is a cooperative, venture of all the participating libraries which transmits the data on short and long distance lines from one library to another.

Role of Netorking in Libraries

The following functions of the library and informations centres can be improved/benefited by using the services of some of the above mentioned computer as well a digital library networks.

- *Library activities:* Inter-library loan, reference and referral service, circulation, document consultation, acquisition of library documents, technical processing (cataloging and classification), collection development, preparation of union catalogs, photocopying and document delivery.
- *Documentation services:* Current awareness and SDI services, list of latest additions, literature searching.

— *Specialised services*: Access to bibliographical databases (inhouse and international), distribution of CD-ROM databases, distribution of inhouse databases, participation in international databases by inputting domestic information, electronic transmission of full text, tele-conferencing.

— *Library management:* Better utilisation of funds, continuing education for users and staff, better management of library and information centres. Now our country is in a position to establish, operate and manage information network to link the information resources available the world over. We hope in the near future that all the libraries in India will be without walls and the resources of all libraries will be available to the whole user community networked digital libraries.

International Digital Library Networks

Some of the leading international computer and digital library networks which are in operation the world over are given below.

— *Internet*: It is an international network spread over a large number of sites all over the world. The three basic Internet applications are e-mail, remote login, and file transfer. Services such as mailing lists, directory, enquiry, usernet news, etc., TELENET, TYMNET, UNINET, BITNET (based in USA) and EURONET & DIANE (based in Europe) are some of the leading international networks which offer e-mail, remote login and file transfer services. A wide variety of public domain (free) and commercial information sources are currently available on Internet, with new sources being announced every day. These include, bibliographical/full text databases, table of contents of journals, discussion forums, preprints, technical reports, directories, teaching and training material, data archives (software, numeric data, documents), library catalog, etc.

— *OCLC'S Online Computer Library Centre, Inc., Ohio, USA*: The largest computer and telecommunications network of

14,000 libraries and information centres in the world contains about 25 million records and nearly 2 million records are added each year. OCLC provides a full range of online products and services. Its main purpose is to build the world's pre eminent bibliographic database and computerised network to compile and share the world's knowledge. Libraries, all over the world, are using this vast database to cataloge 8,000 titles and borrow 10,000 books a day. Through this network libraries benefit from reduction in operational cost as well as increase in access to library materials held in other libraries. Most of the participating libraries in OCLC system are also required to be the members of regional networks of the NELINET for obtaining the necessary services.

— *OLC (Oakland Library Consortium)*: It is a consortium of three libraries located in Pittsburgh (Carnegie Mellon University Libraries, University of Pittsburgh Libraries and Carnegie Public Library). It provides online access to collections of these libraries.

— *LIS (Library Information System)*: LIS of Carnegie Mellon University Libraries, Pittsburgh provides fast and easy access to university-owned library materials as well as to commercially leased indexes and full text databases on CD-ROM. A simple search begins at the search window. Many work stations are scattered through-out the libraries for the use of its readers.

— *ILLINET (Illinois Library Network)*: It provides access to OCLC and other databases for Illinois libraries as well as coordinating other cooperative programs. It allows participation libraries to borrow books through resource-sharing arrangement.

— *NELINET (New England Library Information Network)*: About 200 libraries are participating in this network. It also provides OCLC services.

— *AGLINET (World Network of Agricultural Libraries)*: It consists of a chain of major agricultural libraries in each region or country of the world within the framework of the International Association of Agricultural Libraries and Documentalists (IAALD). The main objective of the AGLINET is to promote mutual and rational exploitation of library resources for the benefit of the world's agricultural development through systematic collaboration among agricultural libraries for the efficient provision for inter-library loan services and bibliographic information.

— *ISONET (International Standards Organisation Network):* The network comprises the National Standards Information Centres and the links between them. It includes the ISO Information Centre in Geneva which has the responsibility to collect, organise, index, and disseminate information for international standardising documents similar to the national responsibility for national documents.

— *ChIN (International Chemical Information Network):* It was launched during 1990 with the support from UNESCO and UNIDO hosted by the International Centre for Chemical Studies of the University of Edward Kardelj Ljubljana, Yugoslovia. The main objectives of ChIN are to bring awareness about new developments and applications in databases, information systems and software in chemistry and related fields, to promote the development and use of chemical information systems and services; to encourage cooperation in information among chemists and chemical engineers, and to develop goal-oriented programmes.

— *DEVINSA (Development Information Network on South Asia):* It is a project conceived in 1981 by the Committee on Studies for Cooperation and Development in South Asia, an organisation of scholars representing six South Asian countries (India, Sri Lanka, Bangladesh, Pakistan, Nepal and the Maldives) to provide information on current development activities and socio-economic research through dissemination and document delivery and thereby to help avoid or reduce duplication of research.

— *APINES (Asia-Pacific Information Network in Social Sciences):* It is presently based at UNESCO's Regional Unit for Social and Human Sciences in Asia and the Pacific,

Bangkok. This network will disseminate information to the scholars doing research in the field of social sciences in the region.

— *RINAP (Regional Informatics Network for Asia and the Pacific):* A project proposal was worked out in joint cooperation with NIC, Government of India, and RINSEAP (Regional Information Network for South-East Asia and the Pacific) to evolve a low-cost RINAP with computer linkages and access to mutually-agreed upon national and international databases.

— *TIPS (Technology Information Pilot System):* It is an UNDP's information network which disseminates commercial data, business and investment opportunities, the latest prices and availability of certain equipments, and offers for joint collaboration. It has 6,000 subscribers and 50,00 entries on technology and trade information, making it one of the biggest databases in the world on trade and technology opportunities in the world. TIPS international operation centre is based in Rome with regional offices in Manila for Asia, and Caracas for Latin America.

— *DIALOGUE Information Services Inc., Palo Alto, California, USA:* It provides online access to vast sources of information covering most of the published literature of the world.

— *STN (Scientific & Technical Information Network):* STN International is a computerised scientific and technical information network offered jointly by the American Chemical Society and the Fachinformation Szentrum Energie, Physik, Mathematik GmbH (Fiz Karlsruhe). The Japan Information Centre of Science & Technology (JICST) will be part of this network in the future. STN offers direct access to a number of databases that are located in different continents.BLAISE (British Library Automated Information Service), ESA/IRS (European Space Agency Information Retrieval Service), etc. are some of the leading agencies which offer online access to various databases.

Digital Library Networks in India

The following are some of the national digital library networks which are in operation/implementation stage in the country.

— *Information and Library Network (INFLIBNET):* In 1986, a national policy on library and information system was formulated wherein it was recommended that the national libraries should form an integrated system for a better coordination of their activities and services. The Planning Commission had set up a working group on modernisation of library and information services for the 7th Plan to suggest measures to network important libraries in the country so that their resources could be shared for optimum utilisation. UGC, under the chairmanship of Prof. Yashpal, formulated the plan in 1988 on Information and Library Network (INFLIBNET) which proposed a mechanism to establish a network connecting libraries in universities' colleges, and institutions affiliated to the CSIR, ICMR, ICAR, DRDO and government departments. When fullfledged, it is envisaged that INFLIBNET will network 184 universities and 23 institutions, deemed-to-be universities, 6,100 colleges and over 200 libraries affiliated to other organisations. It is designed to operate at the national, regional, sectoral and local levels as a multi-service network to provide catalog-based services, access to databases and document supply services and facilities for computer-mediated communication such as e-mail, bulletin boards, etc.

— *NICNET*: NICNET which is designed primarily to be a government information network to promote the collection, storage, analysis, transmission and exchange of data at districts, state headquarters and central ministries and departments at New Delhi for use in planning, management and monitoring of projects and government-sponsored programs. NICNET provides dial-up access to CDROM databases of the US National Library of Medicine, MEDLINE, Biotechnology Abstracts, COMPENDEX, etc.

— *INDONET*: It is a commercial distributed computer network to provide access to the computing power and software resources of CMC Ltd. to users who cannot afford. INDONET has three IBM mainframes at Calcutta, Mumbai and Chennai and smaller computers at Delhi and Hyderabad. The Mumbai node is connected to VSNL's GPSS (Videsh Sanchar Nigham Limited/Gateway Packet Switched Services) enabling computer-to-computer communication via networks abroad. The Department of Telecommunications established during the year 1992 a nationwide Public Packet Switched Data Network (PSDN) called I-NET which have nodes in 8 cities connected through high-speed links.

— *SIRNET (Scientific and Industrial Research Network)* is proposed to interconnect all the CSIR laboratories (22 laboratories have already been connected) and other R&D institutions in India. It is to harness the vast S&T information resources available with national laboratories and inculcate the habit of resource-sharing among them. The ultimate aim of the SIRNET is to link the entire scientific community of the nation with the national library system and the international links to achieve efficient scientific communication. The services proposed to be available on SIRNET are E-mail, file transfer, document transfer, access to indigenous and international databases. INSDOC, New Delhi node of SIRNET has established access to over 1800 international databases on 15 different hosts through.

— *ERNET* was initiated by the Department of Electronics (DoE) during the 7th Plan as a thrust area for setting up a computer network, as a part of UNDP project, for academic and research community with initial participation from five IIT's (Delhi, Chennai, Mumbai, Kanpur & Kharagpur), IISc, NCST, and DOE. The development objective of ERNET is to enhance national capabilities in the areas of design, development, research, education and training on state-of-the-art concepts of computer networking and related emerging technologies. Over 300 institutions in the country reporting a cross-section of universities, government societies, R&D organisations, research institutes are already using it extensively; over 20,000 users use it throughout the country. Services available on the network are e-mail, database access, file transfer, remote login, information retrieval tools; etc.

— *DELNET*: The main objectives of DELNET are optimum utilisation of funds through sharing of resources, creation of commonly usable databases and communication between libraries with the help of automation and networking. It will network 35 libraries in the Delhi area. A packet-switched network is envisaged with each cluster of libraries being serviced by a packet-switching exchange. All databases created cooperatively are expected to reside on a central computer system and dial-up access will be provided to all participating libraries. This network will have e-mail, file transfer, union catalog of serials, database of holdings of individual libraries, bulletin board facilities, etc.

— *CALIBNET (Calcutta Library Network)* is envisaged to cover 38 science and technology libraries in the Calcutta metropolitan area. It will have access to the VSNL, Mumbai through the Indian Public Switched Data Network (PSDN). Each of the participating libraries is expected to automate their book acquisitions, cataloging, serials control, fund accounting and circulation control.

— *MALIBNET (Madras Library Network)* has become operational since May 1993. Currently six major academic institutions are directly linked to the MALIBNET host system. Two online databases, namely, Current Serials in Chennai database covering 300 libraries and Contents Database covering articles published in 300 journals available in Chennai libraries have been created utilising the resources available there MALIBNET will offer current serials acquired in about 50 libraries, full journal holdings of about 50 libraries, contents information of about 400 important journals, specialised databases giving abstract of articles, e-mail including international connectivity, document delivery, etc.

— *BSN (Business Subscribers Network)* planned for providing integrated and reliable facilities to business and industrial users, initially 500 subscribers will be connected to this network. Services to be provided include voice and facsimile transfer, teletex, videotex, e-mail and access to remote databases. The central nodes will be at Mumbai, Calcutta, Chennai and Delhi and secondary nodes are proposed to be at Ahmedabad, Bangalore, Hyderabad, Kanpur/Lucknow and Pune.

— *RABMN (The Remote Area Business Message Network):* The Department of Telecommunications was set it up in 1991 to facilitate exchange of messages in chosen user groups. The satellite-based star network has master earth station at Sikanderabad near Delhi and Very Small Aperture Terminal (VSAT) at user premises.

— *BITS*:Under the BITS program, Microvax-II system in ten specialised information centres in genetic engineering, cell culture, virology, plant tissue culture, immunology, bioprocessing engineering, etc., are being linked through micro-earth station and X.25 protocols.

Many more networks are likely to emerge in the near future. For instance, Defence Science Information Network (DESINET), VIKRAM (by the Department of Telecommunications); Oil and Natural Gas Commission Network (ONGC); Bombay Library Network (BONET); Pune Library Network (PUNENET); Transportation Information Service Network (TISNET); Network for Business Commission, PAILET, COALNET, OILNET, BANKNET SAILNET, TIFACLINE, etc.

4

Online Cataloguing

Introduction of offline, computer-produced book and Computer Output Microform (COM) catalogues was a significant step in the evolution of the library catalog, but almost exclusively in terms of production and maintenance. Computer-produced, offline catalogues addressed many of the problems inherent in card catalogue production and maintenance, and many labor-intensive tasks that were fundamental to card catalogues were eliminated with the use of computers and machine-readable records.

With offline computerized catalogues, only one unit entry record had to be created for each item; the computer expanded this record into as many individual catalogue entries as necessary and performed all alphabetization and filing tasks to maintain the catalog. It was also much easier, at least in theory, to change a major catalogue heading; the change could be made once and applied to all effected entries by the computer-quite a difference from manually typing a new heading onto each which a change applied.

As far ass the library user was concerned, the benefits of computer-generated offline catalogues were far less pronounced. The actual format of the catalogue certainly changed in some instances, but the basis content, and the basis avenues through which records in the catalogue could be found, rally did not. The principles used for access to entries in computer-generated book and COM catalogues mirrored those of the card catalog, and the information was often identical and sometimes even less in amount.

From the users standpoint, computer-produced book catalogues were little more than card catalogues in bound volumes, and COM catalogues little more than card catalogues in a box. Given such frustrations as dealing with multiple parts of a catalogue issues in editions and supplements, and equipment breakdowns with COM catalogues, more advantages of computer-produced offline catalogues were not noticeable to the user and, at any rate, could often be overshadowed by the logistical difficulties in using them.

In contrast, many OPACs, represent a radical departure both from card catalogues and from offline computerized catalogues in their implications for the user. Access to records can be enormously broadened in an online catalogue over what had typically been provided in other forms, but these benefits are accompanied by a new set of requirements and demands on the catalogue user. The relationship between user and online catalogue is fundamentally different from that in use of other catalogue forms.

The online catalogue is interactive, not passive, and requires the user to engage in a dialogue quite uncharacteristic of card, book and COM catalogues. Just to look into the catalogue requires new procedures on the part of the user. A search must be physically, not just mentally, initiated by typing onto a keyboard issuing a command through some other means. The system will respond according to the very specific action initiated by the user.

In many instances, the user will then have to initiate further action based on the system's response, and so on back and forth until the user arrives at the desired end of the search or otherwise terminates the dialogue. This interaction and the nature of system responses represent a significant departure for the user from simply thumbing through catalogue cards or pressing a button, turning a knob, or sliding a handle on a microfilm or microfiche reader.

The fact that a online public-access catalogues (OPACs) is intended for users of library materials in perhaps the fundamental distinction between this application of automation and those which serve strictly internal processing functions. Such matters as simplicity of operation or sophistication of retrieval capabilities should be important considerations in the design and selection of any automated system regardless of application, but self-evidence in operation may be less important in a technical processing system in which the library is able to exercise a certain degree of control over the selection, training, and monitoring of system users.

The design of an online catalogue must take into account a quite different set of circumstances. Considerable diversity exists among users in their level of knowledge about library catalogues and in the extent to which they are familiar with the use of computerized systems. The library will usually have little or opportunity to balance its diversity though a planned program of controlled instruction and monitoring.

Most people will not use the OPAC as part of everyday routine, and hence their knowledge and skills will not be constantly reinforced.An example of the well-placed emphasis in discussions of OPACs on users and their interaction with the catalogue is the series of studies sponsored by the Council on Library Resources (CLR) during the early 1980s, aimed at gaining a better understanding of what users want and need in online catalogues, their likes and dislikes, and the dynamics of their interaction with catalogues.

Despite the vast array of differences among existing OPACs and lack of specific guidelines for development, at the base of these differences is a common goal: to design online catalogues that will allow the user maximum flexibility and yet will be easy to use. Investigations like those sponsored by CLR should help to establish a stronger foundation for realizing such a goal. Phrases such as "user friendly" have become almost meaningless because of their sometimes indiscriminate use to describe systems or features that commonsense observation show are 'anything but.' Yet the overuse, and ever misuse, of well-worn phrases does not negate the relevance of the concepts they represent.

The degree to which OPACs are willingly accepted by library users will indeed depend in large part on just how user friendly these systems are. Technical processing systems can be evaluated largely in terms of functional capabilities, or what a system can do. But the circumstances in which OPACs are still used are too different for such a simple evaluation. Equally and perhaps more important is the question of how easily system functions can be learned, understood and applied to the fullest extent by a diverse group of users.

For any given characteristics in their operation, OPACs are still simply too new, and their use still too little understood, to be able to state categorically that one approach is somehow "better" than the other. Fundamental to all of the features described is the most basic improvement that OPACs have made on other forms of the library catalog: the expansion of avenues of access to catalogue records.

Although the purposes of the library catalogue are not case in stone and depend on one's perspective, one set of standards by which library catalogue functions have been measured throughout the twentieth century is the principles of Charles Ammi Cutter as noted in his Rules for a Dictionary Catalogue. Cutter enumerated three major "objects" of a library catalogue. A catalogue should allow someone to find book if its author, title, or topic is known. A catalogue should fulfill a gathering function, showing what a library owns by a given author, on a given subject or in a given type of literature. A catalogue should provide assistance in the change of a book, either as to its edition or its literary or topical character. A fourth commonly recognized catalogue function, although not explicitly noted by Cutter, is collection, having to do with the arrangement and relationship of headings within the catalog. Underlying most of these functions is the fundamental matter of access top bibliographic records in the catalog: the points of entry through which a record for an item may be found. Cutter's first object—the finding function—is the essential basis for access, nut the gathering and collocation functions also have to do with accessibility to records.

The function least directly related to access is assistance in the choice of material, which has more to do with content of a bibliographic record than access to it. Whether Cutter's objects still provide the most viable criteria for defining the purposes of a library catalogue in an online era is debatable, and some have questioned the degree of completeness to which these objects have ever actually been realized in libraries. Cutter's principles stem from a time quite different from the 1980s.

New factors—including but not limited to those of a technological nature—should not be disregarded in defining the purposes of a library catalog. Nevertheless, Cutter's principles serve as a point of departure in many decisions of online catalogues, and concerning access to bibliographic records they still provide a convenient framework for comparing online catalogues with one another and with other forms of the library catalog.

Access to bibliographic records in library catalogues has traditionally been marked by a high degree of rigidity, requiring considerable knowledge and exactitude on the part of the user. Generally, access is gained through four types of bibliographic elements: author, title, series, and subject. Multiple author and subject headings are assigned to an item as rules or judgment dictates, but the number is usually kept to a minimum.

The terminology selected for headings is also tightly controlled, with the library usually trying to establish a one-to-one correspondence between headings and the persons, corporate bodies, or concepts they represent. These practices may be understandable from a practical point of view, but they also impose certain limits on accessibility to records. The user can indeed locate an item in the collection for which the author, title, or subject is known, but only under some rather inflexible conditions. To find a record under the title, the user must know the full and exact wording of the title—not some or most of the words, but all of the words, and in their correct order. For access by author, because of the pre-AACR practice of establishing full and singularly valid forms of names, it has not always been enough to know the from of an author's name as it appears on publications or by which the person is popularly known.

It has been necessary for the user somehow to know the exact from of a person's or corporation's name as it has been established by the library, often on the basis of considerable research. Where there are discrepancies in name form, it has been up to the user to figure out the form selected by the library. Access by subject is even more problematic.

Singularly valid forms of headings are selected from among all possible equivalents, but because of the greater conceptual complexity involved, there is even greater likelihood in subject searching that discrepancies will arise between the terminology selected by the library and the vocabulary chosen by the user. The problem is further compounded by the general conservatism in libraries toward changing the vocabulary used in headings and by complicated subject heading formation and filling sequences. Such practices, which result in a lack of flexibility, are all but dictated by necessity in card catalogues; however, they were also carried over generally intact to offline versions of computerized catalogues as well.

Given the capabilities of computers and the elimination of the need for manual filing, there is no strictly technological reason for some of these practices to have been retained so uniformly. Additional access points, such as by keywords appearing anywhere in titles or assigned subject headings, could have been provided with little or no appreciable increase in human labor.

Similarly, duplicate listings under variant forms of names could have been supplied in the catalogue. These expansions would have required greater sophistication in indexing and would have resulted in a far greater number of entries, and thus larger catalogues, but whether for economic reasons, ties to tradition, or something else, expansions of this type were never characteristic of offline computerized catalogues. Only with the introduction of online catalogues have such expansions taken firm hold, and they are changing the very concept of access to records in the library catalogue.

Some OPACs adhere quite closely to other forms of the catalogue in the ways in which access to records may be gained, requiring just as much exactitude and exhibiting just as little flexibility. These are essentially electronic card catalogues. Other OPACs significantly broaden, and even fundamentally change, the traditional concept of access.

History of Online Library Systems

One of the first online systems was at the Illinois State Library in Springfield, in late 1966, at a time when many other libraries were designing full offline systems. The backbone of the system was an IBM 1620 computer located in the state processing facility. The equipment in the library consisted of IBM 1033 prints and 1031 card readers, which were similar in operation to the 357 Data Collection System, requiring insertion of machine-readable book cards and borrower identification badges. Rather than producing transaction cards or recording transaction data on tape, however, the 1031 at the Illinois State Library transmitted data directly to the computer. By later standard, the online system at the library was primitive.

Although transaction information was conveyed directly to the computer as it occurred, it was stored on a separate daily transaction pack and was merged with the main circulation file only on a once-a-day batch processing basis. The system did not include item-specific online query, so that it was still necessary to use offline batch-produced circulation lists to trace circulation information pertaining to a given item. For these purposes, the system was much like wholly offline batch processing systems. What set it apart from those, however, was its ability to perform two important functions online: checking borrower registration numbers for validity and checking each returned item against an online holds file. Each time a borrower identification card was inserted into the designated slot of the 1031, the borrower number was automatically checked against a computer-stored file of valid borrower numbers. If the borrower's number did not have a counterpart in the file, that fact was generated immediately on the 1033 printer. This was a major improvement over completely offline operations. Where such validation, if done at all, could be performed only by manual lookup in a printed directory of borrower numbers.

The other important online function of the Illinois State Library system was checking holds, and that had equally important implications. When the book card of a returned item was placed in the 1031 for discharge, the call number was checked against an online list of call numbers of items placed on hold. If the cell number of the returned item matched a call number in the holds file, a message was automatically generated on the 1033 printer showing call number, identification number of the patron who had placed the item on hold, and the data when the hold had been placed. In this manner, greater control over holds was realized than was possible in offline batch processing computerized circulation systems.

Another early online circulation system was implemented in late 1967 at Midwestern University in Wichita Falls, Texas. The Midwestern system was unique in that it was, at least insofar as its designers know, the first and perhaps only online circulation system to operate on an IBM 1401 computer, a decidedly second-generation machine.

Like the Illinois State Library system, Midwestern used IBM 1031 input stations and 1033 printers, validated borrower identification numbers, and checked items against an online holds file. But it went further than the Illinois system in several important respects. Not only did the Midwestern systems check borrower numbers during a charging operation for general validation, but it also determined if a borrower had any outstanding overdue items or unpaid fines. If so, the computer generated an immediate list of the charges on the 1033 printer. The system had an online query capability, albeit restricted to searching on a borrower number. The keying in of a number prompted the computer to respond by printing a list on the 1033 containing all items charged to that borrower. But perhaps the fundamental difference in the Midwestern system was that the main circulation file was online in the strict sense of the term, with the file being updated immediately upon completion of each transaction, rather than in a batch mode.

In September 1968, the Booth Library at Eastern Illinois University in Charleston began to operate its own version of a online circulation system using a third-generation IBM 360/ Model 50 computer and the IBM 1031 input stations and 1033 printers. The Booth system had the basic functional characteristic of the Midwestern system, but with an important additional query feature.

The Midwestern system had query capability by patron number; the Booth system supplemented this with item query by call number. By entering a particular two-digit code followed by a call number, a terminal operator could retrieve bibliographic information and current circulation data about a specific item. Queries of this nature were made using an IBM Cathode Ray Tube (CRT) terminal located at the circulation desk. A further extension of this search capability was a scanning command that displayed bibliographic entries in call number sequence.

Since the Booth Library online file was an inventory file containing an abbreviated bibliographic record for nearly even item in the library—not just items currently charged out—the scanning capability allowed shelflist searching of the entire library collection. The structure and search capabilities of this system suggested possible extension as a public-access tool, and in fact plans were announced to locate a public-access CRT terminal near the card catalog in fall 1971. Still, the known item query capability of the Eastern Illinois system allowed more immediate information about the circulation status of an item than was possible in an offline system.

In the early 1970s, a number of academic libraries began to incorporate minicomputers in their circulation operations. A significant feature of these systems was that at least part of the processing hardware was located in the library itself, although a larger computer, outside the library, still played an integral role. Typically, the minicomputer in the library contained certain files for immediate online access and captured transaction data for later batch transmission to as larger computer located outside the library on which the main circulation file was stored. While some of the operations remained offline, this setup realized the benefits of online processing for certain critical purposes. One of the most common minicomputers in this type of configuration was the IBM System/7 in use in circulation control in at least six libraries by early 1974.

In the system operational at the University of Pennsylvania in Philadelphia, five online files were stored in the minicomputer. Each of these contained critical information against which various types of transactions were checked. There were three item files against which renewal attempts and discharges were checked.

A call number file contained the call number of all items placed on hold, the access number file contained a list of all items recalled, and a reserve book file contained all items for which in request had been placed to transfer the item to a reserve book collection upon its return. Another file, against which all patron identification numbers were checked, was the restricted patron file, containing a lost of borrower identification numbers of all users whose further attempts to charge materials were to be blocked for some reason.

The fifth online file was the daily transaction file, which recorded the day's activity. Once a day, this file was transmitted to the main computer, an IBM 370/Model 168, located at the university data processing center, for batch updating of the main circulation file. This transmission, usually involving information for about 3,000 transactions, required about 30 minutes. For the most part, improvements, gained in the Online circulation systems of the late 1960s and early 1070s over what was possible in an offline system were focused on immediate access to information about restricted items, such as holds, and better control of patron privilege.

Although improvements regarding access to information about restricted items enhanced public service by allowing more rapid reshelving of returned items and a better system for regulating holds and ensuring identification upon return, these benefits were not always immediately evident to the average library user. The second common capability, immediate access to Online delinquent patron files, could as likely cause ill feelings as goodwill between the library and its users.

The lack of reliable backup measures, inexperience in dealing with online systems, and continued reliance on batch-produced circulation lists combined to make early online circulation systems less than revolutionary in terms of public service. At least one facility, the Simon Fraser University Library, had so many problems and so much user discontent with its online system that it abandoned online and reverted to its earlier offline system."

Perhaps the outstanding example during the early 1970s of online circulation system that could, in fact, facilitate user services to a degree not possible in an offline system was demonstrated by Ohio State University's Library Control System. The entire philosophy behind the design and application of the system for the Ohio State University libraries was, as described by Hugh Atkinson, "that the system should be one which would speak to the problems of its users rather than simply the problems of the library." These problems included, among others, a decentralized library structure consisting of a main library and more than 20 branches.

Only one catalog—the main library's—contained complete information for all items in all 21 libraries. Similar to several earlier online circulation systems, Ohio State opted for an "inventory" file approach in which the main machine-readable database contained records for all items in the libraries rather than an "absence" file, which would have contained records only for those items in circulation. This principles as fundamental at Ohio State since the system was to be used as a locator file as well as for circulation operations.

A massive conversion effort—perhaps the largest of its kind carried out by any library to that date—was contracted to a vendor, which put into machine-readable form records containing call number, unique item number, author, title, date of publication. Library of Congress card number, language code, from of publication code, and holding for each of 1 million distinct titles and 2.5 million items. The key to the Ohio State system was its items query capability. Searching was possible by call number, title key, and a combination author/title key. When the desired item was retrieved, it was possible to see which library or libraries on campus owned a copy of the item, and whether each copy was charged out. Search terminals were available in the main library and in most of the branches. Thus, the entire union catalog of the libraries' holdings could be assessed from any library in the system.

Although this in itself was a fundamental improvement over the single union catalog in the main library. An item not already checked out in one library could be charged on terminals located in any a copy was found to be available in a different branch library, the circulation attendant could issue a command that would generate a charge slip in the branch library that had the copy. The item would be retrieved in that library and placed on a shelf to await later pickup by the patron.

The online union catalog, showing location and circulation status of each item throughout the system, combined with the capability of remote charging to remove much of the patron uncertainty that was inherent under prior circumstances. The Ohio State University library system, like all other online system, was not entirely free of problems, but many of them could eventually be alleviated by design changes and the system was such an improvement over earlier conditions that the problems were of comparatively minor consequence. The impact of this system on library service was probably best exemplified by the fact that, during the first 18 months it was in operation, circulation at the Ohio State University libraries increased by more than 40 percent. The system was an important achievement owing to its scale of implementation, its query capabilities, and its emphasis on public service problem solving.

The same system was later taken by Atkinson to the University of Illinois and implemented; today it is the basis of an important networking system in libraries throughout Illinois. Apart from circulation, the late 1960s and early 1970s saw the development of a number of online technical processing systems.

One of the earliest acquisitions systems was designed at the Washington State University Library in Pullman and was implemented in 1968; an online serials control system was up and running at University Level in Quebec the same year. Predating both of these was the beginning of a comprehensive online library system at the Redstone Scientific Information Center in Alabama. Some parts of the system were operational as early as 1966.

By the early 1970s, acquisitions, cataloging, authority control, serials check-in, and circulation were online. Offline computerization had been an important development in acquisitions, providing for machine-assisted production of purchase orders, improved methods of fiscal control, and more timely updating and generation of status lists. Still, a significant amount of from handling and paper file maintenance remained in many of these systems.

The online acquisitions systems developed in the late 1960s and early 1970s represented major improvements by reducing the amount of manual handling and maintenance of paper products, as well as further enhanced those functions that had been performed well in offline computerized system. One of the more ambitious projects in the late 1960s was carried out at the Oregon State University Library at Corvallis. Christened LOLITA, this online acquisitions system required nearly seven "staff years" in programming, systems, and clerical labor to develop. It contained three Online files: order/in-process file contained three display screens of information input when an order was placed, and updated as an item passed through the acquisitions and cataloging procedures. The first screen included basic bibliographic data, the second screen contained accounting data, and the third screen allowed for local cataloging information such as call number and location.

The amount of time and file maintenance that this system saved the staff, particularly when compared with a manual system, was considerable. One of the greatest contributions made by online systems in general was the expansion of access points, and these early acquisition systems were no exception. It was possible with an offline system to produce lists or maintain paper copies of order forms by more than one point of access, such as by order number, author, and title if desired, but that merely increased the number of lists to be consulted or files to be maintained.

As a result, the number of listing parameters was usually minimized in offline systems. In online systems, all files and their indexes could be maintained in the computer, and multiple access points to a single record would not mean an increase in hard copy materials to be consulted or maintained. LOLITA, however, only provided to access points, order number and author, to each record in the system.

The early online acquisitions systems retained some of the capabilities that had been included in their offline predecessors, but the newer systems were much improved in quality, speed, and ease of handling. LOLITA, along with several other early systems, provided for handling of partial shipments and authorization of partial invoice payments, capabilities that were handled, if at all, only with some difficult by offline systems. The fund accounting component of LOLITA was also successful.

A year-end encumbrance, could be generated in 20 minutes, and LOLITA was to only much faster, nut also judged more accurate and detailed in a controlled comparison with manual ledgers. Perhaps the most important characteristic of online acquisitions systems was that, in most cases, it was only one part of a broader integrated technical processing system that brought the acquisitions and cataloging functions closer together. The online order record, upon receipt of an item, became an online cataloging record. This greatly reduced duplication between acquisitions and cataloging and also provided an end product consisting of a machine-readable bibliographic record for each item entering the collection.

In LOLITA, the final steps in the online processing after an item had been received were for a cataloger to verify the bibliographic information originally entered by the acquisitions department and the complete the record by adding local cataloging data. The completed record was removed from the online file, but not before it had been copied onto magnetic tape as a permanent machine-readable record. An important feature in the development of online technical processing systems was the incorporation of Library of Congress MARC records. Records on MARC tapes were transferred into the local online systems in various ways.

A common feature across systems was that each new order was searched against a locally maintained MARC file, and when a match occurred, the appropriate MARC record entered the local system as the source for bibliographic information for ordering and eventual cataloging.

One of the most comprehensive uses of MARC records evolved in the University of Chicago Library Data Management System. Orders could be searched against the MARC files, and there was a retrospective searching capability whereby incoming MARC records were searched against the local bibliographic file to identify previously created local records as potential candidates for bibliographic upgrading by the new matching MARC record.

These features in one from or another could be found in other systems, but an interesting feature of the Chicago systems was its use of MARC tapes as a collection development tool. Subject profiles, defined by Library Congress classification numbers and ranges of numbers, could be maintained online, and each incoming MARC tape was matched against them. The result was an offline list of items falling into each subject profile for use in identifying potential orders for the library. The system also allowed access to these lists online if a bibliographer wished. The system also allowed access to these lists online if a bibliographer wished.

Supplementing the LC class number profiles were certain national bibliography online profiles used to identify potential orders from an area studies prospective. In addition to profiles designed to identify items of potential interest for the library, the University of Chicago system also included a capability designed to assist in better control over blanket orders from publishers.

The first four digits of an International Standard Book Number (ISBN), MARC field 020, are unique to each publisher. Each record on the MARC tapes was automatically searched on these first four digits at Chicago. The system could then generate lists of items published by each publisher with whom Chicago had a blanket order arrangement, and these lists could be used to assist in monitoring receipt of blanket order items

Left with an alternative of in-house, single-library development projects, only the largest and most well endowed libraries could have used an online system for any technical support systems during the 1970s. As early as 1967, however, a second alternative was being formulated, and the outgrowth of this and similar efforts was the evolution of four system—OCLC, RLG, WLN, and UTLAS—whose use by the early 1980s, extended into several thousand libraries on the North American continent.

Although some libraries continued to develop their own in-house systems for certain library functions, it was apparent by the mid- 1970s that automated cataloging in particular was evolving in a different direction. The basis of this transformation was the Ohio College Library Center (OCLC), a system based on the simple premise that, recognizing minor local variations, cataloging data for a given item were essentially similar from library to library. The Library of Congress MARC project had been as major breakthrough in the concept of shared cataloging information in an automated environment, but the general pattern of sharing had been unidirectional and on an institution-by-institution basis.

MARC tapes were sent from the Library of Congress to subscribing institutions, each of which then loaded the tapes and manipulated the data on its own computer. The idea that evolved for OCLC was a central file of cataloging records that could be maintained on a single computer system and accessed through terminals sharing dedicated communications line connected to that computer. Not only would this enable libraries to share a MARC file, but it would centralize development costs of the system and virtually eliminated the need for each participating library to use the host institution's computer system.

Because the Library of Congress cataloged only portion of the universe of materials received by libraries, and since the MARC tapes included only the OCLC online system was the capability for allowing original input of records, using the MARC format, by the participating libraries themselves. The impact of this is seen by the fact that even by the end of the decade, less than one-fourth of the master bibliographic records in the OCLC database had been supplied by the Library of Congress.

OCLC was chartered in 1967 and Frederick G. Kilgour named as its executive director. System production first began with offline batch processing in 1970; 54 member academic libraries in Ohio submitted punched IBM cards with Library of Congress card numbers of items for which they wanted catalogue cards produced. The punched cards were searched against a file consisting of the Library of Congress MARC records, and when a match occurred, catalogue cards were generated and sent back to the requesting library within two weeks.

In 1971, OCLC went online, installing terminals that allowed each library to search the growing OCLC On-Line Union Catalogue (OLUC), the bibliographic database of the system. The library could order catalog cards merely depressing a couple of command keys on the keyboard attached to the CRT display terminal. During the first several years of OCLC online operation, a number of far-reaching decisions were made that would enhance-and sometimes plague—the cooperative effort.

The display format revolved around the concept of a bibliographic 'master record'; in theory there was to be only one record in the database for any given bibliographic entity. When this master record for an item was retrieved by a library, any of the MARC fields could be modified to reflect local practices with respect to subject headings, forms of name entry, local call number, and so on; virtually any element in the record could be modified.

All local changes were reflected on the catalog cards printed offline at OCLC and mailed to the library (and eventually on the library's magnetic tapes of its cataloging activity when this service became available). These modifications, however, were not stored permanently online for the library. Therefore, when a library retrieved a record it had previously used for cataloging, the bibliographic master record was displayed online, without the local modifications that the library had previously made. The lack of capability to permanently store local information was probably justifiable in OCLC's initial stages.

The amount of storage required to maintain this data for each cataloging use of each record by each library would have been enormous, especially since most members of OCLC at that time had a low incidence of adding copies for titles they had already cataloged once. Nevertheless, it was not long after the system went online that some members began to express concern over the lack of a permanent online record containing local modifications for previously cataloged materials.

A characteristic of OCLC during the 1970s was a perpetual gap between announced plans and actual implementation, and the permanent storage and display of local cataloging data—or at least of a scaled-down version of local holdings from selected fields—perhaps provides the most exemplary illustration.

The strategy initially used in creating the online file of bibliographic master records in OCLC revolved around the creation of as large a database as possible in as little time as possible. This may be overgeneralization, but there is little doubt that it was prevalent enough so that a great many of the permanent master records entered into the database by member libraries in the early years suffered in quality and completeness of information.

Master records, particularly for retrospective cataloging entered into the database, were frequently created from a description taken solely from the shelflist card of the first member library to convert the title. Thus quality and completeness depended in great part on any given library's past shelflisting practices, on the library's policy for input of new records into the database, and, beyond that, on the accuracy of the terminal operator.

The philosophy of rapid creation of a database at the expense of detail and completeness of record could be seen in OCLC's approach in 1975 to providing records for serials titles, for which a specifically designed MARC format had only recently become available. To greatly increase the number of serials records in a short time, tapes of the Minnesota Union List of Serials (MULS) were loaded into the OCLC database.

Although MULS contained accurate information as far as it went, it was primarily a locational tool and provided very abbreviated bibliographic data for cataloguing purposes. Perhaps the greatest quality control complication in the long run was the extreme difficulty of upgrading master records when a mistake was detected or information found to be incomplete.

Written forms had to be completed by a member library and mailed to OCLC; when received, the master record was examined by OCLC staff and modified according to the reported additions or changes. This process was time-consuming and cumbersome for member libraries, and not exactly a foremost staffing priority at OCLC.

The result was that a library could easily retrieve a master record containing an obvious typographical error that presumably had been modified locally by any number of other libraries for their own card production, but that remained in the master record due to backlogs at OCLC in record upgrading. Owing to the prominent role of the OCLC database in the Conversion of Serials (CONSER) project, a limited number of libraries were given the capability of making permanent online modifications to OCLC serials master records from their own terminals, thus bypassing the manual error reporting procedure. This proved a tremendous success. The possibility of enabling a small number of libraries a similar online capability for records in other formats was a topic of discussion for several years, and was finally initiated in mid-1984. The approach used in creating its database and the difficulty in correcting errors in master records earned OCLC a reputation in some quarters as a 'dirty database.' To be certain, many early records in the database did suffer from lack of quality control. An often overlooked factor by critics, however, was that OCLC was an experiment without direct precedent and included among its membership a segment of the library community that had virtually no previous experience with any type of library automation.

OCLC was not the first online system used for collective representation of cataloging data fro a number of independent libraries, but immediate predecessors were based on centralized input and thus centralized control. This was quite different from the structure of OCLC, in which any member library could input an original bibliographic master record for an item. Given this degree of autonomy and decentralization, combined with the lack of previous experience with library automation on the part of most of its members, and a lack of precedence to gauge the implications of shared databases, the early 1970s were an individual and cooperative learning experience for OCLC members which served to demonstrate both the strong points and the problem areas of cooperative ventures in library automation.

During its first year of online operation OCLC remained a cooperative venture of Ohio academic libraries. During 1972, membership was extended to Ohio nonacademic libraries, and in 1973 to libraries outside the state. Although the major computer facilities were to remain centralized at OCLC headquarters, a decentralized approach to the provision of general support services emerged by the mid-1970s. OCLC and various independent state and regional agencies entered into contracts for the brokering of OCLC services and for provision of training and ongoing assistance. Some of these networks had predated OCLC; others were formed in direct response to the need for an agency to provide OCLC services in a particular area. Two exceptions to the general pattern of independent brokering were the formation of OCLC Western, consisting of several branch offices on the Pacific Coast, and OCLC Europe, both being service agencies under the direct administration of OCLC.

The independent affiliate networks, which have usually numbered about 20, have remained administratively separate from OCLC a relationship that has at times worked to the benefit of OCLC and at other times served as a source of conflict. Within four years after OCLC's decision in 1973 to expand its base of participation beyond Ohio, the number of libraries using the system had increased to more than 800.

Increasing numbers of public and special libraries were joining, but the majority of new members continued to be academic libraries. These included many members of the Association of Research Libraries as well as medium-sized university libraries, but an influx of new participants continued from among the ranks of four-year colleges, a pattern that underscored OCLCs role in introducing automation into smaller institutions.

The concept of resource sharing was the basis for the formation of a number of formal cooperative ventures during the 1970s. One such, begun in 1974, was the Research Libraries Group (RLG), comprised of Harvard, Yale, Columbia, and the New York Public Library. Its board goals focused on the sharing of resources, collection development, and preservation and conservation of library materials. RLG felt that a common automated bibliographic system would enhance cooperative efforts among member libraries. By early 1978, the four systems under final consideration for adoption included OCLC, Standford's BALLOTS, the University of Chicago Library Data Management System, and the New York Public Library bibliographic control system.

In spring 1978, RLG announced agreement with Stanford for the use of BALLOTS as the group's automated bibliographic component. Although RLG may merely have chosen what it considered to be the best available system, the choice drew strong reactions from within and outside the group. In June of the year, Harvard announced withdrawal from RLG, although

Director of Libraries Douglas Bryant indicated that the choice of BALLOTS was not the motivating factor.

A wide spectrum of emotions was expressed throughout the library community concerning RLG's decision not to go with OCLC, which many saw as the emerging national bibliographic network. In comparing the online features of BALLOTS and OCLC, there is no question that BALLOTS was the far more sophisticated and flexible technical processing system. Unlike OCLC, it also provided for online storage and display of an individual library's cataloging data in a network environment, as well as other features such as searching by title keyword and subject, not available on OCLC.

Although on a smaller scale than OCLC, BALLETS had also proved capable of serving as a shared system as early as 1975 when seven public libraries in California entered into a networking arrangement with Stanford, and the number of libraries using it has increased since then.

The greatest source of resentment among OCLC libraries about RLG's selection of BALLOTS was probably not so much the choice itself as it was the accompanying implicit, and sometimes explicit, attitude that OCLC and its 'dirty database' were unacceptable, and that the needs of RLG members were somehow quite apart from those of the rest of the library community—including those of many prestigious research libraries that remained ardent supporters of OCLC. Equally crucial in the reaction, OCLC had come to be recognized by then as much more than a shared cataloging database. Because of library identifier symbols attached to each bibliographic record, OCLC had grown into a tremendous tool for facilitating interlibrary lending and, to many, was the most current and reliable source of occasional information available in the United States.

The selection of another system by RLG virtually cut off those libraries and their collections from this source of information and ejected a major obstacle to their participation in resource sharing on a broader scale. To many OCLC libraries and even to those using neither system, this detachment seemed a conscious and motivated effort to minimize the role of RLG members in the broader context of American library cooperation. The reaction to RLG did little at that time or later to discourage the image of elitism.

Full membership in RLG, in essence, required a library to be a member of the Association of Research Libraries (ARL), and this restricted potential membership in RLG to a pool of early 100 libraries. RLG permitted other libraries to apply for participant status, meaning a library could use and contribute cataloging data, but the feeling was that this did little to soften the image of elitism.

BALLOTS, which in the RLG environment became the Research Libraries Information Network (RLIN), may have been functionally superior to OCLC as a technical processing system, but not all of its distinctions were carried over into the new network. At Stanford, the system had been, and remained, a full technical processing system, which traced an item and built on its online record from the initial point of ordering to its final point of cataloging. Although any RLIN member library had searching access to Stanford's IPF, there was no capability for other members to build a similar file for their own institutions. Thus, one of the strongest features of the original BALLOTS, which provided the continuity for its realization a more complete technical processing system, did not exist under RLIN in its earliest manifestation for any library other than Stanford.

During the 1970s, work was also being conducted at the Washington State Library on the design of an online bibliographic system. Supported by a $1.2 million start-up grant from the state legislature, the system went online in 1978, the Washington Library Network (WLN) was being used in 12 public and 9 academic libraries in the state, along with 2 libraries in Alaska. Later that year, 3 libraries in Idaho and 1 in Oregon joined WLN.

From the start, it was apparent that WLN was a well-designed and highly sophisticated system. It included retrieval of local information, subject access, and, not long thereafter, authority control. WLN took a cautious approach to building its bibliographic database. As in RLIN and OCLC, Library of Congress MARC tapes were loaded, but unlike the other two utilities, WLN established a standing policy to centrally review all records input by member libraries. In January 1979, the library press reported that the National Library of Australia had signed for membership in WLN had sold its system software to the National Library.

All three of the major utilities—OCLC, RLIN, and WLN—were based on a centralized computer system linked through telecommunications lines to terminals in member libraries; none of the utilities up until that time had attempted to transfer any part of its system for use in another computer.

In 1978, it was not entirely clear to American library community what role WLN would assume in national bibliographic networking. Although WLN was focusing on regional cooperation in the Pacific Northwest, OCLC had also been a geographically limited system at one time, and BALLOTS had been implemented in a single library. It seemed possible that a third nationally competing system may have been emerging in the form of WLN.

In 1979, however, the network reaffirmed its regional emphasis, adopting a policy that expansion outside the Pacific Northwest would-be restricted to sale of the WLN software in a manner similar to what had taken place with the National Library of Australia. In the years immediately following, a number of such transactions occurred, including sales to the South-eastern Library Network (SOLINET), the University of Illinois, and the University of Missouri. Membership in the WLN network in the Pacific Northwest had increased to 60 members by 1980 and, as OCLC had done slightly more than two years before, WLN modified its government structure to reflect the expansion of its membership base beyond a single state.

Although its impact in the United State has been limited, the University of Toronto library Automated System (UTLAS) was a fourth major online bibliographic networking system to have emerged on the North American continent during the 1970s. Implemented in an online networking mode during the mid-1070s, UTLAS had increased its membership to more than 200 libraries by the end of the decade. UTLAS membership was limited primarily to Canadian libraries, with some important exceptions.

In 1980, the network signed its first member in the United States, the Rochester, New York, Institute of Technology. The following year, UTLAS signed a million-dollar agreement with a Japanese firm to broker UTLAS in Japan. The system did not make concerted efforts to expand into the United States, but it is noteworthy that in 1981, in a comprehensive comparison of the four major utilities, the University of California at Berkeley ranked UTLAS first in overall technical capability. The University did not, however, opt for UTLAS. In 1984, UTLAS opened a U.S. branch office in New York, and it will be interesting to see what impact this will have on its position in the nation.

Over the years, each of the four bibliographic utilities has strived to become more than simply a shared cataloguing database. Development efforts by one or more have gone into acquisitions subsystems, serials check-in capabilities, circulation systems, interlibrary loan communications, online union lists, provision of Computer Output Microform (COM) catalogs, and terminal compatibility for searching other databases. WLN, OCLC, and RLIN made a tremendous impact on librarianship in the United States during the 1970s in terms of providing online cataloging capabilities, but their impact in circulation control, acquisitions, and serials check-in was negligible. Some libraries continued to develop their own in-house systems to handle these functions. However, another alternative emerged, particularly in the area of online circulation, in the form of commercial vendors of automated library systems.

Automation via unit-record equipment had been almost the exclusive domain of IBM. Remington Rand offered unit-record equipment comparable to IBMs, but its impact on the library market was negligible. IBM continued its domination into the early 1960s, when offline computer processing came into use in some libraries.

As the decade progressed, however, computers manufactured by other firms began to appear in universities, corporations, and municipal facilities. By the end of the decade, IBM was still the predominant name in computers for library applications, but it no linger maintained the exclusively it had once enjoyed. During its years of dominance, IBM had been responsible in devoting time and effort to assist in applying its equipment to the library environment.

Libraries certainly did not receive an undue share of attention, but IBM representative were often assigned to help libraries with implementing applications, and the corporation published descriptions of and guides for use of its equipment in library applications. The company also sponsored seminars, the most notable being a symposium held in Endicott, New York, in 1964. Although IBM and its new competitors expressed at least nominal interest in library applications during the 1960s, it was evident that this was an infinitesimal share of the total computer market.

According to estimates in the early 1970s, less than one-tenth of one percent of the computers in the United States were being using by libraries in the way. To make these facilities still less conductive as a market, even those with computers were inevitably using equipment purchased by host institutions for a variety of applications, the foremost usually not being those of the library. Libraries had little control in either the selection of equipment or in the decision to replace one manufacturer or model with another.

As long as large-scale, multipurpose mainframes were the only available computers, libraries were essentially at the mercy of their host institutions. Although some libraries established excellent relations with their computer centers and did play a role in automation decisions, procurement was an unpredictable and uncontrollable environment for many. The advent of minicomputers radically altered the computer field for libraries, enabling at least the large ones to perhaps purchase their own equipment and create a more predictable environment.

A number of libraries did purchase their own equipment and designed applications software in-house in the 1970s, but another alternative began to emerge in that decade—the library-specific commercial vendor of automated library systems. In terms of the total computer market as viewed by larger corporations, libraries were too few to attract a great deal of attention, but the potential volume demonstrated a suitable market for smaller and specifically library-oriented commercial ventures.

One early commercial venture came from Computer Library Systems, Inc., later shortened to CL Systems. Inc., and later again simply to CLSI. The company's first automation efforts involved acquisitions systems, and one of its first installations, in 1972, was at the Cleveland Public Library, which had been using a batch processing system on IBM equipment for eight years. In a description of the CLSI system at Cleveland Public, Richard Palmer observed that, over a five-year period, the cost of the new online system was expected to be less than one-half the cost of the IBM batch processing system, had it been continued. In addition, the new system offered broader and more library-specific features.

CLSI soon turned its attention toward circulation control. Its LIBS 100 system and other vendor-supplied systems introduced subsequently come to be known as "turnkey," a reference to the premise that, upon delivery and installation, virtually all that was required to make the system work was to plug it in and turn it on.

Although in practice this has not always exactly proved to be the case, the idea was essentially sound and formed the basis on which these systems would become cost-effective alternatives to in-house development. As so many libraries had learned in implementing their own online or even batch processing systems, the cost of design and development were considerable.

With a mass-marketed system, such up-front development costs could be distributed among many customers and hence would be far less for each library then independent design and development. With a turnkey system, programming expertise was not required of the library staff or even at the host institution. Perhaps most importantly, the library's minicomputer could be operated and maintained within the library itself, and the software was marketed by vendors whose entire business was specifically library applications. Other vendors joined CLSI in the online circulation control market during the early and mid-1970s, nut for several years the field was fairly unstable. Various companies entered and left the market, were purchased by other companies, and radically redesigned their systems.

By 1975, five commercial vendors were offering turnkey automated circulation systems with varying degrees of online and offline capacity. Two years later, three of them had cased marketing efforts in the United States and another had been sold and its system totally redesigned. CLSI provided the only continuity in this short span of time. The year 1977 was pivotal, however, in that several new vendors of circulation control systems entered the market and would prove more stable than most of their predecessors. Among these were Data Phase, Geac, and Universal Library Systems. Entering the 1980s, CLSI was still the leading force in the commercial market, with 177 installations and more than 300 other libraries remotely accessing computers located at one of the installation sites.

The fastest growing computer was Data Phase with 50 installations, followed by Geac with 22. Gaylord, active since 1978, had 11 installations by 1981. Although not actively marketing in the United State since about 1977, the Plessey online circulation system popular in Great Britain had 9 users in the United States and Canada. With the exception of early CLSI efforts, commercial activity in online acquisitions and serials control has lagged behind circulation control and did not really begin to make an impact until the late 1970s and early 1980s. The primary source of commercial developments also differed between the two areas.

For the most part, vendor-supplied online circulation control systems have resulted from new commercial ventures into the library marketplace. In acquisitions and serials control, in contrast, many of the earliest efforts came from long-established library vendors; book jobbers for acquisitions and subscription agents in serials control. Baker and Taylor's offline BATAB system was available to libraries since the 1960s, and by the late 1970s the system had been redesigned, enhanced, and offered online as LIBRIS.

Around the same time, Brodart also announced availability of an online acquisitions system. By the early 1980s, book jobbers had been joined by other vendors, such as Ringgold and Innovative Interfaces, in offering online acquisitions, as well as by each of the four bibliographic utilities. In addition, several vendors of circulation systems were in the process of testing acquisitions modules, promising even more competition. Commercially available online serials control systems have appeared comparatively recently.

Two major subscription agencies, Ebsco and Faxon, each announced plans for an online system in 1981, capable not simply of ordering, but encompassing functions such as check-in and claiming, and not limited to titles ordered through the respective agency. Ebsco eventually abandoned development of its own online check-in component, while Faxon did incorporate one into its online system. Also in 1981, the MetaMicro Corporation of San Antonio, Texas, announced a serials control software package for minicomputer application, although active marketing of this system eventually ceased. Activity in the not-for-profit sector also showed signs of life in the early 1980s, exemplified by marketing of the CHECKMATE serials control system by the California Library Authority for Systems and Services (CLASS) and by OCLC planning efforts to make its rather dormant serials check-in subsystem more attractive.

Changes in the OCLC sub-system were made in 1983, but had a negligible impact in attracting new users. An interesting activity occurred with CHECKMATE, as Ebsco began to market that system when it abandoned development of its own online check-in module. Although the bibliographic utilities emerges during the 1970s as the clearly predominant supplier of automated cataloguing systems, there were a few commercial attempts to penetrate the cataloging market. One of these was the BIBNET system, announced by Information Dynamics Corporation in 1974.

BIBNET was to operate similarly to OCLC in a number of ways: it was principally intended to be a shared cataloging database; it was to contain member input master records as well as LC MARC records; the master database was to be stored on centralized computers; and library identifier symbols were to be affixed to each bibliographic record as an aid to interlibrary loan. Several features of BIBNET were planned conspicuously different from OCLC and attempted to answer some of OCLCs more pressing problem areas.

Keyword-in-title search capability was to be available, along with plans for the eventual introduction of subject searching of the database. BIBNET users would be encouraged to access the system though a minicomputer housed in the library to facilitate local production of offline products and to reduce telecommunications cost. By using a minicomputer, libraries could retrieve records from the master database, copy them onto a cassette tape, and then break the telecommunications link. Master records copied onto the cassette would then be displayed on a CRT terminal connected to the minicomputer, modifications made to the records, and the revised records copied into a second cassette. Catalog cards and other offline products could be printed locally, based on the modified records on the second cassette.

Although access to BIBNET could be gained through means other than a minicomputer, the front-end interface was strongly promoted as the most useful for allowing flexibility. Information Dynamics had ambitious intentions for BIBNET. Not only was it to contain post-1968 LC MARC records, but there was a plan to centrally input access points into the online system for more than 3.5 million Library of Congress manual cataloging records created between 1953 and 1968.

When a library retrieved such an index entry, it could notify Information Dynamics through the system that it would like a full record in the database for that title. Information Dynamics would then create a record in MARC format for the title requested and load it into BIBNET within four days. BIBNET'S entry into the marketplace coincided with the rapid and successful expansion of OCLC. The system simply never established a firm position.

A more successful venture was launched several years later by Informatics, Inc., with the introduction of MINIMARC. It was minicomputer-based, but with no pretense as a networking system. The entire LC MARC database was supplied on floppy diskettes. The library retrieved these records locally on its minicomputer and modified them according to need. For titles not found on the LC MARC database, the library could create and input records into its own working file. Catalog cards and other offline products could be locally produced.

Since a premise of MINIMARC was local processing, the system did not incur the telecommunications charges as did use of a bibliographic utility, and the overall cost were not as per-unit-dependent. On the other hand the initial investment could be as tenfold that of joining a bibliographic utility, and monthly maintenance and other costs were substantial enough to make participation in a utility more economical for smaller libraries. A limiting feature of MINIMARC was that, as a nonnetworking system, its core database was restricted to LC MARC records and was therefore smaller than those of the bibliographic utilities. Since its emphasis was so much on being a local system, it did not serve in any capacity as an interlibrary loan locational tool.

In 1981, however, Informatics, RLG, and the California Library Authority for Systems and Services (CLASS) announced availability of an interface whereby MINIMARC users would be able to search the RLIN database through their MINIMARC system equipment, an arrangement that would enhance MINIMARC as a local system with access to a broader utility.

By 1981, more than 30 libraries had installed MINIMARC, and the number had increased steadily since then. Another successful commercial venture into automated cataloging was the Carrollton Press REMARC project. In 1980, Carrollton announced a five-year project in which it would convert more than 5 million Library of Congress cataloging records, not included on MARC, to machine-readable from.

Libraries could submit brief data to Carrollton, in either machine-readable or nonmachine-readable form, to match against both the LC MARC database and the REMARC database being created by Carrollton. For items for which a record could be found, Carrollton would supply machine-readable bibliographic records containing relatively complete LC cataloguing data.

In addition to MINIMARC and REMARC as alternatives to the bibliographic utilities, a number of commercial book jobbers and COM vendors were maintaining machine-readable cataloguing databases for their customers. These were really a quite different matter, since initially with these stored databases, a customer did not have direct online access to its own database. This circumstance has been changing, as some of these vendors now provide online access.

Online Public Access Catalogues (OPACs)

Online Public Access Catalogues (OPACs) are IR systems used by end-users. Potential OPAC users form a very large population with extremely varied needs and backgrounds. As designers of computerised IR systems, and as specialists in information handling, processing and retrieval, we must be aware of the problems users encounter when interacting with our systems. We should shift our interests from catalogue use studies to catalogues as IR public systems: their usability and ease of use; HCI aspects; end-users; and, ultimately, user information-seeking behaviour.

There is now a well-known history of OPAC design develop-ments and Hildreth has classified them into three generations. The initial OPAC generation was derived from circulation or cataloguing systems, and gives rather limited access to the bibliographic information. It is essentially based upon pre-coordinate IR principles. Their interfaces simulate traditional catalogues in their forms of access by providing mainly phrase access to separate indexes. This is appropriate for known item searching.

The second-generation OPAC systems are more similar to the commercial IR systems; they provide keyword or free-text access, corresponding to post-coordinate IR principles. Their interfaces are generally command driven, making use of Boolean logic which is well suited for subject searching. The indexes to be searched have to be specified by the user in the search formulation.

The first kind of design improvement found in third generation OPAC systems was to combine the features of the first two OPAC generations by providing both phrase searching and keyword searching. In terms of interface this is often achieved by a simplified command language which facilitates user interaction. It leads users through menus and question/answers as well as commands; the interface has improved help screens and instructions and operations are simplified. This is typified by recent developments of a few systems, such as MELVYL, LCS/WLN at the University of Illinois, and CARL, which now also provide access to other kinds of bibliographic information through their OPAC: accessing monographs as well as journal articles becomes more integrated.

MELVYL gives access to the Medline files, CARL searches newspaper clippings, and LCS/WLN uses a PC front- end interface to traditional online systems. This latter system assists users in the use of the command language; it helps them to build a search strategy offline, with a wealth of help screens and detailed instructions; it executes the resulting search strategy online; it downloads the retrieved references on the PC; and it offers to locate the journal titles in the Illinois University Library catalogue. Obviously, offering command languages to OPAC users is a long-awaited and welcome trend.

Nevertheless, it still presents problems with lack of ease and simplicity of use for a large proportion of users. Many end-users would not necessarily want to plough through the lengthy text of LCS/WLN University of Illinois front-end's numerous screens. Other systems, either experimental or operational, are trying to overcome these problems using such means as retrieval, linguistic and semantic aids. Some of these improvements are also referred to by Hildreth. These will be reviewed briefly, starting with 'mechanical' devices and moving towards more 'semantically oriented' devices. Whilst the former try to improve the mechanical matching processes, their interface design does not employ knowledge of the subject area. The latter, however, make use of subject knowledge actively to offer contextual and semantic support in order to assist user interaction.

There have been a few attempts at incorporating the knowledge learned from IR research and experimentation to improve conventional Boolean retrieval systems. The most well-known systems are CITE and Okapi. They have implemented implicit Boolean searching on natural language input, weighting and ranking techniques, and relevance feedback from the user. Thus, they enable the user to search without necessarily being knowledgeable about Boolean search formulation and reformulation. Okapi also offers 'intelligent search sequencing'. This follows automatically various search trees, which combine phrase and keyword access and search various indexes simultaneously or consecutively, particularly for author/title searches. It therefore goes beyond an initial matching between the user input and the database indexes. Okapi attempts various further matches using all the information available from the system and the user. The system retrieves as many references as possible without the user having to reformulate his search. Depending on the result, it gives the user either short or full records, or indexes to browse.

More recent work done at the Polytechnic of Central London consisted of implementing automatic spelling correction and stemming. The automatic spelling is achieved using sound-matching algorithms and corrects miskeyings and other misspellings by mapping orthographically-related words. The sound-matching algorithm reduces words phonetically by representing them by their most significant characters. The automatic stemming links morphologically related words, hence providing a form of implicit truncation. The Okapi '86 team went some way into considering to what extent a word should be stemmed: keeping the longest possible suffix to start with, then stemming further. Both 'strong' and 'weak' stems are generated and a combinatorial method is used for term weighting so that the output is ranked. Weak stems get higher weights than strong stems. Spelling variations (e.g., UK and US forms) are incorporated into the weak stemming procedure. When a word does not stem to anything in the index, it is then sound matched and looked up in the index for the nearest match.

These design features are basically mechanical devices to improve the system matching processes. They are intended to provide the users with as much and as good retrieval as possible, without them having to learn the search mechanics (e.g., truncation) to do it. The burden of the search interaction has therefore shifted from the user to the system. Some of these features have semantic implications; for example, the implicit truncation may bring in semantically related words, although the underlying mechanism uses morphological principles. Other design improvements are more definitely aimed at improving the semantic aspect of the searching process.

LCS/WLN at the University of Illinois has implemented a way of leading users from retrieved information to related information that was not initially formulated by the user. It does this by linking relevant records retrieved with free-text words to other records, using their subject headings. It is an interesting attempt at relating free text to controlled vocabulary. This assists the user in navigating through the natural words and the subject authority entries of the database. CITE, implemented at the National Library of Medicine, also has the same feature: from the user natural input it gives a list of the relevant medical subject headings (MeSH) to be 'weighted' by the user (rather than by the system, as in Okapi). However, the system assumes that the user will be familiar with the medical terminology and the structure of MeSH.

Well-known suggestions by Pauline Cochrane Atherton and Irene Wormell are to add the back-of-the-book indexes, tables of contents and chapter headings to enrich the subject description of monographs. These have not yet been implemented. Another area for subject access and semantic improvements is the use of classification schemes. A very interesting experiment was carried out by Karen Markey and Anh Demeyer at the Online C = Library Center (OCLC). Using the Dewey Decimal Classification (DDC) Schedules and Relative Indexes machine-readable file provided by Forest Press, they tried: (a) to enrich the vocabulary of the database, and (b) to provide for systematic access through the DDC Schedules.

By means of a rigorous experimental set- up they proved that the classification schemes and indexes did enrich the database vocabulary and retrieved records not found with the control OPAC system. With the DDC-based experimental OPAC, the user input is related to the class number(s) under which it appears; the system also displays the *context* of the search input within the classification scheme, emphasising different 'perspectives' under which that topic is classified. The class number of retrieved and relevant records could also be used for expanding and retrieving other records, as a search 'pivot' (in the same way, LCS/WLN at Illinois University uses subject headings). This design idea has not been implemented. Work is also currently being done on the use of PRECIS (PREserved Context Indexing System) as subject authority or online thesaurus by Juliet Congreve at the Middlesex Polytechnic. Without actually implementing a full online thesaurus, it is possible to improve the semantics of the system. Okapi '86 does it in a simple way, using look-up tables which handle semantically-related words.

A semantic tool can range from a simple stop-list of words to a full subject authority control list. Okapi '86 look-up tables contain three types of entries: stopwords; terms to be treated as equivalent (child' and 'children'); and certain compound words to be treated as single terms (e.g., 'industrial relations' and 'Great Britain'). This was found to provide more precise and unique matching than stemming. Other semantically oriented work has been done by Michael Lesk, using the eighteenth-century short title catalogue database at the British Library. He uses various dictionaries (e.g., *The Oxford English Dictionary* (OED), Collins and specialised dictionaries) to expand the user query. An inverted file of dictionary definitions is kept, along with the number of overlapped words and their frequencies to enable a weighting procedure.

The point of using and linking dictionary definitions is that it gives a large quantity of words which a thesaurus would not offer, and also a wide range of different meanings for the words. The dictionary definitions are called in if the user word(s) do not appear in the fie, and bring in related words. If the user input retrieves only a few references, the system gets relevance feedback from the user and expands the query, using the dictionary definitions, to suggest other records to the user. Hildreth states that, librarians should learn about (a) the potential of online retrieval, (b) catalogue access issues, and (c) user-system interface problems and promises.

Most IR systems still do little to help the user transform an information need to the explicit descriptions understandable by the system. To optimise retrieval results in subject searching, more than one search approach may have to be employed in the overall search strategy. This quotation from Chan, referring to the use of various subject aids seems very appropriate: the process of seeking and identifying information to assist with a problem typically follows a more circuitous, cyclical and unstructured path than the one provided for by strictly matching devices. The remaining research quotation is, 'How do we choose among all these numerous design features?' A way of illustrating this problem is to refer to a recently designed operational OPAC system. This system features Boolean searching on keywords, relevance feedback based on free- text, mixed with Universal Decimal Classification (UDC) numbers.

User Interaction

Any improvement in design must also be accompanied by an evaluation of its use and success or failure with the users.

Furthermore, any design decision should stem from an understanding of user interaction problems. We have seen many information system which a panel of experts would undoubtedly rate technical successes however, upon talking to users in the organisations, we hear a different story ... 'products should be more carefully matched both users' skills and their psychological needs'. Evaluation of OPACs has in the past chiefly concentrated on impact studies, public usage, technical and IR performance and use patterns.

Impact studies look at how well users react to and accept these new computer systems as compared with traditional catalogues, and if they prefer them or not. Public usage studies are concerned with which types of users use or do not use the OPAC and the reasons why. These two types of studies are usually carried out using the traditional methods of data gathering, i.e., questionnaires, surveys and focus group interviews.

Technical performance studies look at the computer workload, the response time or the required number of terminals. IR performance studies compare search keys versus keyword searching, title searches in OPACs and in card catalogues, or retrieval results using different features. Use pattern studies monitor the number of known-item versus subject searches, the utilisation and success of various search criteria by users, or the pattern of users' errors in searching the OPAC. These studies use the transaction log analysis method and controlled experiments. The transaction log analysis enables us to monitor *real* usage and gives data on use patterns. Many case studies of individual systems can be found in the literature. Some cover several of these aspects; see Mitev and Efthimiadis, for example. However, on the whole, they tend to be specific to a system and to a library context. A few studies compare the use of two systems in an experimental manner, in order to support the choice of a system by a particular library.

Of special interest is a recent study: which compares keyword subject searching on six operational British university OPACs available through JANET (Joint Academic NETWork). Two specimen subject searches were carried out on the six OPACs. The number of items retrieved on each were compared, together with whether they were retrieved using title keywords or Library of Congress Subject Headings (LCSH) keywords. The various searching features are surveyed and conclusions are drawn on their merits. In terms of evaluating the user interaction, several areas have been explored: ergonomic studies (screen displays, legibility, typing), ease-of-use studies (ease of searching, usability, search satisfaction), and studies of information seeking behaviour.

Work on the comparative ease of use of two types of user interface has been done. A menu-driven user interface giving access to a hierarchical classification scheme and a command-driven interface were compared in a natural setting. It was concluded that users would rather employ their own words than go through several screens of classified data to choose their topic. This last group of evaluation studies has made use of controlled experiments, protocol analysis and talk-aloud methods. This area is by far the least explored.

Human-Computer Interaction

We know that any system architecture has significant and widespread implications for user friendliness, but we know, very little about how to make fundamental architectural decisions differently as a result of an emphasis on human factors. On the whole, HCI research has only touched upon a few aspects of the user interface design. It has looked at hardware problems (keyboard and screen design) and at the very surface of software problems. Beyond the description of these aspects, HCI is not so much concerned with artificial intelligence (AI) (the task of building a computer to reason as we imagine people do) as with what might be called artificial personality (how to make the computer behave the way we want it to). Ideally, the interface design should be dissociated from the rest of the system to allow for flexibility, adaptability and change. The design of many interactive systems is often influenced by our beliefs about the human mind as well as by the traditional (and still essential) criteria of functionality and efficiency.

The user interaction has been divided into four levels by Moran: a task level (the IR task in our case); a semantic level (how the objects and the operations on these objects are defined and represented); a syntactic level (what the things are called); and a physical interaction level (how the users can act upon these objects, operations, etc.). The ease with which the user can interact with the system is also split according to these levels: how well the task is analysed and dealt with by the system and communicated to the user; how well chosen the objects and operations are in order to perform the task; how well expressed this choice is; and how easy it is to manipulate them. It is important here to stress the existence of the first two levels (task and semantic). These are often neglected. The last two levels (syntactic and physical) are more often dealt with, perhaps because they can be seen. They are also more easily modified; one can experiment with them and compare them. Although less obvious, the other two levels (task and semantic levels) are just as crucial for a good interface, perhaps even more crucial than the syntactic and physical operation levels.

Direct Manipulation

The interface should be unobtrusive, not interfering or intruding. If the interface itself is noticed, then it stands in a third-person relationship to the objects of interest, and detracts from the directness of engagement. This idea of 'direct engagement' or 'direct manipulation' is related to (if not issued from) the recent WIMPS developments.

Users interact directly with objects represented graphically on the screen, instead of having a conversation about these objects in order to act upon them. The interface is itself a world in which the user can act, and which changes state in response to user actions. The world of interest is explicitly represented. The interface is not an implied intermediary between the user and the world about which things are said. Although this feeling of direct engagement is of critical importance, the actual requirements for producing it are little known. The purpose of the system is to serve the user, not to use a specific technology and not to be an elegant piece of programming. Metaphor crucially depends on knowing enough about the attributes of the objects in both the central domain and the domain to which it is being likened, to determine what it could possibly make sense to import.

The computer is capable of using many arbitrarily complex mappings between symbols—including those displayed on the screen—and the objects, situations and events they refer to. The relationship between what appears on the screen and, for example, a file being edited, is non-trivial: if it is a copy that is being manipulated (although this is not apparent). Failing to save it, a common mistake, may result in the loss of many hours' work. Such relationships become more sophisticated with the use of icons and customised direct manipulation workbenches.

There is potential for confusion between actions performed on the object itself and its manifestation in one of several displays. The relationship between what happens to an object and what happens to its screen manifestation has to be accepted by a novice user as arbitrary. One example of the use of icons in the context of OPACs is the system designed by Benest et al. at York University, Department of Computer Science. In it, the user is first offered a *picture* of the indexes the user can search. Each index is represented as a book on a shelf, and the user can select one with a mouse.

The chosen index is then displayed on the screen as an open book, two pages at a time, and the user can flick through these pages of index-entries alphabetically There is a way of skipping to a particular letter if required, by selecting a letter among an A to Z sequence on the side. Once an index entry is selected, the book is located on a physically simulated bookshelf. The physical sizes of the books are related to the actual number of pages, format, etc. The authors envisage that the spine could be used for giving further information in the future.

The user can browse through the classified items on the shelf. If a book is selected, there is a book emulator, and pushing buttons will flick and jump through its pages. Pages may be annotated with a highlighting pen and book-markers can be inserted. References within the main text may be selected, causing the full reference to be displayed in a nearby window. Selecting a reference within the list of references causes the display of those page numbers on which the reference occurs. The use of icons in this system is based on the idea that the physical presence of a book, particularly its front cover design, provides the reader with an overall impression of its contents. Spatial awareness is seen as providing recognition clues.

A first remark one can make about this system is that its form of access is phrase searching. Even if it offers sophisticated graphics, it is at heart a first-generation OPAC. It does not make use of the potential power of computer retrieval capabilities. Furthermore, one can question the use of these pictorial representations. Is it pertinent to the user to have books physically displayed on the screen? Is the traditional way of searching bookshelves in any way related to searching a computer? Is it a relevant way of representing and referring to the process of searching monographs online? It could be seen as a diversion from the primary aim of an IR system. One could comment that it may be over- simplifying the issue of ease of interaction, as if ergonomists decided to paint telephone sets pink to make them more user-friendly. Users of such a system might very quickly get frustrated with its apparently simple representation of the IR task, and with the poverty of its retrieval features. This kind of approach is only tackling the representation of objects and operations on these subjects, i.e., Moran's semantic, syntactic and physical interaction levels. To put it differently, the task is assumed to be of a certain nature. The designers have a preconceived model of what the task should be. This might not be necessarily related to the computerised IR task. Nevertheless, this system offers an unusual approach to reading full text and physically annotating pages. It also provides for browsing a classified sequence of books, whichever selection criterion was used to retrieve them.

With user interfaces and their quality of HCI, one has to be aware of the fact that the feeling of directness can depend on how much practice the particular user has. Users may adjust themselves to the interface and, with sufficient practice, may view it as directly supporting their intentions. This gives credit for the work the use has done. Nevertheless, this notion of direct engagement is of interest. One can see that for IR, the use of command languages is like having an intermediate layer between the user and the actual task. Command languages force the user to think about the mechanics of how to ask for something; they are noticed, distract from the task itself, render the interface 'visible' and suppress this sensation of directness.

Another interesting notion found in the direct manipulation literature is the following: 'the expression of a direct manipulation output language must be such that the user can assume that it, in some sense, is the things it refers to'. Furthermore, the nature of the relationship between input and output languages must be such that an output expression can serve as a component of an input expression. 'Input and output languages of the interface should be interreferential, allowing an input expression to incorporate or make use of a previous output expression. . . . This is crucial to create the illusion that one is directly manipulating the objects of concern.' This seems to apply immediately to retrieval systems. Parts of document(s), individual word(s), sentences or groups of word(s) displayed could be used directly as something to be input for another search. This could be done, for example, by pointing and 'picking' them on the screen and carrying them across another area of the screen. The user would not have to input them again.

Expert Systems

The possible contributions of AI to the design of online IR systems have already been examined for some time. AI first, then expert systems or intelligent knowledge-based systems, attempt to overcome barriers to database access by casual users; the AI approach tries to build a better database system with understanding of the user, his requirements and natural language communication. It tries to put all the load on the computer and make it clever enough to deal with the casual user. The HCI approach, in contrast, attempts to remove as much of the load as possible from both human and computer and share what is left between them, through user- computer interaction or 'negotiation'. AI has not been extremely concerned with HCI and ease-of-use problems (natural language interfaces are often assumed to solve that problem). Rather it has concentrated on the issue of computer understanding of users' general reasoning processes, especially knowledge representation and infe-rençe mechanisms, in order to simulate them in the machine.

Expert systems have a more pragmatic approach. They concentrate on limited domains as opposed to general problem-solving mechanisms. They build specialised know-ledge bases and inference engines; this knowledge is generally acquired from human domain experts using knowledge elicitation techniques. It is formalised using knowledge engineering methods, so that it can be implemented on a machine, often using an expert system 'shell'. However, the sometimes excellent decision-making performance provided by expert systems does not necessarily guarantee user acceptability. Expert system users still have HCI needs. Moreover, for some major practical applications the interface should be developed ahead of the reasoning part of the system. Berry and Broadbent even predict that, 'there will soon be more power associated with the interface of an expert system than with the knowledge base and inference engine'.

There have been various attempts at incorporating expert system techniques in IR systems, such as CANsearch EXPERT, Expert System Assistant, etc. A recent paper by Brooks reviews the current developments in this area. There was a special issue of *Information processing and management* on expert systems in 1987. The reader is also referred to Belkin and Vickery for a thorough theoretical review of research into document retrieval and knowledge-based systems, within the conceptual framework of 'intera-ction in information systems'.

The first category of intelligent IR systems might be more appropriate classified as 'front-ends'. These systems' inter-faces assist users with search strategy formulation. They use improved retrieval techniques, i.e., term weighting, document ranking and relevance feedback. These techniques are now being incorporated in OPACs. In other systems (e.g., EXPERT) searches are carried out using a common command language which the system translates into the appropriate query language command. EXPERT embodies a number of rules for deciding which database to search, how to select synonyms and how to combine terms. It enables users to represent their search topic; it assists users with selecting a database to search; it automatically constructs a search strategy from the topic representation and executes it; and it uses relevance feedback to reformulate the search strategy. So far; these interfaces are concerned with mapping the user's input into appropriate search terms, constructing a search strategy and carrying out the search automatically. This deals with the automatic query formulation.

The task of assisting with the online search itself, where the role of the interface is to monitor and advise the user rather than to do the search, has been neglected. For example, the problems with EXPERT are: it is unable to formulate database-dependent strategies; it is unable to suggest search terms; and, perhaps more importantly, it lacks sufficient user involvement in search strategy reformulation. Apart from its use of production rule techniques, EXPERT seems to be little more than a gateway plus relevance feedback retrieval system. With the exception of the construction of search statements and assistance with database selection, the intellectual effort is still largely on the user's side. An exception is IIDA (Individualised Instruction for Database Access), developed within a training/teaching context. IIDA examines commands and responses, looking for errors or indications of problems and detecting faulty search patterns. However, it is more of an intelligent tutoring system, which trains inexperienced searchers in the use of Boolean command languages. These systems still envisage the IR task as a strict matching process, and the underlying dominant searching model is the Boolean retrieval model. The designers have a limited preconceived idea of Moran's task level.

A second category of projects is trying to develop intelligent interfaces for online IR systems, based on expert system techniques. Expert systems try to embody and use some of the knowledge and skills of a human expert in such a form that the system can offer intelligent advice or take an intelligent decision about a processing function. The system, on demand, should be able to justify its own line of reasoning in a manner directly intelligible to the enquirer. The domains to which expert system techniques have been successfully applied, though, are areas such as medical diagnosis and geological prospecting. These areas are of a very different nature from that of an interface to an IR system. Another critical difference is the very wide subject domain covered by most document retrieval systems.

Little work has been done on expert systems which can cope with domains which are broad and not very detailed, and which involve large numbers of concepts and relations. Also, IR systems depend heavily on language. Information conveyed by a document is conveyed by the specific linguistic expressions of that document. The successful use of expert system techniques in our field may not be possible until such techniques have been further advanced. Still, it might be useful to look into it, as we can gain insight into possible design developments. This could be helpful for several reasons: the interactive nature of OPACs, the complex nature of the IR task, and the fact that it is impossible to train the large population of OPAC potential users to the thorough understanding and manipulation of command languages. An interesting example is described in Shoval that this system is designed to assist users with the selection of terms. It employs a knowledge base which contains the knowledge available to the human expert—a thesaurus and additional knowledge of terms, meanings and associations.

The usual hierarchical and synonymity relations found in thesauri are enhanced by the addition of two other types of relation, generator and modal. Generator relations link the components of multiword phrases; modal links are used to express more general relations. The user decides which terms represent his query and enters them one by one. The system then conducts a search of its knowledge base and additional terms of probable relevance are selected.

An evaluation process is applied to distinguish terms which are most representative of the user's request. This system employs more powerful term selection heuristics than EXPERT, and does so as a *cooperative effort with the user.* Whilst the system 'knows' about the vocabulary of particular subject domains and some of the relationships between the concepts, it does not appear to embody knowledge about how these terms are applied by the indexers to documents in the database. Thus, however well the final set of terms may express the user's request, it is no indication as to whether useful documents will be retrieved using these terms.

CANsearch enables medical practitioners to access directly the online databases which cover the cancer literature. The MeSH thesaurus is not easy to use and indexing policies are complicated. CANsearch helps further, by assuming that a cancer therapy search topic involves certain facets. It uses these facets as a framework, guiding the user through relevant sections of the MeSH thesaurus.

The user touches the screen to select the appropriate facets. The facet structure also guides the combination of terms with Boolean operators to form a sophisticated search strategy. CANsearch incorporates subject knowledge, indexing knowledge, knowledge of the query language and knowledge about searching. In terms of IR for both these systems (Shoval and CANsearch), the domain is narrow enough to be well represented and structured. These systems go a long way in terms of semantic or contextual assistance. Obviously that would be much more difficult with an OPAC and its large subject domain. In terms of HCI, Moran's task level is taken a step further than a straight matching process; the IR task is seen as involving semantic/contextual help as well. It is pleasant to use (touch-screen hardware), but users have to go through the same long sequence of facets to choose their topic from, every time they use the system.

The last IR system considered using expert system techniques is PLEXUS, designed under a British Library Research & Development Department grant at the Central Information Service of the University of London. PLEXUS was designed to help librarians to deal with referral queries about a particular domain, 'gardening'. It has a dictionary of terms, a database of referral resources and a hierarchical classification of the subject domain (by facets using the Broad System of Ordering (BSO)). The user is asked to describe what the gardening problem is about; the input is stemmed; and semantic categories, synonyms and pointers to the BSO classification are found. The system then displays concepts in the domain (a section of the BSO classification) from which the user can browse and select terms. If the model is incomplete, rules direct what questions should be posed in order to elicit the missing information.

The search employs knowledge of search strategies and tactics to broaden and narrow the search if necessary (enter broader descriptors, exclude concepts, add synonyms). The result is a Boolean search strategy, which is modified automatically if the user wants more or less information. Perhaps the most interesting aspect of PLEXUS is the fact that it constructs a user model: by a series of questions it assesses the level of experience of the user, his gardening experience, geographical location, previous searching habits, etc. It will use this information when giving results, for example, by giving introductory manuals if the user is non-expert at gardening. Again, this system deals with a very narrow knowledge area, and user queries are maybe more of a problem-solving nature than of a strict reference retrieval nature. Neverthe-less, it provides an interesting semantic/contextual approach to IR. The underlying task model is complex. Perhaps more interestingly, the task interaction/ negotiation with the user is fairly sophisticated. The designers had not foreseen that the interface design would assume so much importance when they started off, and they did pay a lot of attention to it: their system offers much more of a search 'conversation' about the task with its users than most systems.

OPACs have started incorporating some intelligent IR devices. Maybe OPAC design should gain from the experience of providing a semantic/contextual intelligent approach, as illustrated in other IR expert systems in the previous section. This semantic/contextual approach should not merely aim at improving the retrieval process (recall and/or precision). It should be envisaged as a means of assisting the user in his negotiation of a search, or task dialogue, with the system. In contrast to traditional IR systems, OPACs' coverage is very broad. Perhaps this contextual approach could be of prime importance. Our having borrowed design concepts from traditional IR systems shouldn't make us lose sight of the contextual nature of our systems. Broad subject IR systems such as OPACs, full text and mixed media databases are characterised by the fact that the structure of the information is not known *a priori*, unlike expert systems domains. This prevents advance knowledge of the types of questions that will be asked, unlike the situation found in hierarchical and relational database management systems, or in narrow domain expert systems.

It is much more difficult to explore and design expert systems for reasoning on open-ended domains. Nevertheless, current efforts at using expert systems techniques for retrieving information, even on small domains, have shown that the semantic/contextual approach is vital. This should be borne in mind when examining OPAC designs. Eastman's paper examines similar issues, although from the evaluation viewpoint. More specifically, she mentions the classificatory nature of online catalogues as opposed to other IR systems; how expert system techniques have been used for classification problem solving; and she even considers the problem structure of classification systems for catalogue selection to be a subclass of expert systems, and more so than traditional IR systems. 'The general architecture of the operation of a classification system is broken down into three major steps: abstraction of the problem data, heuristic matching of the abstraction in a specialisation network and refinement into specific solutions. . . . The architecture of a number of expert systems can be viewed in this way.'

Dewey Decimal Classification and Online Cataloguing

The Dewey Decimal Classification (DDC) was first published by Melvil Dewey in 1876. It is now in its twentieth edition. It is basically a theoretical scheme, designed to contain room for all knowledge, without attention to the subject emphases of the holdings of any one library. Although its use in North American libraries, especially academic libraries, diminished during the 1960s and 1970s, it is the most widely used library classification system in the world. It is used by over 85 per cent of all types of libraries in the United States and Canada, including almost all school and public libraries, and about two-fifths of all academic libraries. It has been translated into thirty-four languages, from German to Gujarati.

The DDC uses a pure notation based on numbers, and is divided into ten main classes:

000-099	Generalities, including Knowledge, Library science, Bibliographies
100-199	Philosophy; Psychology
200-299	Religion
300-399	Social sciences, Statistics, Customs, Etiquette, Folklore
400-499	Language
500-599	Pure sciences
600-699	Technology, Manufacture
700-799	The arts; Recreation and performing arts
800-899	Literature
900-999	History, Biography, Geography

Further subdivisions are again in groups of ten:

300-309	Social sciences in general
310-319	Statistics

320-329	Political science
330-339	Economics
340-349	Law
350-359	Public administration
360-369	Social problems and services
370-379	Education
380-389	Commerce, Trade
390-399	Customs, Etiquette, Folklore

Still further subdivisions are also in groups of ten:

370	Education
371	Generalities of education
372	Elementary education
373	Secondary education
374	Adult education
375	Curricula
376	Education of women
377	Schools and religion
378	Higher education
379	Education and the state

Numbers divided beyond three figures become decimal numbers:

378	Higher education
378.1	Organisation and administration of institutions of higher education
378.11	Personnel administration
378.111	Academic personnel
378.14	College year
378.142	Summer school

Like any classification scheme, the DDC has advantages and disadvantages when examined with automation in mind. Among the positive characteristics that make it a possible candidate for, use in automated subject retrieval are:

— It obeys many logical principles of a well-designed classification scheme, for example, that the whole of a subject should precede its parts.

— It has, with some exceptions, an expressive notation in decimal form. These three facts (logic; expressive notation; decimal numbers) facilitate hierarchical search and permit truncation. The truncation technique is commonly found in keyword retrieval systems. When it is applied to notation, it makes the notation an even more powerful retrieval tool with which the depth and breadth of a search subject can be quickly and easily amended.

— Truncation—in this case, right truncation (that is, truncating the right side of a notation)—applied to an expressive notation allows a search to be extended or broadened, with more material to be retrieved.

— The DDC uses standard subdivisions, whereby to each subject, broad or specific (Social sciences, Education, Secondary education, Teaching French in secondary schools) can be added generally consistent symbols that indicate the format in which the subject is being treated or the geographic area with which it is concerned.

In spite of its many excellent features, the DDC has disadvantages. It is old, having been created over a century ago and then for a library that by today's standards would be regarded as very small. Originally designed for filing entries (document surrogates) in paper-based files, the DDC was developed primarily for use in shelf arrangement, not for use in a computer. A classification scheme, especially one that is to be used as a retrieval device in an online catalogue, should be consistent in structure and notation, although inconsistencies can sometimes be circumvented by sophisticated algorithms or retrieval programmes. While the DDC is in some respects a remarkably consistent scheme— far more so than the LCC—it also contains some inconsistencies that make the creation of menus, the display of arrays, and the use of truncation not only less than automatic, but often difficult to achieve. Also, while it has in several places a structure that resembles the more versatile and precisely structured faceted classification schemes, it is overwhelmingly enumerative, with the typical limitations of enumerative schemes.

Since the DDC was created over one hundred years ago, its basic structure reflects the knowledge, attitudes, emphases, and political situation of that time. One example is the topic of Psychology which is still placed in the middle of Philosophy instead of with Medicine and health, to which it belongs according to current thought. The use of arrays and scrolling is not aided by this structure. Since the DDC was created before many of today's scientific and technical achievements were invented, and before many of today's social concepts were developed, the scheme originally devoted proportionally far less space and detail to the social, pure, and applied sciences (300s, 500s, and 600s) than today's state of knowledge requires.

New fields can be, and are being, inserted, thanks to the DDC's hospitality. However, because of the limited notational base of ten, the resulting numbers are often quite long which is more of a problem for humans than for computers. The notational base, however, also causes some new topics to be inserted in ways that cause problems in logical relationships and, therefore, online classed searching ability.

While one can always quarrel with the logic of any classification scheme, the DDC is generally considered to be reasonably logical and effective for a general library in its grouping of related concepts and in its separation of unrelated ones. However, while it breaks down each major topic reasonably, the relationships among the major topics themselves are often tenuous. This is true for any classification scheme. For example, while the concepts of Education and Commerce are broken down more or less reasonably, there is little obvious logical connection between the last notations in the 370-379 group and the first few notations in the 380-389 group: 379.982 (Government control of public education in Greenland) and 380.1 (Commerce) are hardly logically connected. Scrolling of class notations or of entries in call number order can, therefore, be limited to searches within any one major topic, such as Education.

In an online system that permits broadening and narrowing a topical search by moving up and down the hierarchy, and that permits broadening a topical search through truncation, two of the most important features are a consistently logical structure and a consistently expressive notation. This requires that topics at any one level in the consistently logical hierarchy have a notation that has at least one more symbol at the end than the notation for the topic at the immediately more general level. While the DDC does fairly well both with respect to logical structure and expressive notation, there are quite a few exceptions that make truncation and hierarchical display based solely on the notation less than automatic, and that affect hierarchical online searches negatively.

Relocations

For users of any living classification scheme, like DDC or LCC, a big obstacle to consistent retrieval is that, over the years, the locations and notations for many concepts were changed. This principle of the integrity of numbers had great appeal, partly because it was made at a time when librarians who used an older method of shelf-bound classification had to reclassify their collections from time to time to accommodate growth. Integrity of numbers has two effects.

First, once a work has been given a symbol, that symbol will not have to be changed, because it will continue to appear in later editions of the classification scheme and will, therefore, be used for new books on the same subject.

Second, patrons who search for a topic will find both old and new material on that topic in one place. The problem with this principle is that knowledge does not stand still. Therefore, notational symbols may have to be changed if a helpful and current arrangement of the schedules, of the books on the shelves, and of the entries in a classed file is to be achieved.

New discoveries and changing relationships within agriculture, or astronomy and astrophysics, or sociology, provide several examples of how much topics and relationships can change in the course of a few decades. However, if the notational symbols are changed in new editions of a classification schedule, old and new books on a topic will not necessarily be shelved or listed together.

The relocations of individual topics, the introduction of new notations, and the deletion of old notations have a profoundly negative effect on the thoroughness of subject searches, both manual and automated. Since libraries cannot reclassify substantial portions of their holdings whenever a new DDC edition is published, or whenever a new quarterly issue of *LC Classification Additions and Changes* appears, they either reclassify very selectively or not at all. Although most patrons are not aware of it, this means that a searcher who finds a suitable class symbol has a fair chance of finding only recent material, or only older material, or only part of the topic that is being searched. This is not conducive to thorough, or especially to historical, research. Especially invidious are partial relocations, that is, changes in which the notation remains but part of its meaning has been altered, so that the user who looks at the shelves, or at the entries in a classed file, does not realise that the total number of entries under one class number really represents two different subject concepts.

Users doing a subject search must be unusually sophisticated and alert to recognise such scope changes in a class notation. The problem has existed for over a century. Online catalogues are likely to show it more clearly but can, if properly programmed, also provide the necessary linking between old and new notations. This will involve an enormous amount of historical research, and will probably be economically feasible only if the linking is done once and for all by the organisation responsible for the classification scheme, on the basis of its schedules, rather than individually by each library on the basis of its own classifications decisions. This means that the wording linking old and new notations must be cautious, because a library may or may not have reclassified its older works, or may or may not have used the new notation for newer works.

LCC and Online Cataloguing

The LCC began to be developed some twenty years after the DDC was introduced to the public in 1876; most of its schedules were developed between 1898 and 1910. Unlike the DDC, it was not designed as a theoretical scheme suitable for all general libraries, but as an in-house scheme designed to reflect the emphases and purposes of the Library of Congress. As a result, it devotes proportionally greater space to the social sciences, especially history, political science, and law, and relatively little space to philosophy, religion, and the humanities. The Librarian of Congress was rather astonished when, soon after the scheme began to be developed, other libraries began to express an interest in it.

Like the DDC, the LCC is an enumerative scheme but, unlike the DDC, LCC has no synthetic features whatsoever. It is probably the most enumerative general scheme ever published. Its enumerativeness and detail are shown by the fact that all of its schedules together take up about three and a half feet of shelf space, whereas the twentieth edition of DDC takes up only slightly more than five inches. The LCC uses a mixed notation of letters and numbers, and is divided into 21 classes.

A General works

B Philosophy; Religion

C History: Auxiliary sciences

D History: General and Old World

E-F History: America

G Geography; Anthropology; Folklore, etc

H Social sciences

J Political science

K Law

L Education

M Music

N Fine arts

P Philology and literature

Q Science

R Medicine

S Agriculture

T Technology

U Military science

V Naval science

Z Bibliography; Library science

Each class, with the exception of classes E, F, and Z, is divided by a second, and sometimes also by a third, letter into subclasses. Class Q, for example, is divided into:

Q Science (General),

QA Mathematics

QB Astronomy

QC Physics

QD Chemistry

QE Geology

QH Natural history (General)

QK Botany

QL Zoology

QM Human anatomy

QP Physiology

QR Microbiology

The subclass CC (Physics) consists of the following major divisions:

QC 1-75 Physics in general

QC 81-114 Weights and measures

QC 120-168 Descriptive and experimental mechanics

QC 170-197 Atomic physics. Constitution and properties of matter

QC 221-246 Acoustics. Sound

QC 251-338 Heat

QC 350-467 Optics. Light

QC 474-496 Radiation physics (General)

QC 770-798 Electricity and magnetism. Nuclear and particle physics. Atomic energy. Radioactivity

QC 801-809 Geophysics. Cosmic physics. Geomagnetism

QC 851-999 Meteorology, Climatology.

Further subdivision is by cardinal (not decimal) numbers from one to approximately 9999. When the notational base gets squeezed over the years by insertion of too many new topics, the system sometimes employs decimal numbers, but not in a hierarchical sense. Still further subdivision is not by classification principles but alphabetically. Depending on the context, alphabetical subdivision may be by topic, geography, language or nationality, or other attributes.

The use of cardinal sequential numbers, and of decimals that have no hierarchical meaning, results in a notation that is not expressive. To use another example, the notation LC 1503 (Vocational education of women in the United States) does not express that it is, conceptually, a subdivision of LC 1500 (Vocational education of women in general). As a result, it is impossible to broaden a search by means of truncation. Nor is it possible to narrow down a search automatically, that is, to make the search more specific by asking the system to "explode" a notation by showing the original notation with the addition of digits that indicate the next more specific level of the hierarchy.

LCC's device of arranging geographical subdivisions of a subject alphabetically has been mentioned. LCC uses also a second device that impedes hierarchical geographical searches: in many schedules it uses not one but several class numbers for various levels of geographical division. Therefore, the cities of a region are not listed as subdivisions of that region, unlike in DDC.

The LCC scheme is hospitable: it permits insertion of new topics by means of gaps in the lettering and in the numbering. In the main classes, letters I, O, W, X, and Y have not been used, and gaps are also left in many subclasses. While each schedule (letter) of LCC is structured on the basis of the subject concerned, a general arrangement pattern of seven categories does exist. The first six categories deal with the physical format in which the topic is being treated—such as serials, collections of articles, or dictionaries—or the manner in which the topic is discussed—the philosophy of the topic, the study and teaching of the topic, general works on the topic, or laws and regulations on the topic. The seventh category consists of topical subdivisions, such as the brain as a subsection of the section. The nervous system, which is, in turn, a subsection of Human anatomy. Many topical subdivisions are themselves subdivided by their own seven categories. Logically, theoretically, and by definition, classification involves hierarchy. To permit hierarchical searches, from broad aspects of a topic to more specific concepts, and vice versa, the whole must precede its parts, as in DDC, and the parts must progress in some standard, logical sequence, either sequential or by inherent logic. LCC's method of dividing many topics alphabetically rather than in classed fashion has been mentioned.

In 1964, the Classification Committee of the American Library Association's Resources and Technical Services Division reported approvingly: "LCC has the advantage of not being logical in exposition, as a rule, and while it is practically impossible to memorise, it is easy to expand without upsetting existing classified books. The advantage of nonlogical classification is apparent in dealing with rapidly advancing subjects."

LCC and Online Searching

The LCC notation is much less suitable to direct use for retrieval than an expressive notation like DDC's. By "suitable" is meant not just the ability to reach a notation via a subject heading, author, title, or keyword, but the ability to use the notation itself as a scrolling device; as an indicator of subject scope, subject hierarchies, and subject interrelationships; and as a retrieval device either by itself or through the use of Boolean formulae that combine a notation with a subject heading, name, keyword, or other term. Like the DDC, the LCC suffers from the disadvantage of age. It too was not designed for use in a computer. It is a completely enumerative scheme with the typical limitations of such schemes. Miksa discusses the various new ideas which LCC introduced in the development of classification practice, but unfortunately most of these ideas make it extremely difficult, if not impossible, to use LCC for real information retrieval in a computer, other than just for browsing in the shelflist, without editing or computer-coding virtually every notation. The factors that affect adversely LCC's use for online information retrieval are:

— A structure that is sometimes illogical in not grouping some topics and their subdivisions together.

— A structure that often omits hierarchical levels and thereby makes hierarchical searches via the notation difficult or less effective.

— A structure that is often illogical in grouping topics related only in a superficial way, and that thereby often makes use of the notation as a collocative device difficult, if not impossible.

— Extensive use of alphabetical rather than logical subdivision.

— A nonexpressive notation that does not make it possible to narrow down or to broaden a search automatically via the notation, and that can also cause problems in scrolling.

— Lack of a unified index.

— Printed schedules that have not yet been converted to machine-readable format, except for some experimental work. This conversion is going to be a major, problematic undertaking.

From an online information retrieval point of view, LCC's advantages are less compelling than DDC's advantages:

— It is maintained by a well-funded, leading organisation, the Library of Congress. It is, therefore, a live scheme that, within limits, keeps pace with progress, adding new topics as needed, and changing others as needed.

— It is hospitable.

— As Chan pointed out, it uses in some subjects very specific notations which should help to pinpoint a search. For example, some literature notations provide unique locations for individual authors and even for some individual works; geography numbers for individual cities and even some city districts exist.

— The LCC notation can be found in almost all MARC records.

— The LCC is at least somewhat familiar to many users of academic libraries. They tend, therefore, not to be in awe of it, although they typically do not know it well enough to take real advantage of it, or to circumvent its pitfalls.

— People whose interests involve only very few highly specific LCC notations strongly support its use.

5

Metadata Library

Today's changing scenario in the publishing and information technology fields have forced library and information professionals to accept the changing demands placed on the profession today. There is a marked shift from the need of information in academics quality to industry and business houses today. The nature of writing has shifted from single discipline to multideciplinary subjects, the value of using management techniques for continuous improvement in quality and reliability has forced us to take a serious view on how libraries and information centres the world over have to reorganise to meet the new challenges of the information technology, publication industry as well as the user demands.

The information resources are customised for specific missions that have traditionally separated, although common technologies, such as printing, photography, and computing, are found across all settings, breaking down all physical barriers between resources. Digital libraries have obvious roles to play in formal learning by providing teachers and learners with knowledge bases in a variety of media. One clear difference between traditional libraries and digital libraries is that digital libraries offer greater opportunity for users to deposit as well as to use information.A digital library is viewed as an electronic version of a public library. By replacing paper with electronic storage, it will lead to three major differences: storage in digital form, direct communication to obtain material, and copying from a master version. These differences will lead to a plethora of further differences so that eventually the digital library will no longer mimic a traditional library.

Digital libraries 'does not mean libraries' in the classical sense, but a network of multimedia systems. A typical digital library is a media server connected to high speed networks. The dawn of information revolution is considered to be one of the marvels of the twentieth century. The new technology has not only transformed the shape of modem libraries but also created very many exciting possibilities and opportunities. With radio, television, computers, communication satellites, cable TV, multimedia, local and wide area networks we are often referred to be living in an "Information Society". Unlike traditional libraries, digital libraries don't reside in a building. In addition to traditional text-based information data accessible through the digital library system includes non-text information (photographs, drawings, illustrations, work of art); streams of numeric data (satellite information, cosmological data); digitised sound and moving visual images and 3D representations (holograms).

In the context of digital imaging, librarians face greater challenges in capturing, storing, formatting, retrieval and reproduction of non-textual information, because it is a new area of developing sources of information and experiences are few. In particular, the technical aspects of digital imaging are far beyond the scope of most of our libraries. As the arrival of digital libraries is imminent, librarians are forced to re-educate themselves to meet this new challenge.

The collections of libraries and archives, the primary repository of analog form of information constitute print (documents) image form (map and photographs) and sound formats (records and videotapes). In other words, the principal categories of information sources are text, video and voice. The visual representation of objects, colours and shapes has always been an integral part of human culture. Hence the representation of visual phenomena through photography, motion film and video have become part of our daily lives. For information to be communicated broadly, it needs to be stored outside the human memory. Today, we have moved beyond text and language, into the storage and communication of images of this visual world.Now consider the imaging aspects of non-textual data. Looking back, recording of original non-textual (image) data was manual until the development of photography. The invention of silver-based film and photographic process added a new dimension to information acquisition, as it was possible to accurately capture complex visual images. Later on, electromagnetic media opened up new possibilities in capturing information through video tapes.

Image information stored in these analog formats could not be processed easily and this led to the birth of magnetic and optical media. Modern information systems are now able to represent the information electronically (as digital signals) and to manipulate automatically at high speeds. Such information represented digitally, in two states, or binary form is often referred to as *Digital information*. Magnetic tapes (serial access), magnetic disks (direct access), and optical disks form the basic recording and storage media in digital forms.The capture of data for electronic storage and digital processing is accomplished by manual (keyboard) and automatic (image processing) techniques. Interestingly, it is observed that two-thirds of the information cannot be digitised by keyboard transcription because they contain drawings, signature, images, etc., or because keying-in would be highly uneconomical. Hence, imaging process becomes the primary modes of converting analog image data into computer readable digital format.

With numerous advantages it is clear that digital image databases will be used to greater extent in the future. In the building of image' database includes phases such as scanning source material, interfacing the images with a database tool or delivering the images to the user. The power and attraction of digital image databases are attributed mainly to the synergy between the two complex technologies, namely, computerised search/ retrieval system and digital imaging. Each of these disciplines—cataloging on one hand, imaging science on the other hand—has long been a speciality of its own.

Digital Records

Records are a by-product of doing business and they have an important role to play in doing it electronically. A simple way of defining a record is as a document that has taken part in a business process, and thereafter provides evidence of the transaction of that business. Records document business activity of all kinds, and are critical to corporate, democratic and historical accountability. They constitute a vital part of organisational and collective identity and memory, and provide important sources of value-added information. As records provide evidence of social and organisational activity, they need to be managed in ways which take account of their evidential nature as well as those characteristics they share with other information resources.In networked environments, records, like other information resources, need to be adequately identified, described and authenticated. They need to be readily accessible via common user interfaces to authorised users, and retrievable for as long as they are required, then to be disposed of in a systematic way. Terms and conditions of access, including freedom of information law, privacy protection and confidentiality requirements, need to be managed and monitored. But records, as accountability traces and evidence of business activity, have additional metadata requirements. Authoritative well-structured metadata which specifies their content, structure, context and essential management needs must be embedded in, wrapped around or otherwise persistently linked to them from the moment they are created if they are to continue to function as evidence.

The explosive growth of interest in the Internet in recent years has created a digital extension of the academic research library for certain kinds of materials. Valuable collections of texts, images and sounds from many scholarly communities—collections that may even be the subject of state-of-the-art discussions in these communities—now exist only in electronic form and may be accessible from the Internet.A number of well-designed locator services, such as Lycos, are now available that automatically index many of the resources available on the Web and maintain up-to-date databases of locations. But indexes are most useful in small collections within a given domain. As the scope of their coverage expands, indexes succumb to problems of large retrieval sets and problems of cross disciplinary semantic drift. Richer records, created by content experts, are necessary to improve search and retrieval.

Formal standards such as the TEI Header and MARC cataloging will provide the necessary richness, but such records are time consuming to create and maintain, and hence may be created for only the most important resources. An alternative solution that promises to mediate these extremes involves the creation of a record that is more informative than an index entry but is less complete than a formal cataloging record. If only a small amount of human effort were required to create such records, more objects could be described, especially if the author of the resource could be encouraged to create the description. And if the description followed an established standard, only the creation of the record would require human intervention; automated tools could discover these descriptions and collect them.

In US, the Online Computer Library Center (OCLC) and the National Center for Supercomputing Applications (NCSA) convened the invitational Metadata Workshop on March 1-3, 1995, in Dublin, Ohio to address this issue. Fifty-two librarians, archivists, humanities scholars and geographers, as well as standards makers in the Internet, Z39.50 and Standard Generalized Markup Language (SGML) communities, met to identify the scope of the problem, to achieve consensus on a list of metadata elements that would yield simple descriptions of data in a wide range of subject areas, and to lay the groundwork for achieving further progress in the definition of metadata elements that describe electronic information. Goals of the workshop included fostering a common understanding of the problems and potential solutions among the stakeholders and promoting a consensus on a core set of metadata elements to describe networked resources. Since the Internet contains more information than professional abstractors, indexers and catalogers can manage using existing methods and systems, it was agreed that a reasonable alternative way to obtain usable metadata for electronic resources is to give authors and information providers a means to describe the resources themselves.

The major task of the Metadata Workshop was to identify and define a simple set of elements for describing networked electronic resources. To make this task manageable, it was limited in two ways. First, only those elements necessary for the discovery of the resource were considered. It was believed that resource discovery is the most pressing need that metadata can satisfy, and one that would have to be satisfied regardless of the subject matter or internal complexity of the object. Secondly, the discussion was further restricted to the metadata elements required for the discovery of what were called document-like objects, or DLOs by the workshop participants. It was believed that DLOs are still the most common type of resource sought in the Internet and that whatever solution could be proposed for DLOs could be extended to other kinds of resources. More importantly, the likelihood of making progress on this challenging problem would be increased if attention could initially be restricted to something familiar. DLOs were not rigorously defined, but were understood by example. For example, an electronic version of a newspaper article or a dictionary is a DLO, while an unannotated collection of slides is not. Of course, the crux of the problem is that in a networked environment, DLOs can be arbitrarily complex because they can consist of text with callouts to images, audio or video clips, or to other hypertext documents.

The Metadata Workshop participants made no attempt to limit the complexity of DLOs, except to say that the intellectual content of a DLO is primarily text, and that the metadata required for describing DLOs will bear a strong resemblance to the metadata that describes traditional printed texts. The goal was to define a core set of metadata elements that would allow authors and information providers to describe their work and to facilitate interoperability among resource discovery tools. But because the core elements do not yield a complete description of objects in a networked environment, careful consideration was also given to mechanisms for extending the element set.

Dublin Core Metadata

The primary deliverable from the workshop was a set of thirteen metadata elements, named the Dublin Core Metadata Element Set (or Dublin Core, for short). The Dublin Core was proposed as the minimum number of metadata elements required to facilitate the discovery of document-like objects in a networked environment such as the Internet. The syntax was deliberately left unspecified as an implementation detail. The semantics of these elements was intended to be clear enough to be understood by a wide range of users.

The discussions at the Metadata Workshop revealed several principles that should guide the further development of the element set. Adherence to these principles increases the likelihood that the core element set will be kept as small as possible, that the meanings of the elements will be understood by most users, and that the element set will be flexible enough for the description of resources in a wide range of subject areas. These principles are intrinsicality, extensibility, syntax independence, optionality, repeatability, and modifiability.

— *Intrinsicality*: The Dublin Core concentrates on describing intrinsic properties of the object. Intrinsic data refer to the properties of the work that could be discovered by having the work in hand, such as its intellectual content and physical form. This is distinguished from extrinsic data, which describe the context in which the work is used. For example, the "Subject" element is intrinsic data, while transaction information such as cost and access considerations are extrinsic data. The focus on intrinsic data in no way demeans the importance of other varieties of data, but simply reflects the need to keep the scope of deliberations narrowly focussed.

— *Extensibility:* In addition to its use in dealing with extrinsic data, extension mechanisms will allow the inclusion of intrinsic data for objects that cannot be adequately described by a small set of elements. Extensibility is important because users may wish to add extra descriptive material for site-specific purposes or specialized fields. In addition, the specification of the Dublin Core itself will change over time, and the extension mechanism will allow revisions while maintaining some backward compatibility with the originally defined element set.

— *Syntax Independence*: Syntactic bindings are avoided because it is too early to propose formal definitions and because the Dublin Core is intended to be eventually used in a range of disciplines and application programs.

— *Optionality:* All the elements are optional. The Dublin Core may eventually be applied to objects for which some elements have no meaning. It also seems counterproductive to mandate complex descriptions if the creators of the content are expected to provide the descriptive material. A simple description is better than no description at all.

— *Repeatability*: All elements in the Dublin Core are repeatable. For example, multiple author elements would be used when a resource has multiple authors.

— *Modifiability:* Each element in the Dublin Core has a definition that is intended to be self-explanatory. However, it is also necessary that the definitions of the elements satisfy the needs of different communities. This goal is accomplished by allowing each element to be modified by an optional qualifier. If no qualifier is present, the element has its common-sense meaning; otherwise, the definition of the element is modified by the value of the qualifier. Qualifiers will be typically derived from well-known conventions in the library community or from the field of knowledge appropriate to the resource. Qualifiers are important because they give the Dublin Core a mechanism for bridging the gap between casual and sophisticated users.

The Dublin Core Metadata Initiative describes the Dublin Core metadata set as facilitating discovery; this term is often applied to the process of looking for resources in a broad cross-domain universe.

Functions of Metadata

In a digital library, metadata may be needed to help the user not only select an item appropriate for the current purpose but also to use it. Such metadata may include structural metadata that permits navigation among components of a single intellectual "object" or information about terms and conditions in a machine-parsable form that can be used to limit access to authorized users. Metadata is also required to manage content and to record information that will support future preservation activities. Metadata that leads users to resources in digital libraries (discovery, finding, collocation, navigation) and lets them choose resources for the task at hand (identification, selection).

The networked world has changed the expectations of information users by removing physical constraints. In the physical world, few question the practice of storing maps or manuscripts separately from books or locating the specialists who help users access and use the resources in different areas of a library or in different libraries.In the networked world, the digital libraries hold the potential to brings resources of many types together to the user's laboratory or desktop (or even palmtop). Some users will want first to cast a wide net as they trawl for information and then to draw it tight and precisely around the most relevant and usable resources for a particular purpose. The wide net calls for interoperability and commonality across domains and custodial communities, while assessment of fitness for a particular purpose often calls for rich and domain-specific metadata. One characteristic of a digital library is the accessibility of the content to the user.

In the traditional library, subject to the physical constraints of weight and distance, the user who selects lots of items that turn out not to be fit for the purpose at hand will incur a high cost. If users can delve straight into the content to aid the act of selection, some metadata conventionally recorded to support selection may be less essential. Users and builders of digital libraries also recognize the potential for navigation among related items. This feature was the fundamental function underlying the initial success of the World Wide Web.

Online, citations can lead directly to cited works and works can link directly to datasets or models they describe. Reference links and thumbnail images change the architecture for research and information seeking. Users can navigate using relationships between metadata records and relationships between resources from their desktop. The functions that metadata must support may not change in a digital library, but, in the new architecture and with new tools, it seems likely that metadata practices must evolve to provide the functionality cost-effectively in the new market. Content is also accessible for building services in a digital library. Metadata or surrogates can be derived or extracted from content files.

Today, a thumbnail is essentially part of the descriptive record for an image. In the collection of negative strips from the Farm Security Administration, many of the images were never captioned; access to the uncaptioned images within American Memory is primarily through navigation. Contact sheet displays of thumbnails are ordered using the processing number sequence on the negatives.

Automatic summarization and analysis of other forms of content is an active research area. The value of including basic metadata in the header of text marked up in SGML or XML is also well recognized. Text conversion projects following the Text Encoding Initiative (TEI) guidelines often use a mapping between elements in the header section of the marked up file to fields in a MARC catalog record. In some cases, the TEI header is derived from the catalog record; in other cases, a catalog record is derived from the header. For material published in digital form, the publishing community will maintain basic bibliographic metadata for its own purposes, including promotion and business-to-business dealings with booksellers.

It will be inexpensive to include it in file headers. For example, the Open eBook Publication Structure specification includes tags for "publication metadata."

In a digital library, searchable text can minimize the need for metadata (particularly when items do not merit the expense of individual cataloging). American Memory has a popular collection, American Life Histories, for which the only item-specific metadata is a title (a display string needed for result lists) and an identifier; the text itself is searched to provide intellectual access. Creators of non-text materials also recognize the value in embedding such metadata within the files. Today, cameras can record the date and time of an exposure. If there is not already a camera with built-in GPS to record location, there will be very soon. Proposals for new digital file formats, such as JPEG2000 (for images) and MPEG-7 (primarily for sound and video) include the ability to embed descriptive metadata within the file.

Metadata Schema

The educational community has been active in exploring the functional needs of educators for finding and using instructional materials. Resources are available because of economic incentives to establish and manage online learning environments and government efforts to improve education. Some information tasks call for rich metadata. For example, a teacher may be looking for material to help him explain a very specific topic in a particular class. The teacher wants to be confident that the material makes appropriate assumptions about what the students already know, has already been used successfully in the classroom, will occupy an appropriate amount of class time, and will work on the equipment available. This level of specificity may be available in a service built by and for educators.

A metadata schema for instructional resources has been developed by the IMS Global Learning Consortium, Inc., a global consortium with members from educational, commercial, and government organizations. Another area with specialized metadata needs is that of geospatial resources. The ability to build maps dynamically or relate geospatial facts from distributed sources of information is enhanced by commonality of metadata. Such capabilities can support government tasks such as emergency management, city planning, and tracking air quality or global climate change. The Federal Geographic Data Committee has developed a Content Standard for Digital Geospatial Metadata. There is worldwide standardization activity in this area in relation to metadata schemas and to the content standards for elements. The activity involves government, commercial and educational sectors.

As with the instructional metadata schemas, the functionality required by the creator and user communities, rather than traditional libraries, is driving these activities. The Visual Resources Association has developed a two-level hierarchical model for describing objects or visual works (such as paintings, sculptures, or buildings) and images of those works. A single set of metadata elements, the VRA Core Categories 3.0, can be applied to the works and to the images. This approach follows the so-called "1-1" principle, distinguishing characteristics of the image surrogate clearly from characteristics of the work. This principle emerged from the Dublin Core community but has provoked considerable controversy. It can not be applied in existing "flat" bibliographic systems without creating awkwardness and confusion for users through multiplicity of records and a burden on cataloging processes by requiring replication of work-level information in records for each surrogate image. A system that takes advantage of the two-level structure must allow searching across all records but present results that pull in work records automatically when a "hit" is at the image level.

The metadata schema used by the Art Museum Image Consortium (AMICO) has a similar hierarchical structure. The Visual Information Access (VIA) system at Harvard University uses a three-level hierarchy. Although the Encoded Archival Description (EAD) standard has been used primarily for describing collections of papers and records that have not been digitized, it too provides a hierarchical structure for description at different levels. The EAD metadata structure has been used effectively as the basis for digital library services, for example at the University of California, Berkeley (and now at the California Digital Library) and Duke University.

A more complex conceptual model has been proposed by the Documentation Standards Group International Committee for Documentation of the International Council of Museums (ICOM-CIDOC). The CIDOC model is an object-oriented reference model that expresses a much more complex knowledge universe than the simple relationship of a descriptive record to a resource or even of a hierarchical structure of related descriptions and resources. It allows for descriptions not only of works, images, document, (conceptual objects) and objects (physical entities), but also of people (actors), places, and periods (time-spans). This model will form the basis for the Cultural Materials Initiative digital library project at the Research Libraries Group.

Full use of such a model will integrate gazetteers, biographical dictionaries, and encyclopedias, going well beyond the traditional use of authority records and thesauri. One example of a digital library enriched by integrating the use of reference resources such as biographical dictionaries and the Thesaurus of Geographic Names is Perseus, housed at Tufts University. In this digital library for the study of the ancient world, the books "talk" to each other. Names of places and people been identified automatically in the text and can be used as links to related information elsewhere in the corpus. This includes automated disambiguation of different places with the same name and of references to people who share names with places). Some of these rich metadata schemas or models have great potential for enriching the interaction with knowledge for users through collocation and navigation using the relationships expressed in the models and supporting knowledge organization systems, such as gazetteers, name authority files, and thesauri. The models are, however, unfamiliar and will require new tools to implement and deploy. The web sites that present them usually have FAQ (Frequently Asked Question) pages that emphasize that most features are optional. There is plenty of evidence that, unless there is strong economic motivation, introductory guidelines and basic tools are needed before complex standards gain broad acceptance.

Part of the genius shown by Tim Berners-Lee in his original standards for the World Wide Web was the simplicity of the specifications. The conceptual model could be explained on one slide and fleshed out in three more. Implementing a server was a few lines of code; a young programmer built a graphical interface (Mosaic) as a side project and the rest is history. The other aspect of Berners-Lee's genius was the instant integration of legacy content by supporting earlier Internet protocols now seldom mentioned (gopher, wais, news). Real-world experience with the simple (e.g. HTML) has led iteratively to better understanding of which extensions to its functionality are most essential.

Complex metadata schemas present a challenge for those with valuable legacy metadata to migrate or metadata maintained in rich, but different schemas. It is relatively easy to "dumb down" metadata records from a rich schema into a simpler one, for purposes of interoperable retrieval, while still maintaining the full richness in a master system. Transforming from one rich schema to another is usually more expensive and the benefits may not be obvious to the institutions or individuals most likely to bear the cost. At the other end of the spectrum, some digital library activities are focusing on allowing users to find resources across an information universe that spans communities, nations, types of information, and types of institution. The Dublin Core Metadata Initiative has been building consensus through a series of workshops and working group activities since March 1995. From the start this has been an international effort to develop a common core of semantics for resource description. The path has not been easy.

The Dublin Core Element Set (Simple Dublin Core) was submitted to NISO as a draft standard this year. The set has 15 elements; all elements are optional and all repeatable. The elements themselves are unlikely to be sufficient as an internal metadata schema for any particular project or application. Some proponents see the elements as the basis for a schema that can be extended by adding or refining elements; others prefer to see the set as a view of a richer, more complex description. This view can be used as a framework for mapping different element sets into a common set for indexing and searching. The DCMI has also developed a model for extending the simple element set while maintaining the objective of interoperability. Elements can be refined.

Tom Baker describes Dublin Core as a pidgin language in a discussion of simple and qualified Dublin Core. The existence of the 15-element set has provided an important focus for other interoperability initiatives. Simple Dublin Core was recently adopted as the core metadata record format for the experimental Open Archives initiative. This initiative is testing whether a simple mechanism that allows service providers to harvest metadata records from content repositories will facilitate and stimulate the development of valuable services that draw on content from many repositories. An initial impetus was the belief that access services could benefit from harvesting records for e-prints and other "grey" literature. Records will usually have links back to the host repository through persistent identifiers for the full content. The concept also allows the development of comprehensive search services that include significant web-accessible resources currently hidden from the "spiders" that crawl the web on behalf of search engines. The so-called "deep web" includes the content of most digital libraries, such as American Memory, whose web presence is largely ephemeral, with records retrieved from a database in response to each search and displays generated dynamically. The Open Archives harvesting framework includes the ability to harvest records in other metadata formats.

The Open Archives initiative is based on the premise that simple records provide the first step to cross-domain discovery. Service-builders can choose to harvest records in a richer schema when available. Specifications for records marked up in the Extensible Markup Language (XML) must be made accessible for any schema used. Cross-domain discovery is the development of a very basic profile for the Z39.50 information retrieval protocol for cross-domain discovery. This specification also supports Simple Dublin Core marked up in XML as a transfer format for records. In many ways, the stimulus for this activity is the success of the World Wide Web. People clearly find value in web search engines, whatever their shortcomings. An enormous mass of information accessible from a single search box has clear appeal; many people prefer to try several queries and skim through pages of hits than to use Boolean queries to increase precision. The computational and linguistic tools built into commercial search engines are enhanced frequently. The architecture of cyberspace has changed the relationship between bibliographic control and access. Today, ironically, resources under good bibliographic control are likely to be less widely accessible than those simply mounted on the web. The motivation behind these simple-minded interoperability efforts is to encourage broad access to resources of value.

Digital Content

The fund of knowledge is represented by a much richer set of resources than static pages on paper, and resources beyond those traditionally found in libraries, even multi-faceted libraries like the Library of Congress. Knowledge has always been conveyed through buildings (and the archaeological sites they become), works of art, physical specimens of flora and fauna, artifacts of different cultures and lifestyles, and human memories. Photography, sound recordings, and motion pictures have added to the fund of knowledge both in their own right as means of expression and as richer surrogates than words on paper. The digital era has added not only reproductions and analogs of older forms of information, but also new digital resources of enormous variety. Some fall into obvious categories. The broad category of datasets includes census and other survey results, gene sequences, images and other sensor data from space, geospatial information that allows maps to be generated dynamically, decades of financial statements for publicly traded corporations, directories of people and places, and structured lexical resources, such as dictionaries and thesauri. More complex digital resources include mathematical and chemical knowledge expressed in structural forms that permit dynamic manipulation, interactive software for education and entertainment, and collections of re-usable "open source" software code.

Digital libraries are being built to manage, serve, and support discovery of all these categories of resource. Some of these digital libraries are extensions of traditional libraries; many have developed from other well-established activities in organizing information. Dynamic information resources, such as the web site that delivers up-to-the minute details of event and results at the Olympic Games challenge all traditional practices for organizing and recording for posterity. However, this too could be represented as a series of snapshots of bit-patterns, a digital resource, a set of computer files.

The metadata required to support discovery and use of digital resources must clearly represent the intellectual nature and genre of the content; in a digital library, the fact that a resource can be represented by 0s and 1s is an assumption, not a useful categorization. Attempts to develop general hierarchical categorizations for genres or types of information have usually failed. The Type working group of the Dublin Core Metadata Initiative developed, with much debate and without unanimity even in a small group, a high-level list of types (the DCMI Type Vocabulary: DCT1): Collection, Dataset, Event, Image, Interactive Resource, Service, Software, Sound, Text. MARC records can hold information about the type of a resource in several ways. Svenonius notes that there are seven different places where a "document type" can be indicated. Each element or indicator has a different set of possible values. Given the different guidelines for use and the different functions these seven elements serve, type information in MARC records has proved impossible to use uniformly within American Memory.

Type indicators in the header are excellent as triggers for systems based on MARC records. They indicate what guidelines have been applied to content fields and therefore can be used to configure appropriate displays or procedures. However, the coded values can not be incorporated into a general keyword index, and are therefore unavailable to a user as a search term as they expect. The current feeling of the Dublin Core Type working group is that some communities will develop controlled lists of terms, but agreement across communities on the important categories or even common definitions for the same terms is unlikely. Lacking initial agreement on an acceptable "standard" typology, American Memory does not have explicit type values in all metadata records. This shortcoming means that searches limited to images may retrieve other categories of content, since the limit is actually by collection and some collections included will have text or sound as well as images. Colleagues agree that adding high-level type information consistently across the metadata records would provide more benefit for American Memory users than any other change.

Interoperability will certainly be well served if descriptive records shared or exchanged always include type information, even if all content within the repository or collection providing the data is of the same type. Based on experience with American Memory, users might be best served by the inclusion of any applicable terms from the DCT1 list and additional terms at finer levels of specificity. The user's objectives are supported not by raw metadata, but through the tools and systems that can take advantage of the metadata. In both library catalogs and digital library services, the functionality for discovery, finding, and collocating is determined not by the metadata but also by the indexes constructed for that metadata. Different systems provide different options for configuring indexes. Public interfaces to library catalogs usually combine different metadata elements into a relatively small set of indexes. For example, a keyword search by subject may find the term in any of the MARC subject fields. Once a record has been retrieved, elements can be labeled more specifically. Some digital libraries, including American Memory, take the same approach.

Individual elements that may be usefully distinguished (and labeled) to support the act of selection are lumped together to support discovery, finding or collocation. The University of Washington Libraries have used collection-specific element sets for their collections of digital reproductions; each set is mapped to the fifteen elements of the Dublin Core Metadata Element Set for cross-collection retrieval. Retrieved records show the specific labels. For example, a collection of pictures of plants has a variety of fields relating to preferred soil quality and climate, whether the plant is native to the state, and other botanical details. For search purposes, these fields are all included in the Description index; on the display they are individually labeled. American Memory uses a similar approach. All descriptive notes are lumped into an overall text index; on display, a summary or abstract is usefully presented first and labeled as such. Many collections in American Memory call for unusual metadata elements, such as musical features for folk songs and descriptions of the key mechanisms in a collection of flutes. For searching, these are all treated as notes and included in the general keyword index. For display, however, the metadata format includes tags that are ignored by the indexer, but provide labels for use in the record display. The indexing approach currently used in American Memory was developed empirically and iteratively, based on data elements usually available across heterogeneous sources and expectations of content custodians and users; it has seven primary indexes that support searching of metadata.

The developers of the Alexandria Digital Earth Prototype at the University of California, Santa Barbara have described the framework they use for querying metadata from distributed sources. Based on experience over several years of working with geo-referenced information, they chose eight search buckets. For the most basic cross-domain discovery, the developers of the Bath Profile for Z39.50 identified Author, Title, Subject, Any. The Bath Profile effort is not strictly a digital library project, but has as an aim, interoperability between library catalog systems and "other electronic resource discovery services." The common text bucket proves invaluable when dealing with heterogeneous data and it is useful to include subject terms in this bucket. Indexing engines designed for full text will find word variants automatically, relieving users from knowing when formal subject terms use the plural form. The distinction between assigned subject terms and textual description is, nevertheless, valuable. In American Memory, it allows us to generate browse lists, which are actually static HTML pages with "canned" searches. The subject index also permits navigation from subject terms on record displays to other records assigned the same terms.

Although American Memory indexes the primary Creator separately from the other Contributors, searching and browsing for creators and contributors is usually done together. Combining the indexes has been considered. In American Memory, the addition of roles to Creators and Contributors proves valuable, particularly for non-text materials. Authorized forms for names are extremely valuable in American Memory. However, names within text are also an important access point. The Alexandria Digital Library is designed for powerful searching by geographic location and date range. Strict machine-parsable content standards are used for those metadata elements. American Memory users would love to be able to search more effectively by date and place. For much content in American Memory, unfortunately, dates of creation for the original item are uncertain and date-ranges recorded are often so broad as to be useless for discovery. For certain collections where chronology is important, normalized dates have been generated and can be used to sort search results.

The Alexandria Digital Library has chosen to index date of creation/publication in the same bucket as date of coverage. In American Memory, there are many instances in which the dates are essentially equivalent. For published books and maps, the distinction is often important, but users may be interested in either or both. The Alexandria Digital Library uses special overlap and containment queries for date ranges and location. Such queries would not be efficient with a full-text engine, but American Memory users would like the capability.

Geographical location is an area in which traditional descriptive practices aimed at human-readable displays do not transfer well to digital libraries. In American Memory's metadata from heterogeneous sources, location may be expressed in many ways: as an informal place-name, as a subdivision in a topical subject heading, as a traditional subject heading or a hierarchical place name. Of these, by far the most useful for manipulating automatically with simple text-based tools has been the hierarchical place name. Users often know that they are looking for an image or for a map and would like to exclude other types of information from the start. Searching by more specific genre terms is also useful, for example for posters or cartoons. As pointed out earlier, type categories expressed in terms that users recognize should be available for limiting or searching. Controlled vocabularies are useful, but are likely to be domain-specific.

The emergence of XML (Extended Markup Language) and its widespread support as a syntax for exchanging metadata and content, particularly for e-commerce transactions and services, is stimulating the development of better tools for transforming and sharing metadata. This, in turn is leading to support for XML from vendors of database software and text-indexing engines. It appears clear that XML will provide the syntax for metadata exchange among digital libraries in the coming years. A few examples of its adoption to support interoperability include: the Bath Profile; MPEG-7; the Open Archives Initiative; and the Federal Geographic Data Committee. XML is also being used as a syntax to represent content objects, such as the proposed Open eBook standard.

American Memory has relied heavily on common indexing of heterogeneous metadata, with different element sets and in two different digital formats (MARC communications format and an XML-like syntax for simple (Dublin Core-like) records. Migration to an XML syntax with a formal DTD or schema is anticipated. Transformations from one XML metadata schema to another (especially from a rich one to a simpler one) can be facilitated using Extensible Stylesheet Language Transformations (XSL/T). This is just one example of the powerful XML-based tools emerging. XSL/T is already in common use for transforming finding aids marked up to the EAD standard (in XML) to HTML for display on the web. XML also includes the ability to mix and match metadata element definitions (semantics and syntax) from other schemas (using the "namespace" feature). As the flurry of XML-related activity on the World Wide Web Consortium web site in late 2000 shows, the general acceptance of XML signals the beginning of a further period of experimentation and development. Among the unanswered questions relating to the use of XML as a syntax for metadata is how soon (or whether) there will be widespread adoption of the Resource Description Framework, an elegant modeling framework for descriptive schemas.

RDF is layered on top of XML, using a particular XML-based syntax for metadata. RDF-specific tools will be needed to take full advantage of its potential for scalable interoperability. Whether the mix-and-match potential of XML namespaces will be widely exploited also remains to be seen. In the past, text-indexing engines, relational database management systems, and SGML-based storage and retrieval systems all offered different functionality to support the finding, collocation, and discovery objectives for digital libraries.

A text-indexing engine can handle heterogeneous metadata and full text in a single system; the capabilities for matching word variants (stemming) have been invaluable for American Memory. Features standard in relational database systems, however, such as sorting by date, have been implemented by additional programming. SGML-aware systems have advantages for substantial bodies of highly structured textual content, such as books and periodicals. Recently, products in one category have found ways to integrate the capabilities of another. ORACLE now has a full text search module, CONTEXT. Some text-indexing engines can now index text stored within relational databases. All such products are announcing "support" for XML. The other area where tools are emerging is in automated integration of thesauri and other knowledge bases to support more intelligent retrieval.

OAI-Protocol for Metadata Harvesting

OAI-Protocol for Metadata Harvesting (OAI-PMH) holds much promise for similar exchanges of metadata describing the collections of museums and other cultural heritage institutions. Materials in these types of collections often are not well indexed by commercial Web search engines. Metadata describing such holdings is hidden in databases, finding aids, and XML documents, or otherwise is not readily available to Web search systems, which typically understand little more than simple HTML. As a result, these materials remain hard to find and out of reach for many researchers. The utility of such a metadata repository will depend on many factors, including the development of more uniform metadata authoring practices across various communities of metadata providers.

Metadata is currently used primarily for a variety of local purposes, and the schemas to which collections conform have been adapted and tailored to meet local needs. Less attention has been paid to using metadata to support universal interoperability. With the advent of OAI and similar protocols, mapping local schemas to more universally standard schemas for the support of interoperability is gaining ground. Even assuming broader and more consistent application of metadata schemas designed to support interoperability, there remains considerable work to be done in learning how best to utilize aggregations of metadata describing heterogeneous information resources.

There is a need to normalize metadata so as to enable more consistent retrieval of results from cross-collection searches. Challenges also exist for presenting search results in ways that provide appropriate contextual information for the records retrieved. As of February, 2002, the Illinois OAI-PMH project has harvested metadata from twenty-five different institutions or consortiums. The resources described range from museum artifacts such as pottery and clothing, to archival manuscript and personal paper collections, to digitized photographs and monographs. The sets of harvested metadata range in size from the largest at 900,000 records to the smallest at 23 records. Some sites include metadata not relevant to cultural heritage mixed with more appropriate metadata. The institutions providing metadata are diverse, including academic libraries, museums, historical societies, public libraries, the Library of

Congress, and special consortia such as the Colorado Digitization Project and the Alliance and Lincoln Trail Library systems in Illinois. Fourteen institutions have provided the Illinois OAI-PMH project team with snapshots of relevant metadata, in a few cases providing an entire database, which has then been made available from Illinois servers in a manner compliant with OAI-PMH.

While all of the metadata harvested from the registered OAI metadata provider sites was in the required Simple Dublin Core format (DC), metadata from the fourteen unregistered sites were given to the project in a variety of formats. These included finding aids formatted in encoded archival description (EAD), MARC format metadata describing bibliographic information, and local metadata schemas stored in HTML files, XML files, or proprietary database structures.To enhance cross-collection searching, local metadata schemas need to be mapped to standard schemas. Even with greater adoption of standard metadata schemas like DC, there remain wide variations in the use of authoring conventions and the depth of descriptive information included when creating metadata to describe cultural heritage collections.

The Open Archives Initiative Protocol for Metadata Harvesting (OAI-PMH) is a new and still evolving protocol designed to allow institutions to share metadata easily. It is hoped that the standard can help increase the discoverability of resources by scholarly researchers. The Protocol underwent one minor revision during its first full year of experimental implementation. Version 2.0 is scheduled for release in May 2002. The fundamental pieces of the protocol are its adherence to well-formed XML, its use of the HTTP standards for data transmission, and its requirement that metadata records shared via the OAI-PMH be made available in the DC metadata schema. One of the common challenges in setting up an OAI-PMH metadata provider service is ensuring that the metadata to be exported is mapped properly into DC.

There are fifteen DC elements: Title, Creator, Subject, Description, Publisher, Contributor, Date, Type, Format,

Identifier, Source, Language, Relation, Coverage, and Rights. Any or all of these elements may be used, and all are repeatable. Because much of the existing metadata about museum and special collections was developed with limited resources, using local schemas and with local needs in mind, the process of mapping to DC can be time and resource consuming and potentially frustrating. There is, however, a growing community of DC users and freely available tools to assist with this process. Harvesting done so far shows that metadata authoring practices differ both in the selection of DC elements used and the depth of information provided even within specific communities. As previously noted, DC elements are both optional and repeatable. These allow a significant degree of variation in the interpretation of which elements to use and how to use them when metadata are created in DC and when mapped to DC.

The Library of Congress American Memory Project, the American Museum of Natural History, the CIMI Demonstration Repository, and the Spurlock Museum to compare the use of DC elements. Within each set of sample records, calculated the percent of records that contain each of the DC elements and the average number of times an element is used in records that contain it. The usage variations are due in part to the intrinsic differences in the collections described by the metadata. However, some variations are clearly due to different decisions made by each institution when determining how to map their metadata into DC. These variations pose a challenge when attempting to build cross-collection search services and determining what depth of detail should be shown in record display. The variations can also influence how a search engine's ranking algorithm orders the result set.

Museums began to use personal computers for tracking information about their collections using a variety of proprietary databases. The use of proprietary software not specifically designed with the museum community in mind can lead to inconsistencies in the way collections are catalogued and tracked. The descriptive elements within a locally created metadata format and the degree of completeness when classifying and cataloging the items can vary widely from one organization to another. This may have the effect of diluting the potential for discoverability as searching aggregated repositories requires some degree of predictable structure and normalization of metadata terms or concepts. At the same time, one should not overlook the value of descriptive, locally created metadata applied to artifacts by professionals familiar with the collection and the museum. This is particularly valuable for collections used primarily by a local community of users. At the University of Illinois Spurlock Museum, FileMakerPro software is used to track the procurement, storage, stage of processing, and display of artifacts. It is also used to maintain descriptive information about the materials. The FileMakerPro database interacts with a Web server to provide public access to a portion of the collection. The decisions made about mapping the metadata were more time consuming than the time spent writing the scripts and manipulating the data. Here is an example of some of the decisions that were made for the cultural materials provided by Spurlock:

— *Subject:* One instance of the DC Subject element was included in each record. The decision was made to concatenate three fields from the original metadata records that could be considered equivalent to DC Subject. Colons were used to distinguish each of the three original strings that were concatenated to create the single DC Subject element. If there were not three values to concatenate, then the DC Subject filed would have two colons next to each other or a lone colon at the beginning or end of the element.

— *Date:* The Date element was qualified as DCQ date.created.

— *Coverage:* The Coverage element was qualified by appending Spurlock metadata field names to the DC element as DCQ coverage.spatial, coverage.temporal, or coverage.cultural.

— *Description:* Key words were added to the Description field values in the original metadata to clarify what was meant by the content of the Description element.

In addition to the mapping given below, 3 fixed DC Type values ("cultural," "physical object," and "original") were included in each Spurlock metadata record exported via OAI. One of the more challenging aspects of implementing the OAI protocol is mapping from metadata schemas designed to describe collections of materials to the DC metadata schema. Finding aids may describe as many as several thousand items or folders in an archive while DC has typically been used to describe individual items. Each EAD record includes metadata describing the entire collection and a "description of subordinate components" which lists the separate series, sub-series, folders and items found in the collection. Some EAD files reach hundreds of kilobytes, or even several megabytes, in size. The challenge is to allow the richness of such a large file to be exposed and made searchable alongside other records that describe a single item or a much smaller collection. Another challenge is due to the very flexible nature of the EAD standard designed to encourage participation by a large number of institutions. It is not surprising that the EAD records analyzed for the Illinois OAI-PMH project reveal many differences in tag structures and encoding patterns between institutions. Despite these differences, the records seem to have enough consistency to make a general cross mapping between EAD and OAI-DC possible. Although the EAD Application Guidelines include two recommended mappings to DC, one for the finding aid itself and another for the resources described in the finding aid, neither mapping will generate records adequate for use in an OAI repository.

While researchers are interested in discovering the existence of actual archives or manuscripts, metadata about the finding aid itself is also necessary in order to point effectively to the source records. For this reason, a flexible approach in mapping an EAD finding aid into an OAI record is needed. This top-level record becomes a base record for the finding aid and must be as complete, accurate, and concise as possible. The base record includes a link to the source EAD file as well as references to related parts of the collection. These related parts are described in other individual records and produce for each component level found within the EAD file's description of subordinate components. Although it is not possible to link these records to each other adequately using simple DC, a sophisticated use of qualified DC fields can produce linked records. This method will provide functional and easily searchable records. Metadata authoring practices as discussed above play important roles in determining the value of a cross-collection repository focusing on cultural heritage materials. Providing context for the metadata, normalization techniques, and developing the search engine and interface also need to be examined and explored for ways to enhance the discoverability of the collected metadata.

One real concern related to the development of cross-collection repository search tools is the context of the original artifact or digital resource. The value of information about the materials that may be found in museum collections and archives is often related to the context and the provenance of the object(s). For example, a photographic slide depicting part of a remaining wall of a basilica dating to the 4th Century would have less value if it were viewed out of the context of the architectural structure it represents. It is not good enough simply to make the slide available for viewing; it needs to be put into a proper context. Ideally, the holding institution of the artifact or digital resource will determine the appropriate context. When the repository encounters URLs embedded within any of the metadata fields, they are mapped to the DC Identifier element. The links sometimes lead to the holding institution or organization's Web site, to the digital display of the resource's record from the holding institution or organization's database, or to an actual display of the resource itself. Given the non-persistent nature of many URLs, it is possible that providing access to them may lead to a large number of dead links over time. With regularly scheduled re-harvesting of the metadata, changes to the URLs should be reflected in the records and therefore allow to avoid excessive dead links. For an example of a repository that has made thoughtful consideration of these efforts, consider the metadata collection contributed to the Illinois OAI-PMH project by TDC, the Teaching with Digital Content project. This project provides a searchable database of images that can be used by K-12 teachers to develop teaching modules that meet specific curriculum requirements. Partners providing metadata for the project include museums, the Illinois State Library, the Chicago Public Library and others. All the metadata has been entered into a database in a format that meets the specific needs of the TDC project and does not conform to DC. However, the display of the records is very clean and consistent and maps well into DC for the purposes of the Illinois OAI-PMH project. With a link directly to the Teaching with Digital Content resource provided from a URL that has been mapped into the DC Identifier field, the context is easily maintained by providing more background information about the record when the user clicks on this link.

Normalization of Metadata

In order to provide context internally and to enhance discoverability of metadata records in a cross-collection repository, some normalization of the metadata is desirable. That normalization can be done on several of the DC elements, including Type, Format, Coverage, and Date. Effective normalization requires to:

— Understand how the element was interpreted by metadata providers and which elements in other metadata formats were mapped to the DC element;

— Identify which - if any - vocabularies were used by data providers;

— Determine whether there is any controlled vocabulary that the project team could successfully apply to all of the data providers;

— Apply vocabulary to the metadata to augment the 'native' vocabulary;

— Build mechanisms into the search interface that would take advantage of the normalization; and

— Gauge the success of the normalization for resource discovery.

The metadata providers used elements in a variety of ways. For example, the DC Date element was used for the date the digital item was created, the date the physical item was created or published, and the date an item was added to a collection. Because OAI-PMH requires use of simple DC, the qualifiers that may have explained these values further were not present. Similarly the variety and specificity or generality of controlled vocabularies also influenced the next steps in the normalization process. Each DC element was examined to determine the focus for normalization for that particular element. While the Date element suggests a need to choose between options like 'date created' or 'date contributed' and the particular format the value is displayed in, the Type element required to focus on the range and specificity of vocabulary used.

Once the vocabulary is developed, the values in the metadata are mapped to the vocabulary terms. The actual normalization of the data is an automated process. Following the mapping, values from the vocabulary are added to each record as additional. After new records are harvested, the system compares the values of specific elements with the mapping already done and adds appropriate terms from the vocabulary where applicable. If a term that has not already been mapped appears, it is flagged and looked at by human eyes. The last step is to provide services so that users can take advantage of the normalization process. The ability to limit searches or sort results by type of resource or to search for specific date ranges or geographic areas is each made possible by the normalization process.

The Process of Metadata Harvesting

Metadata harvesting will be an important part of the interoperability toolkit for libraries. But it is just a first step. Communities that have close affinities with libraries, such as museums and other archival institutions, have good reason to use different descriptive practices. Those practices, and the terminology used: "necessarily depend on conscious or sub-conscious assumptions about who will use it and how". A resource that is of potential use in many contexts may need to be described in several ways and using several vocabularies. In US, the Library of Congress (LC) was an early adopter of the OAI Protocol for Metadata Harvesting to make records for some of its digitized historical collections available for integration into other services. The American Memory team was attracted by a protocol for sharing its resources that promised to be straightforward to implement with no deleterious effect on the primary users. The promise was borne out in practice; the mechanics of harvesting are working well and records for additional collections are being made available every few months.

To non-librarians, the MARC communications format, used by the Library of Congress for its catalog records, was unfamiliar and often seen as a significant hurdle. The American Memory interface was designed for users to locate individual items, not to download batches. On several occasions, LC made an entire collection (records and images) available on an "as-is" basis. Assembling batches for download and explaining what was being delivered was time-consuming, but for an entire collection and a partner with the ability to handle the metadata as it came, it was feasible. Often, what was requested was a substantial subset of a very large collection. LC did not have the resources to do the selection or build a custom batch for download and the requesting institution did not have the capacity to receive the full collection and sift through it. Neither party had the tools or resources at hand to transform the metadata from one form to another. Many worthwhile requests for material to repurpose led to nothing because the effort involved in responding to such requests on an ad hoc basis was simply too great.

During 1996, two task forces of the newly-formed Digital Library Federation (DLF), a group of 15 research libraries engaged in projects involving digital content, met several times to consider recommendations for descriptive metadata and for an architecture to provide common access to the growing pool of resources digitized by member libraries. Both task forces found a variety of practices and local imperatives that would have to be accommodated in any shared approach. For example, three institutions were taking different "standard" approaches to the description of photographs. At LC, the Prints and Photographs Division uses MARC records and follows Anglo-American Cataloging Rules (AACR2) supported by additional rules for describing older and unpublished visual materials. At Harvard, there was strong support, for example from the Graduate School of Art and Design, for the tiered approach represented by the Visual Resources Association's proposal for a core descriptive framework that distinguishes between records for underlying works and records for images of those works.

At the University of California, Berkeley, a commitment had been made to archival practice rather than item-level cataloging for reasons of economy; collections of photographs would be described in archival finding aids, to be marked up in SGML (now XML) using the Encoded Archival Description Document Type Definition (DTD). Practices and technical capabilities also varied widely across university campuses; libraries could not dictate practice to academic departments doing their own digitization or creating their own digital content unless they could provide resources or services to offset the costs of compliance. Rather than attempt to establish a single architectural design, DLF chose to start by promoting exploratory discussions, prototyping, and standards development for components that would be required in any architecture, such as authentication of users, and linking from references to cited articles. Several DLF organizations joined in a proposal to the Mellon Foundation for a project based on a pooled collection of finding aids and a common structure for complex hierarchical objects representing digitized manuscripts, photographs, and other archival objects.

Out of the experience with this XML-based metadata structure has come the more general METS standard, which is now being explored by many institutions as a mechanism for encoding the structure of complex digital objects. However, by 1999, the goal of shared access to the high-quality digital resources in the collections managed by DLF member institutions seemed no closer. Ironically, the convenience and effectiveness of the Internet search engines, such as Lycos and Google, meant that random Web pages were more conveniently available to the students and researchers these libraries served than the resources they carefully selected and cataloged. Rather than being in static HTML pages that could be indexed by the search engines, the managed resources were hidden behind a database query interface, part of the "hidden" Web.

Open Archives Initiative (OAI)

Open Archives Initiative (OAI) and its early history is well documented elsewhere. Services could be specialized, for example, by discipline or by intended audience, or comprehensive and cross-domain. The content described could be digitized historical materials as easily as e-prints. The protocol to support collaboration among organizations building collections of papers and reports deposited by authors could be applied by libraries and museums wishing to build virtual collections of cultural heritage materials. Technology for collaboration can be independent of any particular incentive to collaborate.The enthusiasm from that first meeting led the Library of Congress to play an active role in the Open Archives Initiative. The metadata harvesting approach proposed had a great deal in common with the initially ad hoc approach LC had taken in integrating into American Memory materials digitized by institutions with awards through the LC/Ameritech competition. Based on LC's experience with the competition, many characteristics of the initiative and the harvesting protocol were immediately appealing. These included:

— the emphasis on keeping technical barriers to entry low for those with valuable resources to share through metadata;

— the recognition that requirements for interoperability should not place unacceptable loads on the primary services of institutions choosing to provide access to their content;

— a planned period of practical experimentation followed by review;

— the combination of a very generic common denominator metadata schema that would be mandatory with the ability to exchange records in more specific schemas;

— the potential to integrate, for purposes of discovery, resources from libraries, museums, historical societies, and other cultural heritage institutions with a variety of descriptive traditions;

— suitability for use in any future program similar to the LC/ Ameritech competition or for any organization wishing to repurpose records or content from American Memory;

— and an opportunity to make the resources digitized for American Memory more broadly available and useful, by allowing others to harvest the records conveniently and integrate them into services aimed at different audiences and taking advantage of new technological developments in information retrieval.

From a longer-term perspective, it seemed likely that a simple mechanism for metadata harvesting could provide a substantial body of metadata to support deeper collaborative exploration of interoperability. Interoperability involves agreements at several levels. In the context of the NSDL, the NSDL core integration team identified three levels of agreement needed: technical, content-related, and organizational. Costs of complying with agreements at any level inhibit adoption but without agreements the functionality that can be achieved is limited. A simple protocol for harvesting metadata seemed to offer low-cost participation at the technical level. If a large pool of metadata records were available for harvesting, pragmatic exploration of costs and benefits of fuller agreements at the other levels could follow. Content-level agreements would cover metadata schemas and guidelines for the content and encoding of values for metadata elements. The experience with integrating the heterogeneous records for collections digitized through the LC/ Ameritech competition led to some sense of what minimal normalization was necessary for metadata records to be useful in American Memory. However, a larger "marketplace" of metadata and services established with the use of metadata harvesting might lead to broader consensus as to what is most important. Organizational agreements would cover matters such as governance of a consortium building and running a service based on metadata harvested from members.

By November 2000, with strong encouragement from Winston Tabb, the Associate Librarian for Library Services, the Library of Congress had committed itself to early implementation of the Open Archives Initiative Protocol for Metadata Harvesting (OAI-PMH) as a data provider using selected collections from American Memory as a test. The Library of Congress has been distributing catalog records since 1901, first on cards and since around 1968 in machine-readable form; making records for digitized content available for harvesting continues the tradition of adapting to new opportunities provided by new technology. Tabb also saw participation in the initiative, and other activities supported by DLF, as important for the Library of Congress, particularly in the light of criticisms of isolation in the recent report, LC21 A Digital Strategy for the Library of Congress.

The commitment was possible because the barrier to entry appeared low enough not to draw significant resources away from American Memory itself. This assessment proved true in practice. The first implementation took about 40 hours of programmer time, including analysis and testing. Mappings and conversion tools that were already used for American Memory or managed in LC's Network Development and MARC Standards Office (NDMSO) were reviewed, updated, and used to advantage. These included Perl language routines for parsing MARC records, a one-way mapping from MARC to simple Dublin Core, and a table to translate characters from the ALA character set used in LC's MARC records to UNICODE.

The first records to be made available would be those already upgraded to serve both in LC's main catalog and for indexing in American Memory. These already supported links to the content based on persistent identifiers resolved using a Handle Server, developed by the Corporation for National Research Initiatives (CNRI) and deployed at LC. Procedures for updates to American Memory could be easily extended to update the OAI data-provider service. The computer processing required to support harvesting requests was not expected to have a perceptible effect on response time for American Memory users. Also in late 2000, the DLF put out a call to members asking for lists of digital content for which they were willing to share metadata through the harvesting protocol.

At LC, this call was passed on to the custodial divisions responsible for content in American Memory described by records in the MARC format. Another mechanism to broaden access to their content was greeted enthusiastically, particularly because the links from the metadata records would bring users to the LC site, where more context for the collections would be available and users could follow leads to other related materials. At the January 2001 public release of version 1.0 of the protocol, David Woodward was able to announce that LC's data-provider service, for which he was the programmer, was up and running with records for two American Memory collections of digitized historical materials available: roughly 3,000 records for maps, and 200 records for ballroom dance instruction manuals. The records were harvestable in two formats, the full MARC records in a simple XML schema established for OAI-PMH and in unqualified Dublin Core in the XML schema.

Version 1.0 of the protocol was released in January 2001 with the expectation that there would be a period of experimentation for at least a year. Starting in September 2001, a technical committee was established with membership drawn from institutions actively using OAI-PMH to make metadata available or to harvest metadata and build a service.

LC was invited to participate, not only because of its experience as an OAI data provider, but also because of the importance in the library community of MARC records as a carrier for metadata. The outcome of this process was version 2.0 of the harvesting protocol; the differences are outlined elsewhere. There are many differences in detail, but the underlying philosophy of a low barrier to entry remained. Proposals were accommodated if there was sufficient support, several through optional extension features. LC is taking advantage of the option to provide descriptive records for "sets" of records that can be harvested as a group. Among the additions proposed but not adopted was support for distributed querying. Proponents were encouraged to participate in the activity now known as ZING (Z39.50-International Next Generation). This activity includes a number of initiatives by Z39.50 implementers to make the accumulated wisdom and functionality embodied in 20 years of experience more broadly available and lower the barriers to implementation. Simple Dublin Core was retained as a mandatory metadata format, because no other obvious candidate exists.

Version 2.0 of the OAI-PMH protocol proved as straightforward to implement at LC as the initial version. Based on experience over the first year, a revised architecture was developed to support more convenient and robust updates and additions. LC's OAI service divides records into OAI sets on the basis of American Memory collections or groups of collections. As of late 2002, there were ten sets, with one set being the aggregation of four photograph collections also available as separate sets. The implementation of OAI-PMH is programmed in Perl, taking advantage of the popular CGI.pm library to process and respond to HTTP requests. SGML processing routines from James Clark were used to handle the character conversion. For the first version, responses to the Identify and ListSets verbs were both in static files. ListIdentifiers requests were answered from an index, stored as a file, which mapped record identifiers to sets. The OAI verbs that return records access the source files of MARC records in the standard (ISO 2709) communication format, with dynamic conversion (using Perl) to XML.

The principal change when implementing version 2.0 was to use three tables in a relational database (using MySQL) in place of the simple set-identifier index. The tables represent OAI sets, OAI items, and the set-item links that indicate set membership. Sets can be added and related information edited through a Web form. Perl is still used for the HTTP processing, querying the MySQL database, and dynamic conversion from the source MARC records. Implementation of the new version at LC took roughly 60 hours of programmer effort, including analysis and testing. It was completed during the beta-test period and in operation before the official release of the protocol in June 2002.At NDMSO, the year leading up to the release of version 2.0 of OAI-PMH saw related developments in response to industry trends and requests from the library community. The trends included the growing adoption of XML following the stabilization of the XML schema definition language in May 2001 and the emergence of compliant software tools, the desire in libraries for a "lite" version of MARC encoded in XML, and the interest in metadata harvesting as part of the interoperability toolkit for libraries. NDMSO has developed two MARC-related XML schemata.One of these schemata is recommended in the new OAI release as a replacement for the original oai_marc schema. This MARCXML schema can be used to encode any MARC21 record. Like oai_marc, the tagging of this "slim" schema indicates the structure of a MARC record in fields and sub-fields, allows round-trip conversion without data loss, and will not need modification with the minor changes to the MARC standard that happen routinely. In February 2003, LC's cataloging distribution service made test files available in MARCXML for evaluation and prototype development.The second schema, known as MODS (Metadata Object Description Schema), is still at an early stage of development. Introduced in June 2002 and revised in early 2003, it is intended as a multi-purpose bibliographic element set for library applications. Unlike MARCXML, MODS includes only a subset of MARC elements and sometimes regroups them. MODS uses familiar words as element names rather than relying on MARC's numeric tags to convey semantics. In Fall 2002, LC made its OAI-harvestable records available in the MODS format in addition to MARC21 and simple Dublin Core.

These records provide richer semantics than Dublin Core and will support experimentation with the new format. The implementation uses an XSLT stylesheet to convert MARCXML records to MODS. NDMSO intends to maintain a suite of such tools for manipulating and transforming records between MARC and MODS. Implementing OAI-PMH as a data provider has had several beneficial side-effects for LC. Program code for converting records in the MARC Communications Format to an XML format can be used in many circumstances. Experience gained with special characters has been applied in other contexts through the development of mappings among MARC 21 characters, UNICODE, and character entities for HTML and SGML. Unusual characters in LC's records have also helped harvesters test their handling of UNICODE. Having records formally validated and tested by automated transformations by harvesters picks up errors that may be hidden by local interfaces or simply not noticed. This finding is consistent with experience with the LC/Ameritech competition. When records were brought into American Memory and subjected to different indexing and display routines, errors exposed were often found to cause undetected anomalous behavior in the original system too.

The Library of Congress has registered its OAI server for American Memory collections in the central OAI registry, which means that others can harvest and re-purpose records without LC being aware of it. This is nothing new for LC. Its records are available for copying from bibliographic utilities, such as OCLC and RLG; users of Z39.50 have been able to download records directly from LC's main catalog for well over a decade. Indeed, one of the key benefits to LC from the harvesting protocol is that no special arrangements have to be made when others want to get the records and use them in another service. LC has a particular interest in the use of its records in services with a focus on cultural heritage or humanities scholarship, and services that integrate materials from libraries, museums, historical societies and other archival institutions. The Research Libraries Group (RLG) has harvested records (in the MARC format) for several collections for integration into its cultural materials service. Dublin Core records for all collections are harvested by two services described elsewhere in this issue: OAIster at the University of Michigan and the University of Illinois-Urbana Champaign (UIUC) Cultural Heritage Repository. Records have also been harvested by the Perseus Digital Library. The mechanics of harvesting appear to be working well.

Now that records for a substantial body of cultural heritage content are easily harvestable, organizations and communities can begin to build on this base to support learning and scholarship through richer interactions with the resources accumulated in archival institutions. To achieve this will likely require communities to adopt more detailed agreements about metadata or make commitments to federated organization. Costs associated with metadata content can be daunting. Identifying and characterizing a resource and placing it in an intellectual context is expensive. Local needs take priority and upgrading existing records on an individual basis is seldom an option. Few doubt that "better" metadata lets people find what they want more easily, but a compromise between quantity and quality is often necessary. For pictures, music, and other cultural resources that do not include full text or spoken words that can be searched, human expertise is essential to provide summaries, assign topical and genre terms, indicate where and when a work was created, or relate it to other works.

Because of the expense and investment, change in practices is inevitably slow. Most standards and formal consortial agreements allow a great deal of flexibility so that legacy records can be handled. Motivation to modify records or practices, or to develop and test more complex conversion tools, will exist only if there is obvious benefit to the unit bearing the brunt of the workload. The Library of Congress is aware that it could improve the records it makes available for harvesting in a number of ways, with more or less effort, but needs evidence or guidance from service builders to indicate which modifications would be most valuable and which irrelevant. Indications are beginning to surface. Some inferences can be drawn from an analysis from the team building the UIUC Cultural Heritage Repository and the approach to metadata normalization for that service. The section on data content in RLG's description guidelines for participants in the Cultural Materials Alliance indicates the aspects that are most significant in building their service.

The least expensive way to improve LC's records in the short term would be through modifications to the transformation from the source record into formats for harvesting. LC's current transformation from MARC to simple Dublin Core is extremely basic. Element values are copied directly without conversion to another vocabulary or encoding scheme. Where codes are converted to terms, MARC terminology is usually used, because it matches the semantics of the coding scheme. In some cases, this results in terms that do not correspond to common usage or map cleanly to categories in other metadata schemes. Issues and questions that have come up in relation to simple (unqualified) Dublin Core records include:

— *Title:* The mapping to simple Dublin Core omits all title information except from the MARC 245 field. This is on the assumption that multiple titles will be confusing for service builders if the main title cannot be distinguished. However, significant information will be missing. For example, songs are often known by words from their first lines or choruses rather than the title on the published score.

— *Date:* The value for Date is taken from the statement of publication, distribution, etc. This field is intended for human reading, and the cataloging rules provide methods to indicate uncertainty and approximation, or date ranges when the resource being described is not a single item, and even to concatenate several dates for different events. For cultural heritage materials, uncertainty about the date of creation or distribution is common. The result is that the Date element is neither easily machine-processable nor useful for sorting.

— *Description:* For American Memory materials, note fields can be very significant for discovery: they can include summary descriptions, information about provenance, or biographical details. LC has chosen to include almost all categories of notes as Description elements. Some notes may be of little value for discovery, but because the range of information included in general notes is very broad, it is not easy to distinguish notes that are logistical or administrative from those that provide intellectual context for the resource.

— *Creator/Contributor:* The current mapping uses only Creator and includes all values for MARC fields 100-111 (Main Entry Name fields) and 700-720 (Added Entry Name fields). The semantics of the distinction between main entries and added entries in MARC is not the same as the distinction between Creator and Contributor. In particular, since only one main entry name is permitted, authors beyond the first are added entries. The American Memory experience leads us to believe that a distinction based on role with relationship to the resource being described is more significant for cultural heritage materials than either the MARC distinction or the Dublin Core distinction. Unfortunately, neither the unqualified version of Dublin Core nor the approved qualifiers can represent this distinction. Questions to service builders at UIUC and OAIster about their preferences received somewhat uncertain responses.

— *Type:* This element, which corresponds to the genre or nature of the resource, what it is rather than what it is about, is perhaps the most complex of all. Those thinking about the issue for the first time often assume that a hierarchy of genres can be established for general use. All attempts in the library community have failed, and those with experience, including the DC Type Working Group, believe that genre vocabularies will continue to be developed by communities and for specific contexts.

Some of these issues will not be a problem when transforming MARC records to the MODS schema, since MODS inherits the relevant semantics from MARC. This is not a coincidence, since experience with American Memory and mappings to metadata schemes used in other communities were among the inputs to the development of MODS. Others, in particular those related to dates and genres, will continue to be a concern when transforming records from sources based on MARC records and AACR2/ISBD practices.

6

Digital Archives

We live in a time when libraries will see their missions expanded as they continue to collect and preserve analog materials while at the same time participating wholeheartedly in the digital revolution. The users of libraries will demand no less. The library owns precious content that many publishers and entertainment industry producers would be happy to develop. It has reservations, however, for it has had some negative experiences with such partners. These reservations are understandable, but they should transmute not into suspicion but into a strategy for partnership.

The development of the Internet and the World Wide Web is bringing unprecedented changes to the archival enterprise. In describing and making available holdings, archivists have long developed finding aids, printed them and distributed them in person or by mail. Records have most often been used in research rooms; sometimes records are used through photocopies ordered after consultation with an archivist; sometimes records are used on microform ordered by an archivist and accompanied by some form of description. The general pattern, however, has been of direct communication, one-to-one, between archivist and user, with the archivist able to answer questions, clarify the structure of the holdings and in general mediate the research use. The World Wide Web and the Internet have changed that. The new pattern is unmediated communication in multiples. Archivists place descriptions on a Web site, and users from all over the world have simultaneous access without intervention of the archivist. Copies of documents placed on the Web site may be used in the order the archivist envisions, or may be used in random sequences over the course of the research. These four great engines of change are reflected in the work of the archival profession at large.

In beginning online archival collections were most often presented in one of two ways: as an online exhibition or as a simple database of independent archival documents. Following the "exhibition" method, institutions presented archival collections online in much the same way as they would present an exhibition of physical materials; narrative descriptions or transcriptions of items were presented with links to digital representations of those items. In these digital repositories, each archival document was treated as a separate entity and basic descriptive metadata elements such as title, author, and date were given for each item. While the "exhibition" approach provided an abundance of narrative contextual information, this method was deemed impracticable for the size of the digital collection. Similarly, a strict database approach was also not favoured, as it did not retain the contextual linkages between the documents.

Archives play an important role as an indispensable instrument for the history of both the whole continent and the individual nations. Consequently they must offer well-organized and structured services in order to give easier access to citizens and researchers. Until recently most archives were very isolated and unprivileged institutions. They have been gradually developed and provided with increased resources, as a result of the growing awareness of the important role they play in society. Yet the present situation is far from ideal. The scarcity of economic resources and the lack of proper archival policies are the main problems. Many archives use microfilming technology to preserve records and a few have now started to implement and develop computerised systems to help with the arrangement and description of archival materials. Almost all the archives issue archival publications and are members of international associations. However, there are less positive aspects: lack of specialised human resources and almost non-existent professional archival education and training. In the absence of qualified personnel the archives are experiencing difficulties in tackling the problems of records and archives management. Another major problem is the uncertain financial background -often archives institutions have very limited budgets which do not guarantee them adequate resources for the implementation of a proper archives policy.

Almost everywhere archives are esteemed only for their heritage value; the role documents play in managing the country's affairs and assisting the decision-making process is forgotten. As record-keeping practices are not changing, there is no incentive to draft new legislation. Standardisation is everywhere less developed in the archive sector than in other information sciences.

Archives have three universal purposes:

— to select the records of institutions, the papers of individuals and families and the artificial collections of documentary materials that have enduring value;
— to preserve them; and
— to make them available for use.

Individual nations and archival institutions accomplish these purposes through programmes which vary in emphasis and administration. Identifying the varieties of archival practice in Europe and North America requires assembling and analysing a sizeable quantity of data. All European archives owe a debt to the Greco-Roman archival tradition. There are, however, several obvious groupings of archives, either by virtue of the legislative structure of the nation or by tradition. All archives, however, whether in governments, businesses or private organizations, must soon manage electronic records. At the European Summit on Archives in 1996, delegates agreed that the three principal issues for European archivists are the management of electronic records, training for personnel and preservation of the European archival heritage. Consequently, the critical issue for most European archives is providing guidance to the records creators, in particular in the area of electronic records, not in finding ever larger storage facilities for semi-current records. The electronic records issue binds Europe together. Although the development of the computerized office generally occurred earlier in Western Europe, the computerization of Central and Eastern Europe has occurred at lightning speed, as external donors put computers in parliaments and courts and as businesses snapped them up for commercial ventures. This means that the intensity of the computer question, particularly for the very latest systems, is at least as pervasive in Eastern Europe as in the West.

Archival education increasingly is challenged to provide the new skills needed to manage archives in the current information age. Two shifts are occurring simultaneously:

- records are created and maintained electronically in the entities that are the sources of archival holdings, requiring archives to move aggressively to protect the archival information in the complex environment of modern management systems;
- archives are themselves introducing and adapting automation to facilitate work in the archives.

Recent graduates from academic archival programmes emphasizing digital, processrelated information are entering European archival institutions and challenging with their enthusiasm the staff already employed there. Effective in-service training programmes are urgently needed throughout the European archival world in order to ensure that serious divisions of competency do not occur within the professional community. The third major concern identified at the archival summit in spring 1996 was preservation. Facilities are a central concern of archivists everywhere. The nature of archives is that the holdings are continuously expanding, and space utilization is a constant preoccupation.

European archives also 66% of central repositories with temperature and humidity controls, and 49% with microform storage accommodation to international standards. By contrast, state archives in the United States, 92% with purpose-built repositories and 92% with climate controls. All this suggests that European archives have major problems of adaptive re-use of older buildings, and consequently must struggle to maintain adequate preservation conditions for the materials stored within them. The average European national archives had 93,000 square metres of holdings in 1993. In any event, the apparent lack of reformatting capacities in most European archives suggests that original records are made available to users, even those records that are extremely popular, setting up a future need for expensive conservation treatments. Preserving electronic records requires both physical facilities and the management of the physical and logical structures of the item. The technical facilities available in archives to handle electronic records are not as yet widespread. The techniques for preserving electronic records have evolved with the changes in the information industry; the preservation of flat files is well understood, the preservation of relational databases is fast becoming a standard practice and the preservation of electronic mail is rapidly emerging as a basic technique.

The fast advances in imaging technology are currently causing very serious problems for European archives, both because their popularity means that more and more images are created, and because the hardware and software dependency of imaging systems is extremely high and the rate of innovation extremely fast, leaving orphaned systems littering the way. Add to this the developments in the television industry, linking sound, image and text, and the problems mount. At present the only means of preservation is duplication to a current system, assuming that the system on which the image was generated is still operating. And yet it is essential that archives grapple with these issues, for in the long term this is the way records will be created, maintained, and used.

The purpose of an archives is both preservation and use. One of the most significant developments for archives around the world has been the adoption of international standards for archival description, based on traditional archival practices but adapted for using computers to describe the holdings. This is particularly important, because European archivists estimated in 1993 that only about 50% of their holdings were adequately described but 83% were using computers to describe holdings. There is considerable variation between Eastern and Central Europe on the one hand, and the rest of Europe on the other; in the former 55% of the institutions use computers for description while in the latter the figure is 91%.

As computers are rapidly introduced, adopting a standard format that can be shared electronically through the Internet will revolutionize archival use. No longer will users be tied to opening hours or transcontinental mail deliveries for service; neither will they have to consider wide variations in national descriptive practice. The day is approaching when the information about holdings can be searched in compatible versions worldwide. The use of archives is increasing everywhere in Europe, but with particular ferocity in Central and Eastern Europe. As holdings long unavailable are now released for use, scholars and genealogists are streaming into research rooms. The 1993 figures, based as they are on 1992 data, capture only the beginning of this wave.

In 1993, 63% of archives in Europe were operating under legislation passed or revised in the preceding ten years. While avoidance of obsolescence is all to the good, this means that the archivists must learn to interpret these laws, develop a body of practice that accords with them, and consider what further revisions are necessary. Archivists unite in mourning the actual destruction of documents, but the problems of restitution and division have separated as much as they have united archivists. The break-up of the Ottoman and Habsburg Empires, and the fragmentation of the Soviet Union and the Yugoslavia of Tito, to name only a few examples in this century, caused documents of signal importance to one people to be lodged in the archives of another.

Audiovisual Archives

The audiovisual heritage is an important element within the cultural heritage and has achieved prominence in the twentieth century, the first to have been recorded on audiovisual formats. Audiovisuals are not new but have become of increasing importance as art, entertainment and information carriers. In some cases the transmission of sound and visual data has greater value and impact than the printed document - where, for example, there is a literacy or language banier. Audiovisuals may also be the only suitable records for the oral or sonic transmission of culture and the arts, news and other current items.

The spread and development of modern technologies mean an increase in the role of audiovisual data carriers for communication, information and culture. Today's radio and television rely heavily on archive material and it is estimated that more than 60% of radio and television programmes use archival or stock material for programming. The definitions are still being formulated, but audiovisual materials are to be understood as visual recordings and sound recordings irrespective of their physical base or recording process. The carrier usually requires a playback device. This definition is meant to cover the maximum number of forms and formats. Audiovisual materials should not be confused with multimedia; the former provide source material for the latter, and multimedia as such are not archival material. Two features of audiovisual materials add an extra dimension to the principles of collection and preservation: a proliferation both of formats and of systems of production and playback. These cause incompatibility problems between formats and systems.

Archives have to maintain original playback devices and employ technical staff who know how to use and maintain the machinery. Audiovisual archives are storehouses for a large proportion of the social and cultural heritage of the twentieth century. An audiovisual archive is defined as an organization or department of an organization which is focused on collecting, managing, preserving and providing access to a collection of audiovisual media and the audiovisual heritage, applying archival principles. Such archives contain huge treasures of unique material.

Archives of audiovisual materials are relatively new, but they have proliferated in the past few decades. Television was originally recorded on film, but video has been the principal material since the later 1960s. Although audiovisual materials have appeared so recently, time is not on their side and the longer we delay in gathering, conserving and preserving the materials, the less we shall be able to retain. It is vital that steps are taken now to collect and manage audiovisual materials properly before their fragile nature takes a further toll. Already much has been lost owing to ignorance, lack of awareness of the dangers and careless handling.

Audiovisual archives vary in type, purpose and function, and until recently most of them were singlematerial archives: moving image, sound and still-image archives, the latter frequently housed in more conventional archives of print materials.

As the technologies converge so do the archives, to unite effort and conserve resources. Some archives take responsibility for all recorded materials, others take smaller bites and combine one or two of the materials. The larger archives cannot always combine materials in one department; the physical techniques required to deal with each material from the point of view of storage, handling and restoration need different expertise and materials are therefore separated by this parameter alone. Other functions of collection management can be applied to all the materials: documentation and information retrieval, and selection. Storage vaults may have to accommodate more than one material and the resulting environmental considerations will be different from those more stringently applied to individual materials. Alternatively, an archive may decide that it must apply the optimum storage and environmental values which apply to each material: single-material archives are more fortunate in these cases. Academic archives also house audiovisual materials, many in universities for research, and latterly educational materials for distance learning. These may be small and specialized, or have substantial collections and preservation programmes. Specialized or thematic archives concentrate on a particular format, subject-matter or locality, or relate to specific cultural groups. Many of these archives have developed within larger organizations.

Film companies, broadcasting companies and record companies maintain archives primarily for use and exploitation by the parent company. Many of these preserve and restore their materials for re-use, but the archives' main obligation is to the parent organization rather than to preserving the cultural heritage. This may be left to a national archive, which obtains a selection of the production company's material by deposit. Other institutions with archival responsibility include museums, cinematheques, videotheques and national libraries. Most of these are more concerned with maintaining stock for exhibition purposes, and originals may be deposited for long-term preservation in a national archive. There are also collections of last resort which attempt to conserve copies of material in usable condition, but seldom retain archival originals or masters. Audiovisual materials result from a huge level of investment.

Archives in organizations such as broadcast associations or film production companies have commercial backing and motivation, and meet costs from their revenue. Once that commercial motive is fulfilled, however, it is generally acknowledged that, as with other records of the national cultural creativity, the cost of maintaining the collection reverts to government and granting bodies. Many valuable collections have disappeared for ever as a result of production company closures or changes in franchise when materials are not taken over by already overstretched archives. The basic tasks of an audiovisual archive are collection, preservation, documentation and access provision. Methods of collection and acquisition vary, and include the legal or voluntary deposit of collections or individual items, the deposit of in-house productions, donations, special agreements for copying nationally produced materials, and purchase. Other archives collect their own materials in the form of oral or video history programmes, with the purpose of recording cultures, languages and music before they disappear. Closely allied to acquisition are evaluation, selection and appraisal.

The audiovisual archive acquires materials according to a particular remit, balancing new acquisitions against existing stock and the purpose and function of the archive. Storage space and resources being what they are, archives have to select material for preservation on the basis of relevance, uniqueness and quality. Wherever possible an archive should be dealing with original materials, but originals are hard to come by. There is strictly only one original film, video or master sound recording. Such originals seldom survive and there are various forms of tampering with the products - cut/uncut versions, director's/ producer's cut, censored and unexpurgated versions. Owners of original material may be reluctant to deposit their master material in an archive until they have no further use for it, by which time the technical quality has deteriorated.

Three elements in audiovisual documents have to be considered in the selection process: the artefact or carrier, the information content and the aesthetic content, particularly with film and sound recordings. The artefact or carrier will designate the form of the audiovisual and influence selection for technical reasons. Audiovisual archives, therefore, do not have a huge selection of material, but most of it has unique value, and such archives retain more material than many other archives. Some audiovisual collections will include several interpretations of the same work—for example, music recordings—or several records of the same event carried in different documents: a film, video or sound version. Guidelines for archival selection exist, but they are usually those of organizations with their own parameters. Selection of material is dependent upon the function of the archive, the quality of the material and the uniqueness or rarity of the content. Audiovisual archives should concentrate on recordings of national origin. To avoid duplication of effort, material should be offered back to the country of original production or to archives with a more relevant collection remit. The main function of any archive is to preserve the heritage and the artefacts which make up that heritage.

Organisation of Archives

In a well-designed archival network, institutions can share the burden of archiving journals, and libraries and researchers needing to use archival materials can locate and retrieve appropriate copies from a participant in the network. However an archival system is set up, though, it must be clear who takes responsibility for the material being archived and how this responsibility is enforced.

Some authors and organizations may attempt to archive their own material. A publisher may declare that it will archive its own back issues indefinitely, for instance. Many authors have also provided preprints of their papers and journal articles on their Web sites for years. This informal practice is now encouraged by manifestos like the Budapest Open Access Initiative."Self-archiving" can also be done by authors' institutions. For instance, MIT's Dspace repository promises stable long-term storage for the scholarly work of its faculty.Self-archiving, however, will not suffice to preserve scholarly journals, let alone scholarly communication as a whole. It essentially relies on the self-interest of the original creators and publishers to keep the archive viable, but Web sites often disappear when an individual changes institutions or careers. Copies of papers on individual sites are often preprints, so they may lack important revisions and supplementary information that appeared in the journal version.

Publisher-run archives may disappear without warning if they are no longer cost-effective to the publisher, or if the journal or the publisher fails or is acquired by another company. Contents of archives may be changed, corrupted, or withdrawn, either by accident or intentionally. As holders of copyrights to the content they archive, publishers and authors have exclusive rights to disseminate this content unless they grant rights to archives run by disinterested third parties. With exclusive rights comes near-exclusive responsibility for their material. Without very strong certification and backup strategies, self-archiving with this level of exclusivity is not likely to be widely trusted to preserve scholarly information for the time spans researchers and libraries have come to expect. This does not mean that self-archiving is useless, however. Self-archiving can be a backup to trusted archives run by other parties.

Whether run by content creators and publishers or by third parties, archives have traditionally taken full responsibility for the content they archive. They are responsible for quality control, continued preservation, and providing appropriate access. If they themselves cannot maintain the content in perpetuity, they are responsible for finding someone else who can. While they may delegate some of their functions, such as ingestion or migration, to outside service providers, they are ultimately responsible to their clients for making sure these functions are carried out correctly and that the content is preserved for future access. This "integrated" responsibility for preserving and providing access to content may earn the trust of users, since the buck stops, as it were, with a definite party. Publishers, too, may be more willing to grant rights to a specific agent who takes responsibility for their work. Of course, the archive must live up to this responsibility, with its attendant certification and sustainability requirements.

The LOCKSS (Lots of Copies Keep Stuff Safe) project at Stanford suggests a more distributed form of responsibility, similar to the distributed responsibility for print journals discussed earlier. With LOCKSS, no one institution takes responsibility for a journal. Instead, many institutions maintain sites that cache copies of journal content published on Web sites. Content can be accessed from the cache if it is no longer available on the original publisher's Web site. Cache contents are automatically checked against each other on a regular basis, and corrupted or lost copies of items replaced with other copies. The cache correction protocol is slow and relies on records of past holdings. These features make it highly unlikely, given enough participants, that a copy of an object will be completely lost, be corrupted, or become unavailable to any site that originally cached the content. Because the protocol also checks what content a site has previously demonstrated that it owned, the protocol does not "leak" content to sites that were not authorized to see it.

LOCKSS is designed to run on low-cost machines with as little maintenance as possible, making it attractive for libraries to set up LOCKSS caches. If enough libraries continue to cache the same content, that content can be preserved reliably even if no single institution takes final responsibility for it. The system can be queried to see how many sites are caching content. Institutions that see a need for greater reliability, can arrange to put additional copies on caches run at their own site or other sites.In its original form, LOCKSS makes a number of simplifying assumptions about what is being cached, that may not be applicable to all journal archives. For instance, LOCKSS obtains publishers' content by automatically polling their Web sites for HTML and image files, but while those sites may include presentation forms of journals they typically do not include source forms. However, the basic LOCKSS model can be generalized to cover a broader range of journal archiving strategies, especially if caching sites can individually decide what to cache and how.

Useful generalizations of the model include:

— *Introducing an explicit representation of trusted sources for journal content.* The basic LOCKSS model assumes the publisher's Web site is the trusted source for journal content. However, other trusted sources might be needed to provide content not available on the Web site such as source forms for journal content, metadata, and updates and migrated versions of journal content.

— *Caching Archival Information Packages (AIPs).* If AIPs and not just Web pages and images are cached, then a distributed archive can reliably cache both source and presentation forms of content, as well as appropriate metadata and migrated forms. These AIPs would need to come from a trusted source.

— *Identifiers for AIPs and other journal content.* A distributed archiving system requires a consistent way of identifying content so that different servers can check consistency between different copies of the same material. As originally designed, LOCKSS simply uses URLs as identifiers, but this only works for material pulled directly from the Web at static URLs. A distributed archiving system could use AIP identifiers to identify content, but would have to settle on a suitable global scheme for assigning such identifiers. Other globally addressable entities, such as directories, will need globally unique identifiers as well.

— *Metadata*. A distributed archiving system should agree on a common core set of metadata to maintain for journal content, including descriptive and technical metadata, to support searching and browsing and maintenance of particular journal content.

— *Directory services*. Once the metadata above is in place it should be possible for archive users to be able to see what content is in the system, even if they cannot actually view all the content. They should also be able to search and browse it in customary ways, such as looking up an article by its citation, or browsing tables of contents for a particular journal volume. Directory information needs to be updateable as more journal content is added.

— *Versioning*. LOCKSS' cache consistency protocol works well for objects that do not change once they are imported into the system, but a general-purpose distributed archiving system includes several types of changing objects. AIPs for particular journal articles may change as new manifestations of the articles are added (such as through migration) or if publishers issue a corrected version of an article after its original publication. Directories change as new articles, issues, and journals are added to the system. A versioning discipline would allow LOCKSS-like consistency checks for updates and new manifestations of these objects. A new version could be identified as an update of an existing version of an object in the system, and distributed archive sites could decide whether or not to accept the version. The sites could use acceptance criteria of their choosing, such as the trustworthiness of the source and the nature of the differences between the new version and the older version. Some types of updates may be expected to be monotonic: new data gets added, but old data does not get taken away. Sites could also decide whether or not to retain older versions. Most legitimate updates to journals would not occur more frequently than issues of journals are published, a pace which is compatible with the deliberately slow coherency protocol that LOCKSS uses.

— *Controlled expansion of access.* LOCKSS' access control model is also monotonic: if a site has had a copy of some content in the past, it can be given a copy again, if its old copy has been lost or corrupted. Trusted sources could also grant new copies to sites that previously did not have copies of particular content, when this is permitted, without any further changes in the access control model. It would also be useful to be able to designate that certain content could be given to a wider set of sites. The simplest approach would be to include an "open access" flag that could be given to journal content or metadata that can be distributed freely. Trusted sources could set this flag, either on original distribution, or when previously arranged "triggers" applied that opened access to content.

In making these extensions, one must avoid introducing so much overhead into the system that the primary advantages of LOCKSS — reliable distributed archiving with minimal cost and maintenance — are lost. Each of the enhancements mentioned above should not be overly burdensome in itself, but designers of a distributed archiving system should make sure the enhancements are kept as simple as possible.

Service providers help scale up an archival system by spreading out responsibility for archival tasks. They can be useful when an archival function requires specialized expertise or resources. For instance, if a company provides low-cost, highly replicated reliable data storage, an archive might out-source backups to that company rather than maintain backups itself. Or, if content is submitted or stored in a variety of protocols and formats, ingestion and migration of this content might be usefully parceled out to service providers, each specializing in a particular format or data provider, instead of trying to have one organization handle everything.

Service providers often do not need to make the same sort of long-term commitments as archives themselves do, unless their service includes long term information storage. However, they still need to be visible in the design and operations of an archiving system. Archive users may want to make sure they are certified for carrying out their service correctly. Publisher agreements may need to allow them to access copyrighted material, and publishers may want to be assured that they do not distribute or alter this material without authorization. The business model for the archive or archival system also needs to include some sort of compensation for the services of the providers.

Several organizations, including JSTOR, Highwire, PubMedCentral, and various publishers and national libraries, are currently archiving journal material. As the population of archives and archived materials grows, it will be increasingly important for archive maintainers and users to be able to keep track of who is doing what and with what content. A registry of journal archiving activity would make this possible. It would allow users to find content they needed, and allow archive maintainers to find service providers, look up technical information on archiving formats and practices, and track redundant archiving of journal content. Several architectures are possible for such a registry.

Responsibilities of Archives

The archive is responsible for ensuring scholars can access journal content for as long as it is of scholarly value in a form that allows it to be used effectively for research, teaching, and learning. The archive is responsible for respecting the copyrights of authors and publishers in its stewardship of electronic journal content. It is also responsible for helping maintain a healthy climate of scholarship and scholarly communication. It should neither hinder publishers or libraries with overly burdensome procedural and economic constraints, nor hinder scholars themselves with overly restrictive policies for access or deposit. Archives need to be granted sufficient rights to carry out these responsibilities.

Responsibility for Selection

The archive is responsible for identifying journals it wishes to archive and making these selections known to a publisher for the publisher's approval. The selection does not have to be enumerated. For instance, archives that plan to include all electronic journals of particular publishers, could agree that any newly added journal will be included in the selection unless either the publisher or the archive notifies the other that the new journal should be excluded. In such cases, the publisher should also inform the archive about newly added electronic journals or of journals that it no longer publishes.Of course, this notification, and other provisions of information given in this section, can be made simply by publishing the information in an agreed-upon location, such as a Web page or a mailing list.

The archive and publisher also need to agree on what content in the journals is being selected. Normally, the archive should collect at least all issues published from the time the agreement is made. Back issues, where feasible, are also desirable to include. The archive and the publisher also have to agree on a set of formats that will be collected, and protocols for collecting content and metadata. Either the archive or the publisher should be able to request, with sufficient advance notice, that archiving for a journal be cut off: that is, no further issues will be deposited into the archive. The archive is responsible for notifying its clients, including appropriate registries, of its selections.

Responsibility for Ingestion

The publisher is responsible for providing content and metadata for the journal issues being archived. Content should include the journal content as provided to subscribers in presentation forms such as PDF and HTML. Even if an archive does not store presentation forms, it is helpful for an archive to be able to compare any source forms it receives against what the publisher actually supplied to subscribers in the electronic journal. This provision may simply consist of allowing the archive access to the online journal for testing.When the archive is preserving source forms of content, the publisher is responsible for providing them and for ensuring they are correctly formatted; the publisher is also responsible for ensuring the source forms correspond appropriately to the published presentation forms. The publisher should likewise be responsible for providing metadata for the journal content in sufficient detail to allow standard scholarly citations to be built for all articles and other citable contributions. This includes title, authors, issue information, page numbers or other section delimiters where applicable, and other standard identifiers for the content such as ISSNs and DOIs. Abstracts and keywords would also be useful, when available.

The archive is responsible for collecting content and metadata in a timely fashion, checking it for consistency and proper formatting, and either ingesting it into its repository or informing the publisher of any errors or problems with the data. If the archive reports errors the publisher should remedy them, and the archive should then reingest content. Generally, the archive should try to ingest an issue while it is still the current issue. If the archive is harvesting data from the Web or another published source, it should be able to assume the data is in its final form unless the publisher has notified it otherwise. For example, if the publisher posts "draft" or pre-publication material which it then modifies before an issue's "official" publication, the publisher is responsible for telling the archive when and when not to harvest this information.

The archive is responsible for collecting appendices to articles such as datasets, audiovisual clips, program code, and other multimedia when this is within the archive's stated selection criteria. The publisher may need to assist the archive in collecting these appendices. If the appendices have unusual size or format, they might not be required to be migrated as is regular content. "Appendices" external to the journal itself — a Web site referred to by a URL in a journal article, for example — need not be collected. If content is to be collected by harvesting from the publisher's site, the publisher is responsible for allowing access by the archive's harvesters, while the archive is responsible for ensuring the harvesters do not unduly load the archive's servers.

Responsibility for Storage and Maintenance

The archive is responsible for ensuring the long-term persistence and stability of the archived content. It is also responsible for making sure the content does not become unusable due to technological obsolescence. Therefore, the publisher should give the archive the right to store copies of the journal content and metadata, make and store backup copies, and create derivative works based on the original data for the purpose of maintaining their suitability for research and scholarship. Such derivative works could include migrations to new formats, indexing for searching and browsing, and transformations required for emulation. Ideally, the right to create derivative works would also allow enhancements to the content, at least when the enhancements are for services that researchers come to expect in online journals. Such enhancements, for instance, could include converting static images to wavelet-based forms that allow panning and zooming, or inserting hyperlinks to make it possible for readers to go to referenced articles. Users expect that reliable, persistent electronic archives will not lose content. Therefore, the rights above and other intellectual property rights given to the archive should be irrevocable by the publisher, provided that the archive fulfills its responsibilities. Publishers can retain copyright; they just need to assign appropriate rights for the archive to do its job.

Responsibility for Access and Distribution

The archive is responsible to its clients for providing authorized users with its content and metadata, and it is responsible to publishers for providing content only to authorized users. Content provided to authorized users should include:

— Copies of the journal content as originally published for journals archived in presentation form.

— Images of the journal pages in formats commonly readable at the time of access for journals archived in presentation form. This may require migration if common data formats change.

— The text of the journal content in formats commonly readable at the time of access. This may also require migration.

— Where feasible and cost-effective, other journal content, such as data sets and audiovisual materials, in formats commonly readable at the time of access.

Metadata should include at least citation information for the journals and their articles. The archive should also provide reasonable facilities for locating an article or journal with a known citation. It seems relatively uncontroversial to allow general access at least to citation-level descriptive metadata. This allows users to know what is in an archive. Richer descriptions, such as abstracts, may be more controversial, but if they encourage a user to seek out the full content and become more interested in the journal as a whole, providing such detailed metadata can benefit both archive and publisher.Likewise, allowing access to content by the publisher and by the archive maintainers seems uncontroversial. Widening access further, though, proved more problematic. Even providing access to subscribers to the journal for content that was also available on the publisher's Web site raised concerns that the archive would compete with the publisher's own offerings.

The concerns here seemed to be not just possible loss of marketing opportunities on the publisher's own Web site, but also possible degradation of image. The look, the services, and the authority that the publisher took pains to establish on their Web site could be lost on the archive site, thus weakening the "brand" or reputation of the publisher. This seemed to be less of a concern if the archive just offered material that was no longer available on the publisher's own Web site. Concerns about image may also be alleviated if appropriate links are made between the archive site and the publisher's site. Even more controversial is allowing access to archived journal content to those who are not subscribers to the journal. JSTOR and Highwire, two established projects that archive journal content, allow such access after a certain time has passed from publication. The point at which access is opened is referred to as the "moving wall." There are several advantages to this sort of access:

— It satisfies, at least in part, the desire of many scholars that scholarly information should be generally accessible to all for little or no cost, whenever feasible.

— It provides an electronic counterpart to the long-standing custom of researchers obtaining older journal articles by interlibrary loan if their institution did not subscribe to the journal or retain their volumes.

— It avoids the overhead of the archive having to keep track of exactly what users should be allowed to access each item in the archive.

— It allows a wide audience of readers and third-party automated programs to examine the archived content and verify that it is being accurately preserved or report problems if it is not, thus enhancing trust in the archive. This may be especially important when material needs to be migrated to a new format, a process that may risk losing information or usability in unexpected ways.

— It may make it easier for mirror sites and other service providers to access the content.

— It provides an ongoing service of document delivery to the scholarly community, instead of just being an unseen "insurance" policy as an inaccessible or "dark" archive would be. This strengthens support for the archive in that community.

These are all benefits for the archive and its users, but they are not direct benefits to publishers. Of greatest concern was the possibility that libraries would cancel subscriptions to their journals or not sign up for them in the first place if they could have access to the archive without a journal subscription. Martin Richardson of Oxford University Press, for instance, reported that institutional subscriptions to eleven journals made available via Highwire had declined by three percent per year in the three years since they had been placed online, even though they had been increasing prior to that time.

Faced with such declines in subscriptions, publishers might have to raise prices for the subscribers that are left, or cut the budgets to produce the journals. As an alternative to general free access Richardson recommended free access to readers in developing countries and low article pricing for infrequent users of journals. Richardson's report does not prove that opening access caused the drop in subscriptions or that a more distant moving wall, such as the three to five years that is common for JSTOR journals, would not solve the problem. Both Oxford and Cambridge have been willing to experiment with allowing some of their journal content to be accessible to nonsubscribers through JSTOR and Highwire as well as PubMedCentral.

Some may argue that copyright law already specifies a moving wall when works enter the public domain and are available to anyone. However, this moving wall has been extended repeatedly in the United States and is now up to ninety-five years after publication for older publications and works for hire, and to seventy years after the death of the last surviving author for other works. The distance and uncertainty of copyright expiration in these circumstances makes an archive that requires public domain verification before providing access to electronic journal content equivalent to a "dark" archive for most practical purposes.

Other "trigger" events besides a fixed moving wall are also worth considering. For example, opening up access when migration is required would ease user concerns that migration might not be successful. It might also benefit publishers if they found migration too expensive or troublesome to carry out themselves. It is also reasonable for archives to be able to provide general access to content that is no longer being offered online by the publisher or the publisher's agents.

The archiving agreement should not abridge the traditional rights recognized by copyright law. These rights include fair use, first-sale rights, and unrestricted use of public domain material. All of these rights play important roles in scholarship, so archives whose purpose is to support scholarship should avoid restricting them. Some publishers digitizing older material may want to make an exception to this rule for new digitizations of public domain content from early in a journal's run. An archive should weigh this proposed exception carefully. In some cases, a short-term embargo on unrestricted use of this material may be necessary if the only likely digitizer of the content is worried about the investment going to waste, but there is little justification for extending this embargo beyond the same moving wall term that is given to copyrighted content. On the whole, the copyrighted content of most electronic journal archives will usually be much more valuable than recently-digitized public domain content. Users are also much more likely to trust and support a comprehensive and authorized archive of a journal's run than an unauthorized provider of part of the journal's run.

Responsibility for Certification and Evaluation

The archive is responsible for specifying a process for certification of its content and procedures, and for reporting the results of this certification to its clients, including its publisher partners. The RLG-OCLC Trusted Repositories paper notes two basic approaches to certification: an approach based on auditing and an approach based on standards and usage. For a "dark" archive, or an archival system that uses software that is not available for public inspection, certification will generally need to involve auditing, to satisfy the concerns of constituents who cannot examine the content or the software themselves. In a more open system, such as LOCKSS, each site can examine its own contents and the software it is using. In such cases, separate auditing is less important though it may be desirable for the designers of the system to have the code reviewed and certified by an outside party.

Publishers may want to know how the content they publish is being used in an archive as well as the cost of the archiving processes. It is reasonable for an archive to share aggregated usage information with publishers as long as the form of the information sharing protects the privacy of individual readers. If publishers are subsidizing the archiving they also have a right to be informed of the costs involved. Archives and publishers should agree in advance on the data an archive will collect, what an archive can be expected to provide, and for how long an archive should retain usage data.

Responsibility for Sustainability

The archive is responsible for ensuring it has appropriate technology, procedures, and funding for it to continue archiving activities for as long as needed. Responsibility for funding, however, is related to the other rights and responsibilities of an archive. Funding for an archive can come from various sources including:

- — The organization running the archive (self-funding)
- — External sponsors (e.g., private foundations, government grants, marketers)
- — The publishers of the journals in the archive
- — Users of the archive materials (e.g., individual researchers and libraries)

Self-funding is viable for most academic libraries if the archival system is sufficiently lightweight and inexpensive to run and provides commensurate benefits. We can run a LOCKSS server on a commodity PC, for example, and in its current form it requires very little maintenance. Even a more ambitious system, such as the distributed archiving system described earlier, could easily pay for itself if its cost were similar to the original LOCKSS system and it made it easier for us to move older journals to inexpensive remote storage.

Full-service "integrated responsibility" archives are much more heavyweight. According to discussions with its maintainers, PubMedCentral, run by the National Center for BiotechnOlogy Information (NCBI) of the National Institutes of Health (NIH), requires seven full-time employees to run on an ongoing basis.

The project archives fewer than thirty externally published journals, plus a few dozen very low volume journals published by NCBI, and makes extensive use of automation. PubMedCentral staff represent only a small fraction of the staff of the NCBI, itself a small division of NIH. Organizations like this, which have national mandates as collectors and providers of research information, should find it a relatively small stretch to maintain an archive of online scholarly journals in-house and to justify it in their budgets.

Many publishers can fund an archive if the archive provides them sufficient benefit. The costs of funding will ultimately be passed on to someone else. For subscription-based journals, the price of subscriptions may account for the cost of funding the archive. Journals that charge authors for publication might build charges for preservation of the article into the author's fee. Journals published by scholarl societies may have those societies fund their preservation.

Costs for preserving journal material are ongoing but publishers may be unwilling or unable to pay for archiving the material indefinitely. One solution to this problem is to structure publisher funding as an endowment. When a publisher deposits a journal volume or issue in an archive, it would also include a one-time payment to endow the future archive needs of the deposited content. Income from this endowment would fund ongoing archiving, backup, mirroring, maintenance, and migration of that journal content in perpetuity. If the archive decided to transfer responsibility for the content to another institution or back to the publisher, the content's endowment would be transferred as well. If a publisher stopped supporting an archive, the endowments associated with previously deposited content could still fund the preservation of that content.

For the publisher and journal subscribers, the endowment would provide a guaranteed source of funds to ensure the ongoing availability of journal content. Funding would not be dependent on an archive's ongoing revenue stream. By guaranteeing long-term availability of journal content, an endowment-funded archive could ultimately save money both for the publisher and subscribers to the journal. Subscribers who can rely on preserved electronic copies may be willing to forgo print versions or keep them in less expensive storage, thereby lowering their costs. Hence, they may be willing to contribute to an endowment fund via their subscription fees. If the archive is sufficiently trustworthy and accessible, it may even be possible to discontinue print production which would lower costs and subscription fees for the publisher.

For the endowment model to work, however, costs have to be well-understood and kept under control. If the costs can be kept down to a small percentage of subscription revenue, the endowment model may be financially viable. For instance, a journal that costs $350 per volume, with 300 annual subscribers, brings in about $100,000 of subscription revenue. If endowment income were five percent per year, then each one percent surcharge for archiving would pay $50 per year of archiving costs for that volume. So if the true costs to the archive were $150 per year per volume, three percent of subscription revenues would need to go towards archiving.

Unfortunately, this may be an optimistic estimate of archiving costs, which are still uncertain and likely to change as archives develop and as technology changes. Long-term costs may be difficult to measure in the early stages of an archiving project, especially since it may be unclear what costs are startup costs and what costs are ongoing or recurrent, given the fluid nature of technology and archiving standards. Automation of as many tasks as possible may help, as long as the cost of computers continues to decrease while the cost of labor increases. The endowment model also works best when an archive's fixed costs of operation are low compared to costs that vary with the size of the archive, favoring larger archives. For similar reasons, high endowment requirements may also favor larger publishers which might be an undesirable side-effect for libraries already worried about over-consolidation of scholarly journal publishing in for-profit conglomerates. If scholarly archives are ultimately designed to meet the needs of scholars and scholarly institutions, a funding model that relies on publishers may produce a less useful archive than one that is funded more directly by scholars and their libraries.

Funding by users appears to be a viable alternative to endowments by publishers. JSTOR has found success through funding from libraries and other journal users. Libraries pay a one-time capital development fee and an annual subscription fee to access JSTOR content. Publishers are not charged for deposits into the archive. JSTOR has proven highly popular with libraries and their patrons. JSTOR's convenient access is the carrot that encourages libraries to pay for subscriptions that cover both access services and archiving. JSTOR's success with libraries, scholars, and publishers makes a powerful case for this type of funding model. Of course, it is possible for journal archives to have multiple funding sources, but complicated funding models may produce more problems than they solve.

An archive faced with high ingestion costs could depend on users to fund its general operations and development, as JSTOR does, but charge publishers for ingesting their content unless their content came in a prepackaged, easily-validated form prescribed by the archive. In effect, the archive would offer to sell publishers a packaging service for their content. The publisher could pay for the archive to package their content, or pay some other service provider to do it, or do it on its own and avoid having to pay. In any case, the archive's own costs for ingestion would be reduced and publishers would have an incentive to provide their content in accordance with archival standards. Both of these developments would make the archive more reliable and sustainable.

Funding and control of access rights represent a tradeoff. Publishers can provide funds or they can provide access rights to users after a suitable delay. They are reluctant to provide both. Libraries and scholars, on the other hand, may be disinclined to fund an archive that does not give them access except in some far-distant or unforeseeable circumstances. Thus, archives funded primarily by publishers may tend to be "dark," whereas archives funded primarily by libraries and archives should be more open to access by their funders.

Responsibility for Transfer and Delegation

Archives must be ready for unforeseen changes in the scholarly or online community that may render the archive unsustainable or make it far preferable to archive content elsewhere. Therefore, agreements with the publisher should allow the transfer, if necessary, of the archival material and its associated rights to another party that agrees to assume the archive's responsibilities. The publisher, if it is still in existence, may want to stipulate some additional qualities of the new party, for instance, that it not be a commercial competitor.Similarly, the agreement should allow third parties to act as service providers for delegated archival functions as long as the third parties do not distribute archival material or use it for any purpose other than to carry out legitimate archival functions on the archive's behalf.

Functional Modules of Archival Process

The OAIS model breaks down the archiving process into distinct functional modules which manage archival information packages throughout their life cycles. The key modules defined by OAIS and some of their functions are:

- *Ingest*. This includes the archive's acquisition of journal content and metadata, validation of the content, and packaging for archival storage as Archive Information Packages (AIPs).
- *Archival storage*. This includes maintaining AIP data and ensuring the continued survival and integrity of binary representations of archival data.
- *Data management*. This includes, among other things, maintaining metadata on archived content, managing storage, and handling queries on stored data.
- *Administration*. Among other things, this includes migration.
- *Preservation planning*. This includes planning and implementing further development of the archival system, including migration planning.

— *Access*. This includes delivery of content both to end users and to other archives under appropriate access controls.

— *Ingestion*. Ingestion of presentation content and metadata from Web sites helps to construct a modular prototype harvester that could collect metadata and links to content from different publisher Web sites, then deposit the metadata and links into a common data structure that could be browsed and accessed uniformly.

Size of the content varied greatly among journals. For example, PDFs for American Law and Economics Review, a semi-annual journal, took up little more than 2 MB of storage space per year, whereas PDFs for Brain, a monthly medical journal, took up closer to 100 MB of storage space per year. Articles in PDF form were generally easy to harvest, usually as one PDF file per article, although in some instances the PDFs were page-oriented instead and included content from multiple or adjacent items in the same file. Correctly harvesting HTML presentation forms was considerably more problematic. Many of the HTML-formatted articles were clearly generated from source files and included numerous automatically generated links, some of which led to content that was important to the article, such as high-resolution versions of illustrations, while others led to related material that was not part of the article itself. Many of these HTML articles were produced by the same organization, Highwire Press. Ingesting material into an archive, whether manually or automatically, is far from foolproof. When publishers manually send a journal issue to an archive they may accidentally leave out articles, send misformatted files, or even send the wrong files altogether. Occasionally, articles published on Web sites included mistakes. An early spot-check of one mathematics journal article revealed a PDF file in which the last pages could not be read as the file was initially posted. Human checks may turn up some of these errors but can be expensive to perform.

Archived content and metadata are not likely to stay usable forever. Preserving the integrity of the original digital forms of archived electronic journals is not difficult with proper planning and the right to make copies as needed for archiving. The strategies of generating checksums, making backups and offsite mirrors, regularly refreshing media, and conducting regularly scheduled consistency checks and disaster drills are well-known in digital preservation and data security circles. However, more uncertainty exists about whether the digital forms can continue to be understood and used effectively as technologies and expectations change. Data structures and formats based on simple, openly-specified, and widely-used standards are the easiest to preserve, and journal archives should encourage their use. The definition of XML, for instance, is straightforward and widely publicized. Even if XML is eventually replaced by some other standard for structured data, it would not be difficult to migrate XML files to the new standard or to maintain programs that continue to parse XML in its original form.

To understand and use archival files formatted in XML or SGML, though, it is not sufficient to be able to parse the markup; it is also necessary to know what the markup represents. In addition, we need to preserve the DTDs or schemas used, as well as the documentation for defining DTDs, schemas, or whatever syntactic convention next comes along to describe markup formats. Above the level of DTDs or schemas, we need to document and preserve the semantics of the schemas: the meaning of the markup elements and how their composition turns a set of angle-bracketed words and sentences into a journal that speaks from mind to mind.

The semantics may be expressed in English-language descriptions, stylesheets, a program that renders markup as a visual display like that of a Web browser, or all of these. Particularly since some of the syntax and semantics may be specific to the world of electronic journal publishing and archiving, the archival system will need to include a preservation mechanism for both the syntax and semantics of its data.

Preserving format information is not a new idea. The Multipurpose Internet Mail Extensions (MIME) registry maintained by the Internet Assigned Numbers Authority (IANA) preserves descriptions of data formats commonly used on the

Internet, as well as standard methods for encoding, packaging, and transmitting them. The Typed Object Model (TOM), adds semantic capabilities to a distributed format registry mechanism, supporting automated services like migration, format identification, and interpretation of data formats by remote servers. An ideal registry for journal archiving data structures would allow the combination of the prose descriptions and canonical authority of IANA's MIME registry, the computational power of TOM, and the expertise of digital librarians, archivists, and publishers. Preserving presentation forms presents some special problems: they are often complicated, defined by vendors, and dependent on external information in unexpected ways. Fortunately, the presentation forms of most electronic journals are designed to be viewable by ordinary Web browsers without esoteric plugins. The capabilities of Web browsers are well-documented, for the most part, so it should be possible to deal with the formats they handle.

7

Digital Collections and Classifications

The purpose of the library is to constitute a resource for answering inquiries that arise. The term 'inquiries' used here in a very broad sense, ranging from research concerning matters apparently not known to anyone, through learning what is not known to the individual, to perusing texts for vague curiosity and amusement. The intended outcome is that library users will become better informed. Library collections, although ordinarily thought of in terms of books and serials, actually contain a very broad range of materials: manuscripts, archives, photographs, recordings, movies, and much else. Not only will a particular collection include different sorts of objects, but some objects combine textual, visual, audio, and artifactual aspects. Further, the same object can be of interest for quite diverse reasons. Collections of library materials support the purposes of the community served and that those served use the materials in the collections.

In a significant sense library materials are used as evidence in learning—as the basis for understanding. One's knowledge and opinions are affected by what one sees, reads, hears, or experiences. Textbooks and encyclopedias provide material for an introduction to a subject; literary texts and commentaries provide sources for the study of language and literature; arrays of statistical data provide input for calculations, and inference; statutes and law reports indicate the law; photographs show what people, places, and events looked like; citations and sources are verified; etc. In each case it is reasonable to view library materials as evidence, though without implying that what was read, viewed, listened to, or otherwise used was necessarily accurate, useful, or even pertinent to the user's purposes. Nor need it be assumed that the user did believe or agree with what was read. In this view collections are regarded as selections of material of actual or potential usefulness in meeting the sorts of inquiries regarded as appropriate for the people for whom library service is provided.

Viewing library materials as selections of potential or putative evidence enables us to examine library use more deeply. When faced with evidence people sift, excerpt, evaluate, summarise, and may well add to the cumulation of evidence. Sifting is an inquiry for a local telephone number is ordinarily straightforward—the telephone directory usually suffices. Someone inquiring into the role of women in eighteenth-century England could benefit from a very wide range of materials: helpful evidence might be found in literature, diaries, sermons, pictures, in contemporary materials of almost any kind, and in commentaries of many sorts written in the centuries since. Much of the evidence is likely to be indirect, in the implications of texts and images created for quite other purposes. Excerpting and summarising permit copying and condensing of evidence for the convenience of the inquirer, whether by hand, photocopier, or computer. Evaluation of and inference from the texts, images, and objects in the collections leads to understanding, insights, and new ideas. These, in turn, may lead to new material in new articles or books, which may include commentary on the old, thereby increasing the accumulation for the future.

A fundamental feature of library collection development is the continual effort to make resources of library materials more conveniently available in a manner that corresponds to the local use of evidence. Much of the material assembled in library collections is not raw data but material that has already been processed and refined. This is to be expected. For most inquiries the original data are not what would be most helpful. These two processes, which we shall refer to as 'inter-pretation' and 'summarising', are central to understanding both the nature and the use of library materials. We use the term 'interpretation' in a broad sense, not just as a matter of translation from one language to another but in the sense of explaining: to explain the meaning of, to elucidate, unfold, show the purport of, to translate into intelligible or familiar terms. Some books in a library contain original data, but many, if not most, of nonfiction material involves explanation or interpretation of more detailed material. In the case of foreign literatures, both interpretation and summa-rising can be seen. The original writing is not always the first choice.

The notion of 'summarising' or reducing evidence can be illustrated most conveniently using examples from the sciences. In statistical studies the goal is usually to reduce large amounts of data into progressively smaller summaries: large quantities of numbers can be aggregated into summary tables; tendencies and patterns in the data can be briefly expressed as, for example, an average, a curve representing the relationship between two variables, and so on. Useful though this simplification and diminution in physical size can be, some of the evidence is necessarily lost in the process of reduction. The essence of statistical technique is the desire to maximise the reduction while minimising the loss of evidence.

There is no question that the summarising, condensing, and interpreting of evidence pervades recorded knowledge. In the case of statistical studies, summarising is an apt description of the process of making evidence more convenient and, in-deed, more understandable. In literary and historical studies, however, where words rather than numbers are the principal basis for description, the commentaries intended to render the original more understandable can easily be larger than the original.

Library collections are permeated with these processes of interpreting and summarising. Articles and books summarise, cite, refute, and build upon earlier work. This is especially noticeable in the scholarly literature where the growth of material has created the need for abstracting and indexing services, for guides and reviews. Nor is this only a matter of language, since materials at the forefront of most fields of scholarship are difficult or unintelligible to most nonspecialists because the concepts and specialised terminology are not understood. Hence summaries and introductory works such as textbooks are useful. Collection development needs to be based not only on what a book is about, but also on its suitability as evidence from which people can learn. Given constraints of funding and space, the challenge is how to select from the colossal universe of all possible materials in order to achieve collections that will, it is supposed, constitute the most useful resource for whatever the groups to be served, the pattern of inquiries, and the goals of the library service may be.

Development of local collections in support of the logistic function of collections is essentially a compromise between the physical convenience that can be achieved and the resources allocated to this purpose. The choices of outcomes include the completeness and appropriateness of the range of materials relative to the demand, the standard of availability of the materials in relation to the pattern of demand, and the physical accessibility of the collection.

If material has not been collected at all, it is not available for anyone. Not only must it be collected, it must also be preserved for future use. With the obvious fragility of the photographic media and the gradual self-destruction of most extant books from acid traces in the paper, it is clear that there are massive problems beyond the effects of ordinary wear and tear through usage.

Generally, we use the terms 'library materials' and 'collections' more or less interchangeably. But the distinction is fundamental to any serious understanding of the present and future role of collections. We use the term 'library materials' to denote text-bearing, image-bearing, or other objects of the sort that libraries collect that could be informative for the people that the library seeks to serve. The assembling of collections is a matter of practical convenience, a matter of logistics and convenience. A book does not have to be in any particular collection to be useful. Ideally one would have one's own copies of what one needed and hence neither need nor want to use a library. In practice, however, the cost and bulk of books preclude this possibility, with the exception of a limited quantity of the materials which one might expect to use a great deal. Like compiling a bibliography or a catalogue, the building of a collection is a practical device intended to facilitate access to materials.

The overwhelming preponderance of libraries' collections, even of research libraries, serve the second, logistic purpose in the sense that most of the materials acquired also exist elsewhere in other copies in other libraries. Imagine how much different, smaller, and more economical libraries would be if only the archival role mattered, and just one or two copies were acquired nationwide or worldwide. Therefore, assembling of a library collection can reasonably be regarded as the first stage of the process of retrieving material for use. One might also argue that collections themselves serve as a form of bibliographic retrieval system analogous to the catal-ogue in that by inspecting the array of books on the shelves one can discover works on particular topics. Ordinarily 'retrieval' is thought of only in terms of catalogues, indexes, classification schemes, or other devices that provide pointers to the documents or data that might satisfy the inquiries that arise.

Regardless of the terminology used, the archival role of library collections is, in an important sense, a necessary precondition for, or first stage of, retrieval. Material that has not been collected at all is simply not available for retrieval by anyone. Material that has not been added to local collections is not available for convenient retrieval by individuals at that location. Material that has not been collected locally can still be obtained by purchase, by reproduction, or by inter-library loan, but all of these involve delay and expense, and are best seen as procedures that are corrective of failures in collection development.

The challenge for the librarian is to develop a collection of materials appropriate to that situation, given the inevitable constraints on space, labour, and funds. Most of the effort will be concerned with assembling locally the most suitable collections. Some of the effort should be devoted to arrangements for ensuring that everything likely to be needed by anyone will be preserved somewhere.

Libraries and library users are concerned with ideas and knowledge, but through recorded texts and images—in very large quantities. As a result, any change in the technology of the media for recording or storing texts and images could have enormous significance for libraries. The characteristics of data bases are different from those of paper, and do not fit into current library practice very well. Exploration of the underlying characteristics of the different media seems a good basis for reconsidering the assumptions concerning collections that have been built up on the basis of library materials on paper.

Microfilms and other microforms represented a significant departure from paper materials, yet they differ on only one of the characteristics noted above—special equipment is needed to read them. This adds a requirement for libraries to maintain a new sort of equipment: microform readers and printers. The first major programmes of microfilming library materials began with newspapers in the 1930s. Use of microforms increased greatly in the 1960s as microfiche were used for the dissemination of technical reports by government agencies. Microforms are even more localised than paper materials: not only must the would-be reader and the microform be in the same place, there must also be a usable machine on which to read it at that place. Furthermore, copies are less convenient to make and cannot, like paper, be annotated. They are even less suitable for correction or revision.

Library collections are not expected to be entirely random compilations, but to have some scope or coverage. Some important features of decisions concerning what to include and what not are:

1. Any definition of scope implies that the universe of items that could be included can be divided into more or less definable subsets; and
2. There are gradations of inclusion within the scope. At one extreme there is minimal inclusion: "Even if we were given it, we would not keep it." At the other extreme is exhaustive collecting: "We want at least one copy of everything written by or about Paracelsus." The terminology used for these gradations is not and, perhaps, cannot be completely standardised. A good example is the terminology developed for the American Library Association:
   a) *comprehensive level*: A collection in which the library endeavours, so far as is reasonably possible, to include all significant works of recorded knowledge for a necessarily defined field. This level of collecting intensity is that which maintains a special collection; the aim, if not the achievement, is exhaustiveness.
   b) *research level*: A collection which includes the major source materials required for dissertations and independent research, including materials contai-ning research reporting, new findings, scientific experimental results, and other information useful to researchers. It also includes all important reference works and a wide selection of specialised monographs, as well as an extensive collection of journals and major indexing and abstracting services in the field.
   c) *study level*: A collection which supports undergraduate or graduate course work, or sus-tained independent study; that is, which is adequate to maintain knowledge of a subject required for limited or generalised purposes, of less than research intensity. It includes a wide range of basic monographs, complete collections of the works of important writers, a selection of representative journals, and the reference tools and fundamental bibliographical apparatus pertaining to the subject.

d) *basic level*: A highly selective collection which serves to introduce and define the subject and to indicate the varieties of information available elsewhere. It includes major dictionaries and encyclopedias, selected editions of important works, historical surveys, important bibliographies, and a few major periodicals in the field.

e) *minimal level*: A subject area in which few selections are made beyond very basic works.

The financial consequence of changing from one level of collection to another, especially from level C to level B, or from B to A, can be considerable. So, therefore, is the opportunity cost in that increased expenditure for collection development prevents the use of those resources for other desirable purposes inside or outside the library. There needs to be, therefore, a significant perceived benefit in the accumulation of the collection if there is to be any degree of rationality. A benefit, however, implies a value. Hence, discussion of the scope ought to be related to the choice of values. The collection of books for their own sake—bibliophilia—could be such a value, but it is more likely to be the increase in knowledge of one sort or another within a particular group of people that the library is expected to serve.

If the growth of knowledge is to be the determining value and if resources are limited, the only rational procedure is to relate the scope of the retrieval system to those items likely to facilitate the growth of knowledge in the most cost-beneficial way, insofar as one can. For example, if a copy of a book were never to be used, it is difficult to see how it could have facilitated the growth of knowledge; and, since it took resources to acquire, to process, and to store it, its acquisition was not merely not beneficial, but counterproductive, since those resources might have been used in some other way to foster those values.

The library exists in a political and cultural environment. In this environment the funders, the users, and the librarians have social values that form part of the context of the library's mission. Library collections are constrained to be compatible with those social values. It is for this reason that a library's collection will not always contain the most informative material even where it can be afforded. Funders, librarians, and users would probably prefer their library not to include material that facilitates or encourages topics deemed socially undesirable, such as poisoning public water supplies, dangerous drugs, pederasty, or how to make bombs. There is some tendency to regard such decisions as censorship and outside librarianship, or somehow separate from selection and collection development. Until one can find a library service that has no context, these cultural constraints are best viewed as an inherent part of selection and collection development.

Collection Management

Collection management reflects a shift from 'discrete institutional collections to a wider library world and from narrower issues specific to collection building to a rather daunting range of issues drawn from wider aspects of professional practice'. Technological innovations have made it possible for librarians to view their own organisations in wider contexts, both in terms of access to greater information at the local level as well as to greater information about the world. Collection management involved a range of processes made more efficient by computing and communications techn-ologies—gathering information, coordinating communications, formulating policy, evaluating and planning. While these processes still form the basis of collection management activities, the specific activities which comprise collection management in the year 2000 have evolved during the past decade, and now include assessment of user needs; inter- and intra-library communication; policy development; budgeting and allocation of resources; contract negotiations; macro-evaluation of collections; micro-evaluation for selection, relegation, preservation or withdrawal of stock; and system evaluation. To create an intellectual work, an author undertakes research, draws on personal experience, engages in a creative process, or is involved in a combination of these activities. The task also requires the author to record the results of the foregoing activities in an intellectual work as, for example, a paper for a scholarly journal, an article for a popular magazine or a novel.

After recording an intellectual work the author sends it to a publisher, and, if selected for publication, it is demarcated as an intellectual work by the tangible information package in which it is published. This means that all manifestations of a work are clearly identifiable as a mono-graphic edition, a journal article, a chapter of an edited monograph, or even as an adaptation such as a film production. If the original intellectual work were altered in any way, the outcome would be recognisable either as a new manifestation such as a revised edition or, if the alteration were significant, as a new work in its own right. To create new knowledge an author must still perform research, draw on personal experience, engage in a creative process, or be involved in a combination of these activities and record the results in an intellectual work. The intellectual work, however, is no longer clearly delineated in a tangible information package.

The nature of digital information allows it to be interactive and to be altered or linked to other works. Activity in an online discussion group can demonstrate how one individual's intellectual work can become something quite different in a single day. The lack of a physical presence and the very nature of digital media have several consequences. Intellectual works are not captured in a form that ensures their preservation. A work in digital form is easily altered—text can be added, purged, exchanged, amalgamated; that is, an author can easily create a new manifestation of a work, or another author can easily alter a work subtly or indeed in a major way. When a publisher creates both print and digital versions of a work, the digital version may contain interactive data that can be downloaded and manipulated, as well as video and audio items.

Libraries are striving to respond to the pervasive and persistent growth of global networking and manage the demand for access to this dynamic medium. Working in the trenches of the digital revolution, librarians and information professionals are beginning to offer internet services to patrons; their work marks the beginning of the grassroots implementation of the public digital library. Such efforts do not come without their attendant risks, and it is extremely important that those who are becoming network service and resource providers and content producers clearly understand what is involved in their participation in the digital revolution from an issues and policy-oriented perspective. The concept of the digital or virtual library describes a new organisational form that is expected to be linked in some way to physical libraries.

Although at best an elusive concept, the digital library has acquired the cachet of a powerful memo, driving research and thinking throughout this decade. In fact, the definition of a digital library is by no means clear; despite the awarding of millions of dollars to develop components of digital libraries and several conferences devoted to the topic, there does not seem to be a consensus on the meaning of the term. The emerging field of digital libraries brings together participants from many existing areas of research. Currently, the field lacks a clear agenda independent of these other areas. It is tempting for researchers to think that the field of digital libraries is a natural outgrowth of an already known field. It will be limited if viewed only as a subfield of prior research interests.

Throughout the past few decades, librarians and information professionals have moved to the front lines of the digital revolution as a consequence of their interests and in response to increasing customer demand, providing internet services to a wide range of patrons in a wide variety of settings. Libraries complement both research and education. Predictably, most of the well-publicised work that has been done on digital libraries has occurred in academic settings and has focused on the technical issues involved in digitising, storing, organising, and providing access to the content of these libraries. However, this only represents one of two major streams of work on digital libraries, the high end, well-funded, test-bed projects taking place in research and educational institutions.

A stream of work is taking place in the trenches of the digital revolution, where librarians and information professionals in public libraries are in the midst of attempts to provide to their patrons what certainly will become important components of digital libraries. Their work is typically under-funded and done 'on-the-fly', yet they have the potential to generate some of the most innovative educational uses of the evolving national electronic networked environment for meeting the needs of the widest range of individuals.

Public and school librarians are working typically without a blueprint, under time and economic constraints and, with a few exceptions, with little assistance from the research community. Their efforts do not come without their attendant risks, and it is extremely important that public and school librarians who are becoming network service and resource providers clearly understand what is involved in their participation in the digital revolution from an issues and policy-oriented perspective.

Academic, special, and public/school libraries operate under varying institutional, social, and economic constraints and it is reasonable to expect that researchers and practitioners exploring the possibilities of digital libraries will have access to different resources and will face different problems in their work. One key difference is that the academic digital library projects are taking place under the aegis of the university and the major funding agencies; these projects may allow the public access to their services and resources, but they are not really public. On the other hand, many of the efforts of public and school librarians take place without the same kind of institutional safety net and are intended for immediate public use. They are creating a new organisational form—the public digital library.

As the media continues to define the internet as the broadcast television of the 1990s, the general public discovers the vast world of resources and services on the internet, and politicians attempt to impose a regulatory framework on the internet, public and school librarians find themselves on the front lines of provision of access to the net. As librarians and information professionals begin to offer internet services to patrons, they are in the trenches of the digital revolution and their work marks the beginning of the grassroots implementation of the public digital library. The complexity of the technical challenges that must be faced and overcome in these settings is neither trivial nor easily managed. However, there is an equally challenging set of issues focused loosely around the concept of intellectual freedom which also must be faced and managed.

The collection managers' consideration of the authors of works is primarily in the micro-evaluation component of both the selection and withdrawal activities of the collection management function. In evaluating information packages the selector will at times use the author as a variable for quickly determining the quality of an intellectual work. In general, however, new works or new manifestations of a work are rarely selected based solely on an author's reputation, since in relation to the overall number of authors there are very few who are well known. Evaluation is more often based on the publisher's reputation which is derived over time from the value-adding activities undertaken by the publisher in relation to the intellectual works of many authors.

In many large libraries, selection of information packages for purchase is semi-automatic, such as when blanket orders are established or when selection is outsourced to distributors who create profiles based on disciplinary areas. The collection managers in these situations have made macro-evaluation decisions for ongoing bulk selection in which the publishers or the topic areas, or a combination of both, are considered to be more important as variables than are the individual authors or the individual intellectual works.

In publishing distributors for example, have acted as intermediaries between publishers and libraries in the sale and distribution of monographs. They have served as book warehouses by purchasing multiple copies of monographs from publishers based on the number of libraries they calculate will want to acquire them. In some instances distributors have also acted as outsourcing agencies, managing a portion of the library's acquisitions budget, selecting and purchasing monographs for them based on certain criteria and then distributing those monographs to the library, sometimes with bibliographic information for loading into the catalogue.

For other libraries the distributors has acted simply as a middleman, informing the libraries of new titles of interest, then selling and distributing them to libraries who have selected them and billing those libraries for their purchases. The collection manager's role was to establish and monitor the relationship with the distributors, evaluating the performance and ensuring that the services provided by the distributors met the needs of the users and were cost-effective for the library.

The e-book publisher, netLibrary, has already formed relationships with many publishers of paper-based works with .a view to providing customers with an extensive selection of scholarly, reference and professional books in digital format. When the medium of distribution is paper, the roles of publisher and distributor are distinct. When the content is moved to digital format, the distribution component can be done by the publisher or within another type of publisher/distributor relationship, as is now occurring with many electronic journal titles. Serial publications in paper format have resulted in a distinctive style of publisher/distributor relationship with libraries.

The serials vendor or subscription agent has long acted as a middleman between the publishers and the libraries. The vendor's service to the publishers has involved selling subscriptions, aggregating them and maintaining control over them by collecting payments from the subscribers .and sending renewal notices at the appropriate times. The serials vendor's service to the libraries has involved alerting them to new serials titles, consolidating their subscriptions and payments, notifying them of renewal times, and making claims on their behalf to the publishers.

In the digital environment journal publishers can distribute their own journals directly to their subscribers over the Internet, dissolving the boundaries between the roles of journal publishers and of vendors in their interactions with libraries. How does the blurring of boundaries in the publisher/distributor relationship with libraries affect -the role of collection management staff? First, there are many new products and services from publishers and distributors which collection management staff must evaluate. In some instances there are clearly distinguishable variations between products which make them easy to evaluate, whereas in other instances the mixing and matching of products and services makes the evaluation task more difficult.

The second important impact on the roles of collection managers is that they must now deal with many more types of licensing options which are becoming available for the new types of digital information packages and products. Because of the rapid pace with which these new products are entering the market, the groups involved in licensing e journals have so far had little opportunity to address licensing issues.

In the digital environment, collection managers will have to understand licensing arrangements to ensure that they obtain appropriate access to the products their clients require. While the model agreements will save the library staff and publishers time in their negotiations, they have nothing to do with prices, so collection managers will still have to determine the best prices and decide whether they should be involved in a consortium to obtain the best product at the best price.

The boundaries between publishers and libraries has several impacts on the roles of collection managers. Information products and library collections are already changing, and we see this increasingly in the shift away from the sale of print based resources to the licensing of digital information resources by commercial publishers and in the change in thinking by library managers from ownership of library resources to the provision of access to them. Many librarians believe there is a relationship between providing access to online periodical databases and recent reductions in book circulation statistics. If publishers eventually market information products directly to endusers, libraries will be left with only those patrons who have no access other than the library, those for whom the convenience of atmosphere of the library environment is attractive, or those dependent upon print resources that are inimical to being digitised. If a library should survive the collection managers must:

— act collectively by forming new, more relevant types of consortia to provide a greater wealth of resources more conveniently to patrons

— take the opportunity whenever possible to market the strengths of their collections as they perform user surveys, consult with faculty members, or work on committees or in consortia groups with other librarians/collection manager:

— draw on each other's collection strengths by creating multi-institutional information products based on their collective resources.

They must also work closely with others to blur the boundaries between the librarians, the computing centre staff and the administrators of their organisations. In moving into the role of publishers of e-texts for humanities resources libraries are undertaking a role very similar to that of many research institutions in the past, that is, creating collections of reproductions of historical documents for both access and preservation. The digital publishing of historical documents held in an academic library collection requires a three-way partnership between the library, the computing centre and the academic staff. User studies should be undertaken to determine whether there is sufficient academic need to warrant product development. If there is sufficient need, a collection development plan should be created which would establish a policy for selection of appropriate texts and provide a clear framework for producing and maintaining the digital resources and evaluating the project. The plan should also identify the standards required for creating texts that can be networked, and establish the basis for quality control. The boundaries between libraries have distinguished individual libraries as unique institutions with their own governance as well as unique collections of resources acquired for specific groups of intended users or for specific purposes. However, we are now in an era during which a global library and information infrastructure is evolving.

The growing importance of library consortia is evident by the numerous descriptive articles which have been appearing in the recent literature. Even those writers who highlight the lack of success in cooperative collection development for consortia in the past suggest that the circumstances are right for consortia to perform better. When examining the terms used in our literature for developing and managing library collections, Gorman comments that collection development has given way to collection management and that rapidly shifting emphases, driven in part by information technology and in part by economic factors, further mean that any definitions established today will be different tomorrow.

Content management does not suggest that the format of an information package is irrelevant—it affects the way the content is communicated, and content managers need to select the format most appropriate to the user. By focusing on content in conjunction with user needs, collection managers will identify the resources most important for their users, and will ensure that their users can obtain access to those resources in the most suitable format.

Managing content requires cooperation and coordination across multiple institutions and includes acquiring and providing access to paper-based resources, signing collective contracts and ensuring appropriate technology to provide access to digital resources, creating and managing e-texts, and a host of other activities which span the boundaries between libraries. For collection management staff the blurring of boundaries at all levels of the information chain leads to the blurring of boundaries between their roles and responsibilities in collection management and those of other librarians, and even those of individuals working in other fields. Changes to work practices in collection management are already evident. The team approach to selecting information resources in digital form is a clear case in point. With electronic resources there are concerns about the greater expenses incurred through subscriptions, associated hardware and software interfaces with other online systems, printing costs, changes to strategies for providing technical and public service support, and training programmes for both staff and users.

In the digital environment some of the roles of collection managers will move outside the realm of librarianship. For example, the selection of resources will move from collection development librarians to the users themselves, and collection managers will become 'managers of electronic rights' who ensure that the institution's users have open avenues to the information they need. He contends that in the digital world selection for the local collection is likely to decrease in importance as the primary work of collection development librarians, who are the largest group of subject experts in research libraries. In the digital environment delivery services will, through 'disintermediation', begin to assume or replace some mediation services.

One of the most important conceptual goals that academic libraries need to pursue as information becomes increasingly online should be the elimination of the distinction between academic library collection building and specialised scholarly publication. This distinction is eliminated in the digital environment because academic staff members will select the intellectual works for inclusion in the control zone, thus bestowing the prestige on selected works which was formerly conferred by the publishers of scholarly communication. The libraries' role will be to ensure that this subset of information remains stable and accessible over time through two fundamental library functions: archiving and metadata.

Archiving of digital information, is merely one of the latest manifestations of the eternal dilemma of preservation. Although the digital environment raises new challenges, such as ensuring backwards compatibility and selecting the most important works from the sheer volume of digital information, such technological and selection issues have always been a component of collection management. 'Content rating' should be added subsequent to the act of publication by experts in the field who have determined the work's significance through their own use of it; 'audience level' should indicate the target audience and should be added by the work's creator; and 'use history' should indicate the frequency of use by specific groups and should be generated automatically.

The role of collection development in a research library should be given back to academics, it is unlikely that this will happen. Rather, the creation of the content ratings and the audience level ratings in metadata will be done by experts, but these experts will be collection management staff—the subject bibliographers and selectors who already evaluate information on an ongoing basis. While the creation of metadata is a new role for collection managers, it has long been the role of cataloguers. These professionals have traditionally been responsible for adding access value to selected information resources by creating descriptive metadata (i.e. surrogate records), and by adding subject metadata (i.e. subject headings) as access points to those surrogate records. While it is plausible that academics will be involved in establishing a new form of scholarly communication, there is already a precedent for this role—the peer review process. Academic staff will not want to increase their workloads by undertaking the responsibilities of other members of the academic community, in this case, the addition of metadata which is already the responsibility of librarians.

Digital Classification Systems

New and emerging classes of information systems applications have swept into the lives of office workers and everyday people. These applications ranging from digital libraries, multimedia systems, geographic information systems, and collaborative computing to electronic commerce, virtual reality, and electronic video arts and games have created tremendous opportunities for information and computer science researchers and practitioners. As applications become more overwhelming, pressing, and diverse, several well-known information retrieval (IR) problems have become even more urgent. Information overload resulting from easy creation and transmittal of information via Internet and WWW, has become prominent in people's lives. Significant variations of database formats and structures, the richness of information media (text, audio, and video), and an abundance of multilingual information content also have created severe interoperability problems.

The conventional approaches to addressing information overload and interoperability problems are manual in nature, requiring human experts as information intermediaries to create knowledge structures and/or classification systems. Such manually-created classification systems, which represent subject vocabularies and their relationships, are often used to index and/or organize collections or to suggest search terms during retrieval processes. But as information content and collections become even larger and more dynamic, thus rendering manual knowledge creation to become more difficult, if not infeasible, we believe a complementary system-aided, algorithmic, bottom-up approach to creating large-scale digital library classification systems is needed.

In US, the Information Infrastructure Technology and Applications (IITA) Working Group, the highest level of the country's National Information Infrastructure (NII) technical committee, held an invited workshop in May 1995 to define a research agenda for digital libraries. The shared vision that emerged is an entire Net of distributed repositories, where objects of any type can be searched within and across different indexed collections. In the short term, technologies must be developed to search across these repositories transparently, handling any variations in protocols and formats (i.e., addressing structural interoperability). In the long term, technologies must be developed to handle the variations in content and meanings (knowledge) transparently as well. In a new NSF Knowledge Networking (KN) initiative, a group of domain scientists and information systems researchers were invited to a Workshop on Distributed Heterogeneous Knowledge Networks at Boulder, Colorado, in May, 1997. They considered that scalable techniques to improve semantic bandwidth and knowledge bandwidth are among the priority research areas, as described in the KN report: The Knowledge Networking (KN) initiative focuses on the integration of knowledge from different sources and domains across space and time. KN research aims to move beyond connectivity to achieve new levels of interactivity, increasing the semantic bandwidth, knowledge bandwidth, activity bandwidth, and cultural bandwidth among people, organizations, and communities.

"Knowledge networking" or, using a more general term, "knowledge management" (KM), has attracted significant attention from academic researchers and even executives in Fortune 500 companies. KM is formal in that knowledge is classified and categorized according to a pre-specified - but evolving - ontology into structured and semi-structured data and knowledge bases. Many commercial software systems are considered enabling technologies for KM, including Internet/ Intranet search engines, groupware, electronic document management systems, full-text retrieval systems, database management systems, and electronic mail. Major consulting firms, on the other hand, are promoting KM practices such as organizational development, strategic planning, performances metrics, and methodology. Despite of obvious differences in technologists and consultants views of what KM should be, their calls for advanced classification and categorization technologies to help analyze, organize, and present mission-critical information and knowledge are the same - turning information overload into knowledge assets.

Library classification systems and thesauri often capture nouns or noun phrases and represent only limited relationships (e.g., broader terms, narrower term, etc.). The representations are often coarse, but precise, and they do support their practical goal of supporting indexing and searching, but significant human efforts are needed to create and maintain such large-scale classification systems.Artificial intelligence representations such as semantic networks, expert systems, or ontologies represent another approach to capturing knowledge, e.g., Lenat's CYC common sense knowledge base. Their representations are often richer and more fine-grained and the goal of capturing human intelligence is ambitious and difficult. Due to the granularity required of such representations, knowledge creation is slow and painstaking. Only experimental prototypes in small, limited domains have been created. Their usefulness in large-scale digital library applications remains suspect.

The traditional approach to creating classification systems and knowledge sources in library science and classical AI is often considered top-down since knowledge representations and formats are pre-defined by human experts or trained librarians and the process of generating knowledge is structured and well-defined. A complementary bottom-up approach to knowledge creation has been suggested by researchers in machine learning, statistical analysis, and neural networks. Based on actual databases or collections, researchers develop programs which systematically segment and index documents in various databases (text, image, and video) and identify patterns within such databases. Analyzing databases which contain structured and numeric data (e.g., credit card usage, a frequent flyer program) is often referred to as data mining or knowledge discovery.

Generating knowledge algorithmically from multimedia databases (especially text, e.g., customer complaint email, machinery repair reports, brainstorming outputs) is considered the core of knowledge management. Two stages of such a bottom-up knowledge management approach are often required:

— Object Recognition,

— Segmentation, and

— Indexing:

The most fundamental techniques in IR involve identifying key features in objects. For example, automatic indexing and natural language processing are frequently used to extract meaningful keywords or phrases from texts automatically. Texture, color, or shape-based indexing and segmentation techniques are often used to identify images. For audio and video applications, voice recognition, speech recognition, and scene segmentation techniques can be used to identify meaningful descriptors in audio or video streams.

Symbolic machine learning, graph-based clustering and classification, statistics-based multivariate analyses, artificial neural network-based computing and evolution-based programming are among the popular techniques. Most of these are computationally intensive and are particularly suitable for creating classification systems or knowledge structures from unstructured textual collections. Large-scale image based knowledge extraction is still at an early stage of development due to the difficulty of designing image-invariant content-based segmentation and indexing algorithms.

8

Digital Preservation

Digital information today is produced in highly varying degrees of dependence on particular hardware and software. It is costly and difficult for vendors to assure that their products are either backwardly compatible with previous versions or that they can interoperate with competing products. There may be sufficient demand for entrepreneurs to create and archive emulators of software and operating systems that would allow the contents of digital information to be carried forward and used in its original format. Refreshing digital information by copying it from medium to medium and the possibility of maintaining a complex set of emulators describe two distinct points on a continuum of approaches to preserving digital information. However, neither refreshing nor emulation sufficiently describes the full range of options needed and available for digital preservation.

The problem of preserving digital information for the future is not only, or even primarily, a problem of fine tuning a narrow set of technical variables. It is not a clearly defined problem like preserving the embrittled books that are self-destructing from the acid in the paper on which they were printed. Rather, it is a grander problem of organizing ourselves over time and as a society to maneuver effectively in a digital landscape. It is a problem of building-almost from scratch-the various systematic supports, or deep infrastructure, that will enable us to tame anxieties and move our cultural records naturally and confidently into the future. For digital preservation, the organizational effort-the process of building deep infrastructure-necessarily involves multiple, interrelated factors, many of which are either unknown or poorly defined. One of the biggest unknowns is the full impact on traditional information handling functions of distributed computing over electronic networks.

Digital archives are distinct from digital libraries in the sense that digital libraries are repositories that collect and provide access to digital information, but may or may not provide for the long-term storage and access of that information. Digital libraries thus may or may not be, in functional terms, digital archives and, in fact, much of the recent work on digital libraries is notably silent on the archival issues of ensuring long-term storage and access. Conversely, digital archives necessarily embrace digital library functions to the extent that they must select, obtain, store, and provide access to digital information.

Many of the functional requirements for digital archives defined thus overlap those for digital libraries. Many traditional libraries, archives and museums, as institutions, have taken and may well continue to assume digital library and archival functions. Certified digital archives will have available to them a critical fail-safe mechanism. Such a mechanism, supported by organizational will, economic means and legal right, would enable a certified archival repository to exercise an aggressive rescue function to save digital information that it judges to be culturally significant and which is endangered in its current repository. The current repository may be a digital library, another digital archives, or some other individual, organizational, public or private source of digital information.

Without the operation of a formal certification program and a fail-safe mechanism, preservation of the nation's cultural heritage in digital form will likely be overly dependent on marketplace forces, which may value information for too short a period and without applying broader, public interest criteria. Such development is necessary for and will contribute powerfully to the overall growth of an information-based society and economy. We can afford to continue and increase economic and social investments in digital information objects and in the repositories for them on the information superhighway if, and only if, we also create the archival means for the knowledge the objects and repositories contain to endure and redound to the benefit of future generations.

The digital world is still too new for us to describe fully the life cycle of the information objects that do now or will in the future reside there, but what surely unites the community of actors in their various information-based activities is their common purpose in support of the pursuit of knowledge. The pursuit of knowledge is a process in which the emergence of new knowledge builds on and reconstructs the old. Knowledge cannot advance without consistent and reliable access to information sources, past and present.

It is the archival function in the system of knowledge creation and use that serves to identify and retain important sources of information and to ensure continuing access to them. How reliable the archival process proves to be in the emerging digital environment hinges on the trustworthy operation of digital archives and on their ability to maintain the integrity of the objects they are charged to preserve. For digital objects, no less than for objects of other kinds, knowing how operationally to preserve them depends, at least in part, on being able to discriminate the essential features of what needs to be preserved.

Digital technologies increasingly serve to integrate information resources. Text, numeric data, images, voice, and video have heretofore resided in print or other analog media for storage and transmission. When they are encoded digitally, either by conversion or at the point of creation, these various kinds of resources share layers of technology-a common means of storage and transmission- that allows them to be brought together and used in both old and new ways. Multimedia and hyperlinked objects on the World Wide Web represent some of the new kinds of information and new ways of knowing in the digital realm that bring together the traditional forms of information and transform their use.

The application of computer hardware and software has also generated other new kinds of information objects, including the products of simulation, remote sensing, computer-aided design (CAD) and geographic information (GIS) systems. These objects come into being and exist as creatures of the digital environment; if nurtured well, digital technologies will certainly beget still other kinds of information objects, which we can now only anticipate.

The processes of preserving digital information will vary significantly with the different kinds of objects-textual, numeric, image, video, sound, multimedia, simulation and so on-being preserved. Whatever preservation method is applied, however, the central goal must be to preserve information integrity; that is, to define and preserve those features of an information object that distinguish it as a whole and singular work.

In the digital environment, the features that determine information integrity and deserve special attention for archival purposes include the following: content, fixity, reference, provenance, and context. What digital archives are trying to preserve after all is the intellectual substance contained in information objects. The notion of content, however, is itself a complex idea that operates at several different levels of abstraction. To preserve the integrity of objects in their charge, digital archives must decide at which level, or levels, of abstraction they are defining information content. At the lowest level of abstraction, all digital information objects consist of simple bitstreams of 0s and 1s. One can distinguish objects from one another merely by distinguishing the configuration of bits.

Preserving the integrity of an information object in this sense means preserving the bit configuration that uniquely defines the object. There are various well-established techniques, such as checksums and digests, for tracking the bit-level equivalence of digital objects and ensuring that a preserved object is identical to the original. Defining content as a collection of bits, however, is often too limited and simplistic to be useful. In the digital environment, ideas are typically embedded in particular formats and structures that are dependent on hardware and software technologies subject to rapid change. In addition to character set issues, digital archives must also grapple with the means of representing and preserving textual content embedded in layout and structure.

Markup systems, such as implementations of TeX and the Standard Generalized Markup Language (SGML), do exist as platform-independent mechanisms for identifying and tagging for subsequent layout and retrieval detailed structural elements of documents. The use of TeX and its variants, for example, is relatively common among scholars in some scientific disciplines such as mathematics and computer science, and the federal government and scholarly publishers are increasingly employing the SGML standard in documents that they produce and distribute electronically. Beyond these relatively specialized segments, however, word processing and desktop publishing systems still dominate the market for the creation of documents with complex structure and layout, and the software for such use typically models and stores document structure and layout in proprietary terms.

Although software may provide mechanisms for converting documents to common interchange formats, use of such mechanisms often results in the loss or inadequate rendering of content such as page structures and the layout of headers, footers and section headings. The preservation of images comprises another example of the ways in which content, defined in terms of structure and format, poses integrity problems for digital archives. Image resolution, accuracy of color representation and compression for storage all require attention, but the interaction of these structural factors tends to pit judgments about the quality of content against the need for its efficient archival storage and use. In general, one can express the tradeoffs as follows: the higher the resolution and the richer the color register, the larger the file size and more costly the storage.

At the highest level of abstraction, digital archives define content in a way that transcends the limits of the hardware and software systems needed for reading and interpreting the bits of an information object and for rendering it for use in a specific format and structural representation; that is, they define content in terms of the knowledge or ideas the object contains. The measure of integrity in the preservation process thus turns, at least in part, on informed and skillful judgments about the appropriate definition of the content of an digital information object-about the extent to which content depends on its configuration of bits, on the structure and format of its representation, and on the ideas it contains-and for what purposes.

The process of identifying and preserving a digital information object as a whole and singular work goes well beyond considerations of content. It also depends, for instance, on the way that the content is fixed as a discrete object. If an object is not fixed, and the content is subject to change or withdrawal without notice, then its integrity may be compromised and its value as a cultural record would be severely diminished. The acts of production and broadcast establish radio and television programs as discrete objects. And the act of publication marks a specific version or edition of a literary work. In each of these cases, it is virtually impossible to change or withdraw the cultural record that the release of an information object establishes. On the digital landscape, by contrast, it is still relatively easy for a creator to alter or retract previously released information. Such actions can eliminate or overlay significant content and thereby corrupt the record. To address these problems, a wide range of cryptographic techniques, such as watermarking, already exist for various kinds of digital information objects. These could serve well to mark and identify specific, canonical versions and editions of textual, audio and visual works, and to establish trusted, protected channels of distribution for those objects.

However, the standards and infrastructure and the policies and practices for applying such techniques to the creation of fixed versions of digital information objects still need considerable development. Absent such development and the fixity of information that would result, digital archives face considerable challenges in trying to preserve the integrity of digital objects. Some kinds of digital objects present the problem of fixity of information in yet another way. An increasing number of networked information resources are better modeled, not in terms of versions or editions of works, but as continuously updated databases. The financial communities also depend on large, continuously updated databases. There is no natural way to fix these resources at the database level, no natural set of publication points for the objects as a whole. Their integrity, or singularity, as databases resides in the coherence of the database as a whole and in the continuousness of the updates.

To preserve the integrity of such information resources, the complete record of changes has to be built into the design of the database and fixed at the record level. In the absence of such a preservation-oriented design, digital archives may have no choice but to fix the database artificially in time and capture a series of snapshots of its state at periodic intervals as a way of preserving its integrity. Information objects come into being and acquire their distinctiveness in relation to various other objects in an information space.

There are several factors contribute to the unique identification of digital information objects. Two of the most important factors are the Uniform Resource Name (URN) and the Uniform Resource Locator (URL). The URL refers to the specific place where a digital object resides and is currently the dominant method of object location on the World Wide Web. The weakness of the URL, however, is that it may frequently change, especially as an object migrates from one machine to the next.

By contrast, a name, the URN, is supposed to apply uniquely and permanently to a distinct object and to designate it independently of its particular location at any point in time. URNs today exist more in concept than in practice. Thus, resolving the name and location for variant digital works and thereby providing consistent reference to them means moving from a conceptual design of the relation between names and locations to an operational reality through the implementation of naming authorities, which assign URNs, and and the development of digital services that translate names into currently valid URLs.

For archival purposes, however, there are two other qualities of digital information objects that a reference system must take into account. Provenance has become one of the central organizing concepts of modern archival science. The assumption underlying the principle of provenance is that the integrity of an information object is partly embodied in tracing from where it came. To preserve the integrity of an information object, digital archives must preserve a record of its origin and chain of custody. For some information objects, the formal process of publication creates a trusted channel of distribution and serves to establish a sophisticated record of provenance, at least from the creator through the point of release.

In the digital environment, as in other domains, individuals produce and accrete much information that relates to their private lives and to their public roles and responsibilities, including their means of livelihood. The archival challenge for establishing the provenance of such objects is to find ways to preserve an understanding of the corporate policies and processes and roles and responsibilities thus represented in the information system and its products. In some cases, the instrumentation produces data in the service of individual experiments or of clinical practice; in other cases, remote sensors gather streams of observational data about physical systems in space or on earth.

The investment that digital archives make in establishing the provenance of objects in their care serves to preserve the integrity of digital information in two distinct ways. First, a tracing of chain of custody from the point of creation helps to create the presumption that an object is authentic, that it is what it purports to be and that its content, however defined, has not been manipulated, altered or falsified. The second effect of establishing provenance through a chain of custody is to document, at least in part, the particular uses of the object by the custodians. In thus creating a record of use, the archival concern with provenance is intimately related to the notion of context as a matter of information integrity.

As network-based objects, such as video and records of confidential transactions, make their way into digital repositories, an archival account of their integrity must include an account of the features of the network context that supports their existence. Finally, the wider social environment plays a significant contextual role that contributes to the integrity of digital information objects. Networked information, for example, depends on specific policy and implementation decisions that address the bandwidth, security and other qualities of the network and related technical infrastructure.

Long-term Preservation

Different types of information involved in the long-term preservation of information in an Open Archival Information System (OAIS). Each of these types can be viewed as a complete Information Object in that it contains a data object and adequate Representation Information to understand the data. The Content Information is the set of information that is the original target of preservation by the OAIS. Deciding what is the Content Information may not be obvious and may need to be negotiated with the Producer. The Representation Information for a digital Content Data Object (both semantic and syntactic) is needed to fully transform the bits into the Content Information. In principal, this even extends to the inclusion of definitions (e.g., dictionary and grammar) of any natural language (e.g., English) used in expressing the Content Information. Over long time periods the meaning of natural language expressions can evolve significantly in both general and in specific discipline usage.

As a practical matter, the OAIS needs to have enough Representation Information associated with the bits of the Content Data Object in the Content Information that it feels confident that the members of the Designated Community can enter the Representation Network with enough knowledge to begin accurately interpreting the Representation Information. This is a significant risk area for an OAIS, particularly for those with an expert Designated Community, because jargon and apparently widely understood terms may be short-lived. In such cases extra care needs to be exercised to ensure that the natural evolution of the Designated Community Knowledge Base does not effectively cause information loss from the Content Information.

For an Information Object in general, the Representation Information can also be viewed as being augmented by Access Software that supports the presentation of the Content Information to the Consumer. Examples of this type of software include word processors supporting complex document format representations of Content Information and scientific visualization systems supporting representations of Content Information as a time series or a multidimensional array. The software uses its knowledge of the underlying Representation Information to provide these services. Often required information will be embedded in the software packages used by the Designated Community to present and analyze the Content Information.

A reason for preserving working Access Software arises from a convenience factor. Even with a complete set of Representation Information, practical access to all or part of a digital Content Data Object requires the use of Access Software. Thus a software module that provides useful access to a digital Content Data Object may be preserved in a working state as a matter of convenience. This is not difficult to do as long as the environment, which supports the software module, is readily available. This environment consists of some underlying hardware and an operating system, various utilities that effectively augment the operating system and storage and display devices and their drivers.

A change to any of these may cause the software module to no longer function, to function incorrectly, or to be unable to present results to the application or human user. The complexity of these interactions is what traditionally makes the preservation of working software such an arduous task. In short, the use of Access Software to replace Representation Networks is attractive from the point of view of minimizing the resources needed to ingest data and provide current users with access to data. However the reliance on working software can provide major problems for Long-Term Preservation when that software ceases to function. Indefinite long-term information preservation requires a full and understandable description of the Representation Information.

An important function of the OAIS is deciding what parts of the Content Information are the Content Data Object and what parts are the Representation Information. In addition to Content Information, the Archival Information must include information that will allow the understanding of the Content Information over an indefinite period of time. The specific set of Information Objects, which are required for this function, is collectively called Preservation Description Information (PDI). The PDI must include information that is necessary to adequately preserve the particular Content Information with which it is associated. It is specifically focused on describing the past and present states of the Content Information, ensuring it is uniquely identifiable, and ensuring it has not been unknowingly altered. This information is typical for all types of archives and has been classified in the context of traditional archives. However, the class definitions must be extended for digital archives. The following definitions are preserving Digital Information:

— *Reference Information*: This information identifies, and if necessary describes, one or more mechanisms used to provide assigned identifiers for the Content Information. It also provides those identifiers that allow outside systems to refer, unambiguously, to this particular Content Information. Examples of these systems include taxonomic systems, reference systems and registration systems. In the OAIS Reference Model most if not all of this information is replicated in Package Descriptions, which enable Consumers to access Content Information of interest.

— *Context Information*: This information documents the relationships of the Content Information to its environment.

This includes why the Content Information was created and how it relates to other Content Information objects existing elsewhere.

— *Provenance Information*: This information documents the history of the Content Information. This tells the origin or source of the Content Information, any changes that may have taken place since it was originated, and who has had custody of it since it was originated. This gives future users some assurance as to the likely reliability of the Content Information. Provenance can be viewed as a special type of context information.

— *Fixity Information*: This information provides the Data Integrity checks or Validation/Verification keys used to ensure that the particular Content Information object has not been altered in an undocumented manner. Fixity Information includes special encoding and error detection schemes that are specific to instances of Content Objects. Fixity Information does not include the integrity preserving mechanisms provided by the OAIS underlying services, error protection supplied by the media and device drivers used by Archival Storage. The OAIS needs to explicitly decide what the exact definition of Content Information is in order to be able to ensure that it also has the PDI needed to preserve the Content Information. Once the Content Information has been determined, it is possible to assess the Preservation Description Information.

— *Packaging Information*: The Packaging Information is that information which, either actually or logically, binds or relates the components of the package into an identifiable entity on specific media. For example, if the Content Information and PDI are identified as being the content of specific files on a CD-ROM, then the Packaging Information may include the ISO 9660 volume/file structure on the CD-ROM. The Packaging Information does not necessarily need to be preserved by an OAIS since it does not contribute to the Content Information or the PDI. However, there are cases where the OAIS may be required to reproduce the original submission exactly. The OAIS should also avoid holding PDI or Content Information only in the naming conventions of directory or file name structures. These structures are most likely to be used as Packaging Information.

— *Descriptive Information:* To preserving information, the OAIS must provide adequate features to allow Consumers to locate information of potential interest, analyze that information, and order desired information. This is accomplished through a specialization of the Information Object called Descriptive Information, which contain the data that serves as the input to documents or applications called Access Aids.

A library is not a last resting place for the books contained there but a place where information and ideas live and breathe in new minds. The digital age brings, here as elsewhere, opportunities and challenges. The Library can now provide access to some objects without assuming any responsibility for preserving them. The acquisition of materials and their integration into a library's collections traditionally have implied a responsibility to preserve those items for use by future generations. Its preservation responsibilities using a variety of professionally accepted practices:

— Providing adequate storage conditions (e.g., proper environmental controls and appropriate binding and shelving);

— Reformatting materials from their original fragile formats and media to more stable media (e.g., microfilming newspapers and brittle books, transferring audio recordings to more stable media, and copying content on nitrate and acetate film to more stable polyester film bases); and

— For a small percentage of rare and unique materials with intrinsic value in their original formats, restoring originals through conservation treatments.

Over the last two centuries, it has conducted research and led efforts in areas such as binding and shelving books, proper environmental conditions for storage, use of microfilm for preservation, and mass deacidification of paper. The Library faces challenges in digital preservation that are widely recognized and shared by many other libraries and archives. They include the following:

— *Fragile storage media*—Digital materials are especially vulnerable to loss and destruction because they are stored on fragile magnetic and optical media that deteriorate rapidly and that can fail suddenly from exposure to heat, humidity, airborne contaminants, faulty reading and writing devices, human error, and even sabotage.

— *Technology obsolescence*—Digital materials become unreadable and inaccessible if the playback devices necessary to retrieve information from the media become obsolete or if the software that translates digital information from machine- to human-readable form is no longer available.

— *Legal questions surrounding copying and access*—Libraries, archives, and other cultural institutions have limited and uncertain rights to copy digital information for preservation or backup purposes, to reformat information so that it remains accessible by current technology, and to provide public access.

All organizations with responsibilities for preserving digital information are seeking better technical solutions, model policies, best practices, and clearer guidelines regarding legal and intellectual property issues. In US, Library Congress (LC) providing leadership or contributing actively to solving critical problems of digital archiving and long-term preservation. Until now, LC seems to have assumed a wait-and-see attitude toward its role in preserving digital information created outside the walls of the Library itself; this was probably exacerbated by the absence of a director for the Preservation Directorate. The Library's collecting policies and mechanisms with regard to born-digital materials are closely tied to its preservation capabilities. As long as traditional collecting mechanisms guarantee a steady stream of print, other analog materials, and tangible digital objects such as CD-ROMs into the Library's collections, there is an illusion that little significant content is being lost. The absence of significant digital content in the Library's collections removes a sense of urgency about digital preservation, and the lack of organizational capacity to preserve many types of born-digital information discourages the Library from taking on responsibilities that it is not prepared to fulfill. The methods for doing this include traditional collecting and custodianship and developing relationships with publishers, other research libraries, other national libraries, bibliographic networks and utilities, government agencies, and archives. Traditionally, the acquisition of materials through purchase, exchange, or deposit and their cataloging into the Library's permanent collection entailed a commitment to preserve those materials. In the digital environment, libraries will assume a wider variety of roles and responsibilities with regard to preservation.

One of the first steps that librareis needs to take in adapting its collecting practices to accommodate born-digital information is to delineate clearly its responsibilities for preserving digital information. As libraries identifies the areas in which it will assume the lead responsibility for digital preservation, other organizations can adjust the scope of their digital collections accordingly. Just as the Library cannot ignore the problem of digital preservation, so also it cannot be expected to do it all. If libraries does not set clear boundaries around its digital preservation responsibilities, then many people may assume unrealistically that the Library will be the repository of last resort for everything worth keeping.

In the paper world, each library that decided to provide its users with a given resource both obtained and conserved its own copy of the object. This replication in the paper world served as a powerful fail-safe mechanism, helping to ensure long-term accessibility through the uncoordinated but distributed maintenance of independent copies. In the digital environment, in which much content is distributed through the centralized services of a publisher, it is not clear where the preservation responsibility lies.

Library needs to articulate carefully a policy identifying the subset of digital materials for which it will assume long-term curatorial responsibility, taking into account the following:

— The burden of preserving digital collections is daunting and must be shared with other archiving institutions.

— The archiving and preservation of digital resources normally accessed over the Internet will not take place as a by-product of normal access but must be explicitly pursued. Simply assuming that preservation will be carried out somewhere across numerous replicated research collections will not be a solution for networked resources.

Both considerations argue for libraries to define the scope of their archiving roles, in order that responsibilities be distributed across the archiving libraries of the world. The archiving and preservation responsibility is a long-term one that will serve researchers in generations to come. One advantage of digital materials is the potential to distribute preservation responsibilities among a wide variety of partners so that each institution preserves only a designated portion of the global digital record. With careful planning, coordination, cooperative agreements, and clearly articulated boundaries around its curatorial collection, the Library could assume long-term preservation responsibility for a much smaller portion of the digital corpus than it did for the paper one. Some redundancy is necessary for backup and security purposes, but less redundancy is needed for digital collections than was required in the past because access no longer requires physical proximity to materials.

Even if LC carefully defines its roles and responsibilities along the continuum from serving as a portal to acting as the primary custodian for digital materials, there is an urgent need for it to enhance its technical capacity and expertise in digital preservation. Such preservation will involve a wide range of activities, including the following:

— "Protecting the bits"—The making of backup copies, periodic recopying to new media, and regular checking of object coherence and validity are required to make certain that rarely accessed materials remain technically sound.

Access will be enhanced to the extent that archived materials remain online rather than, say, being stored on media such as tapes, which must be mounted manually.

— Archiving appropriate copies—For many digital materials, the format most useful for current services (say, a PDF file or a GIF image) is not the most robust for long-term archiving (SGML, XML, or TIFF may serve better). A preservation program must encompass the selection and archiving of the appropriate formats for long-term use and then the derivation of current-use copies appropriate to the technological base of today's users. It must also work with users to help them undertake these tasks.

— Maintaining appropriate metadata—All preservation activities will depend on the completeness and quality of the metadata for the objects to be preserved. It will be critical for the Library to monitor developments in metadata standards and follow best practices for metadata as they develop.

— Migrating formats—Even the most careful selection of archiving formats cannot ensure that objects will be useful in the decades to come. It will be necessary to migrate objects periodically from one archival format to another. Such processes must be carefully designed and executed to ensure minimal loss of content (it is impossible to ensure that all such migrations will be loss-free). Some works, such as those that include active software (e.g., Java applets), may raise particularly difficult issues.

— Conducting research and development—Only a handful of institutions are likely to face digital preservation challenges on the scale or scope of those that LC faces in the coming years. This makes it unlikely that LC will be able to import models and solutions for all of its preservation needs. An active program of research and development in digital preservation is needed to solve immediate preservation problems--technical, legal, and economic—at LC and to provide guidance to other libraries and archives.

— Educating the relevant communities—Especially in this transitional period, when digital materials are new and preservation practices are still in flux, institutions and particular communities will need to be educated about digital preservation: What is the state of the art? What factors must be taken into account in planning for preservation? LC is well situated to participate in such efforts and possibly to take the lead.

A robust preservation program will employ curators and preservation staff with knowledge of the formats of materials in their collections and of appropriate metadata standards and practices and an understanding of the issues involved in migrating objects from one format to another. It will require well-developed production services for creating the specified metadata, sound and robust repository services, and periodic quality checking and copying of objects in the collection.

In the future, libraries will also need to make much more extensive use of digitization for preservation. Some professionals consider digital objects—whether born digital or turned digital—unacceptable as preservation masters because their longevity is uncertain. In some cases, however, digital conversion may offer the only viable means of salvaging and preserving certain materials, such as audio recordings in obsolete analog formats. The Library has used digitization to preserve severely damaged black-and-white negatives and some audio and video records on magnetic media.

Strategies for Digital Preservation

Today no one knows how to ensure the long-term preservation of multimedia documents nor how to ensure the integrity of documents that may have many links to other documents that may be anywhere in the world. Given the problems just outlined, the dominant approach to digital preservation has been that of migration. Migration is the process of transferring data from a platform that is in danger of becoming obsolete to a current platform. This process has both dangers and costs. The notable danger is that of data loss, or in some cases the loss of original functionality or the 'look and feel' of the original platform. For these reasons, some have seen emulation as an alternative and superior strategy. The essential idea behind emulation is to be able to access or run original data/software on a new/current platform by running software on the new/ current platform that emulates the original platform. If emulation is to be adopted, the first question is what is to be emulated? Three options are:

— Emulate applications

— Emulate operating sytems

— Emulate hardware platforms

One of the issues for digital preservation is what needs to be preserved in addition to the pure intellectual content of a digital object. In some cases the 'look and feel' of a digital object may be important, as may its interactivity. The fear is that migration to new platforms may lose these aspects, and that emulation may be the only strategy for preserving them. This problem is exacerbated, of course, by the increasing use of more complex digital objects (multimedia and hypermedia). Some analysis needs to be undertaken to provide a framework for examining the issue of when these aspects of digital objects are important, with a view to providing data for a cost-benefit analysis for the justification of the likely additional costs of preserving these complex aspects of digital objects.

Intellectual Property Rights (IPR) issues may well be involved in emulating either operating systems or applications. It seems almost certain that the costs of emulation will mean that emulation will not be an option for every user. This will be one part of a case for wanting trusted organisations that can undertake the work and make this available for others to use. Of course the nature and cost of these organisations are major issues but not issues that only effect emulation.

Preservation strategies have often accepted loss of some of the characteristics of the originals. Rothenberg's attitude seems to be that if we can't have everything, we can't have anything. Rothenberg discusses claims made on behalf of relational databases that this provided a kind of lingua franca; since the same mathematical model underlies them all, any can be translated into any other. This, as he points out, is limited by the fact that some relational databases use proprietary features. There are number of strategies for preserving digital documents. Customers should demand that vendors provide cost-effective migration paths to advancing hardware and software systems. Many vendors do provide a limited form of this capability in that an advanced version of their hardware or software system will provide the ability to migrate a customer's operations from the superseded system to the advanced. However, this type of conversion is generally limited to the previous generation of the hardware or software system and therefore, it is a short-term fix that must be repeated with each successive system upgrade.

The translation of a digital document into successive shortterm standards over its life cycle may result in the loss of the document's original content. Without the original document and the original software to accurately interpret the document, then the format and content of the document may be compromised and the original meaning lost.Dollar and Rothenberg suggested promoting a "trend toward non-proprietary standardized open systems environments, which are designed to overcome compatibility between computer systems and applications and are reflected in international standards". While these open system standards would make digital documents accessible through any software system that conform to the standards, there is still the problem that even the open system standards will change as information systems technologies continue to advance. Thus, over time, as hardware and software systems continue to evolve, it will still be necessary to either migrate digital documents to an updated standardized format or to provide some other method to maintain continual access to these documents. Rothenberg suggested a means of maintaining long-term access to the information contained within digital documents by extending the life of the original computer hardware and software systems on which the digital documents were created. These life-cycle extensions involve the operation and maintenance of antiquated hardware systems and the archiving of the software needed to access digital documents in their native formats.

While maintaining a depository of antiquated hardware might be achievable in principle, it is also plagued with problems. The main drawbacks being the cost of operating multiple information systems and the difficulty in acquiring antiquated hardware system components. These problems make it unrealistic to expect that any organization could effectively and efficiently maintain multiple, aging information technologies in order to maintain access to superseded digital documents. To overcome the problems associated with maintaining aging hardware, Rothenberg suggested the creation and use of system emulators that can imitate the behavior of antiquated hardware systems. This method would allow the operation of superseded software on advanced systems as a way to view digital documents in their native formats. However, in order to emulate an antiquated information system this method requires exhaustive specifications on the original system's hardware. Therefore, this method may require extensive participation by hardware manufacturers. Many manufacturers may be reluctant to supply all of the specifications to software developers because some of the technology may still be in use in advanced systems they have developed.

Challenges of Digital Preservation

The main problem with digital preservation is that digital technology, in comparison to print, is an extremely fragile medium for the cultural memory of the world. The most commonly given example of this fragility is the 1960 United States Census, where raw data stored on magnetic tapes apparently became obsolete and, to all intents and purposes, unreadable by the late nineteen-seventies. Digital information has two main weaknesses:

1. *The storage medium* - digital storage media, whether magnetic or optical, are subject to relatively rapid decay: especially when compared with print.

2. *The hardware and software* - digital information is machine-dependent, and to be 'read' accurately it needs specific computer hardware and software. Unfortunately, hardware and software quickly become obsolescent or otherwise unusable.

Proposed solutions to these problems usually involve periodic 'refreshing' or recopying of the digital information onto new media and the occasional 'migration' of data into new formats. Assuming that some answer can be found to these problems, there remains the important issue of intellectual preservation. The archives community has been addressing these issues for some time now. This has partly been led by the need for electronic records to be accepted in legal evidence but the fact that electronic records are increasingly created in a variety of important situations: government; health-care; business-transactions, etc., has resulted in a renewed interest in authentication and validation issues.

When the library and information community discuss metadata, the most common analogy given is the library catalogue record. Priscilla Caplan, for example, has defined metadata as a neutral term for cataloguing without the "excess baggage" of the Anglo-American Cataloguing Rules or the MARC formats. The most well-known metadata initiative, the Dubin Core Metadata Element Set, has the specific aim of supporting resource discovery in a network environment. The Internet has many virtues, but it was not designed specifically for information retrieval. The search technologies that evolved - Archie for anonymous ftp sites, Veronica for gopher and search engines for the Web - were developed as a response to perceived needs rather than as an integral part of the original concept. Search engines like Digital Equipment Corporation's Alta Vista construct indexes by means of robots which 'crawl' through the Web collecting indexing information.

This is a less than perfect solution as Web sites typically do not contain all the relevant information for automated indexing and if they do it is unlikely to be in a form identifiable to most robots. It is possible that if Dublin Core metadata is attached to or embedded in a large number of Web documents, a new generation of Web robots or harvesters could collect this metadata and make it available through improved search services. Search engines, however, are not the only solution to the Internet resource discovery problem. An alternative approach has been to get people to select resources according to agreed criteria and then make them available via a Web site, where they can be browsed or searched. Metadata formats come in a variety of shapes and sizes. Dublin Core is intended to be a simple structured record which can, if required, be enhanced or mapped to more complex records.

Dublin Core may have a role as a minimal metadata set in order to allow for interoperability between other, more complex, metadata formats. Library and information professionals with an interest in the Internet should be interested in the development of metadata for resource discovery. Clifford Lynch points out that if the Internet is to continue to thrive as a new means of communication, "something very much like traditional library services will be needed to organize, access and preserve networked information". Metadata does have an acknowledged role in the organisation of and access to networked information, but it could additionally be important in the general area of digital preservation.

Society has vital interest in preserving materials that document issues, concerns, ideas, discourse and events. Custodians of the cultural record have always had to manage the inherent conflict between letting people use manuscripts, books, recordings or videos, and being sure that they are preserved for future use. For works printed on acidic wood pulp paper, as most books have been since 1850, they measure the remaining lifetime of those materials in decades, not centuries. In 1993, forty-five percent of U.S. workers were using a computer; the number is surely larger now. Virtually all printing and a rapidly increasing amount of writing is accomplished with computers. Professional sound recording is digital, and digital video is on the verge of moving from experimental to practical applications. As a means of recording and providing access to their cultural memory, digital technology has numerous advantages and may help relieve the traditional conflict between preservation and access. For materials stored digitally, users operate on exact images of the original works stored in their local computers.

Separating usage from the original in this way, digital technology affords multiple, simultaneous uses from a single original in ways that are simply not possible for materials stored in any other form. Digital technology also yields additional, effective means of access. In full text documents, a reader can retrieve needed information by searching for words, combinations of words, phrases or ideas. . Readers can also manipulate the display of digital materials by choosing whether to view digital materials on a screen, store them on their computer or external media, or to print them. Digital technology, however, poses new threats and problems as well as new opportunities. Its functionality comes with complexity. Anyone with a compass (or a clear night to view the position of the stars in relation to true north) could theoretically set up or repair a sundial.

A digital watch is more useful and accurate for telling time than a sundial, but few people can repair it or even understand how it works. Reading and understanding information in digital form requires equipment and software, which is changing constantly and may not be available within a decade of its introduction. Who today has a punched card reader, a Dectape drive, or a working copy of FORTRAN II? Even newer technology such as 9-track tape is rapidly becoming obsolete. They cannot save the machines if there are no spare parts available, and they cannot save the software if no one is left who knows how to use it.

Rapid changes in the means of recording information, in the formats for storage, and in the technologies for use threaten to render the life of information in the digital age as, to borrow a phrase from Hobbes, "nasty, brutish and short." Some information no doubt deserves such a fate, but numerous examples illustrate the danger of losing valuable cultural memories that may appear in digital form. In 1976, the US

National Archives identified seven series of aggregated data from the 1960 Census files as having long-term historical value. A large portion of the selected records, however, resided on tapes that the Bureau could read only with a UNIVAC type II-A tape drive. By the mid-seventies, that particular tape drive was long obsolete, and the Census Bureau faced a significant engineering challenge in preserving the data from the UNIVAC type II-A tapes.

By 1979, the Bureau had successfully copied onto industry-standard tapes nearly all the data judged then to have long-term value. Though largely successful in the end, the data rescue effort was a signal event that helped move the Committee on the Records of Government six years later to proclaim that "the United States is in danger of losing its memory." The Committee did not bother to describe the actual details of the migration of the 1960 census records. Nor did it analyze the effects on the integrity of the constitutionally-mandated census of the nearly 10,000 records of aggregated data that the rescue effort did not successfully recover.

Instead, it chose to register its warning on the dangers of machine obsolescence in apocryphal terms. With more than a little hyperbole, it wrote that "when the computer tapes containing the raw data from the 1960 federal census came to the attention of NARS [the National Archives and Records Service], there were only two machines in the world capable of reading those tapes: one in Japan and the other already deposited in the Smithsonian as a relic". In 1964, the first electronic mail message was sent from either the Massachusetts Institute of Technology, the Carnegie Institute of Technology or Cambridge University. The message does not survive, however, and so there is no documentary record to determine which group sent the pathbreaking message. Satellite observations of Brazil in the 1970s, critical for establishing a time-line of changes in the Amazon basin, are also lost on the now obsolete tapes to which they were written.

Similarly, in the late 1960s, the New York State Department of Commerce and Cornell University undertook the

Land Use and Natural Resources Inventory Project (LUNR). The LUNR project produced a computerized map of New York State depicting patterns of land usage and identifying natural resources. It created a primitive geographic information system by superimposing a matrix over aerial photographs of the entire state and coding each cell according to its predominant features. In the mid-1980s, the New York State Archives obtained copies of the tapes containing the data from the LUNR inventory along with the original aerial photographs and several thousand mylar transparencies. Staff at the State Archives attempted to preserve the LUNR tapes, but the problems proved insurmountable. The LUNR project had depended on customized software programs to represent and analyze the data, and these programs were not saved with the data.

Even if the software had been retained, the hardware and operating system needed to run the software were no longer available. Today, information technologies that are increasingly powerful and easy to use, especially like those that support the World Wide Web, have unleashed the production and distribution of digital information. Such information is penetrating and transforming nearly every aspect of culture. If they are effectively to preserve for future generations the portion of this rapidly expanding corpus of information in digital form that represents their cultural record, they need to understand the costs of doing so and they need to commit ourselves technically, legally, economically and organizationally to the full dimensions of the task. Failure to look for trusted means and methods of digital preservation will certainly exact a stiff, long-term cultural penalty.

Index